The Men's Section

D1363819

HBI Series on Jewish Women

Shulamit Reinharz, General Editor
Sylvia Barack Fishman, Associate Editor

The HBI Series on Jewish Women, created by the Hadassah-Brandeis Institute, publishes a wide range of books by and about Jewish women in diverse contexts and time periods. Of interest to scholars and the educated public, the HBI Series on Jewish Women fills major gaps in Jewish Studies and in Women and Gender Studies as well as their intersection.

The HBI Series on Jewish Women is supported by a generous gift from Dr. Laura S. Schor.

For the complete list of books that are available in this series, please see www.upne.com

Elana Maryles Sztokman
The Men's Section: Orthodox Jewish Men in an Egalitarian World

Sharon Faye Koren
Forsaken: The Menstruant in Medieval Jewish Mysticism

Sonja M. Hedgepeth and Rochelle G. Saidel, editors, *Sexual Violence against Jewish Women during the Holocaust*

Julia R. Lieberman, editor
Sephardi Family Life in the Early Modern Diaspora

Derek Rubin, editor
Promised Lands: New Jewish American Fiction on Longing and Belonging

Carol K. Ingall, editor, *The Women Who Reconstructed American Jewish Education: 1910–1965*

Gaby Brimmer and Elena Poniatowska, *Gaby Brimmer: An Autobiography in Three Voices*

Harriet Hartman and Moshe Hartman, *Gender and American Jews: Patterns in Work, Education, and Family in Contemporary Life*

Dvora E. Weisberg, *Levirate Marriage and the Family in Ancient Judaism*

Ellen M. Umansky and Dianne Ashton, editors, *Four Centuries of Jewish Women's Spirituality: A Sourcebook*

Carole S. Kessner, *Marie Syrkin: Values Beyond the Self*

Ruth Kark, Margalit Shilo, and Galit Hasan-Rokem, editors, *Jewish Women in Pre-State Israel: Life History, Politics, and Culture*

Tova Hartman, *Feminism Encounters Traditional Judaism: Resistance and Accommodation*

Anne Lapidus Lerner, *Eternally Eve: Images of Eve in the Hebrew Bible, Midrash, and Modern Jewish Poetry*

Elana Maryles
Sztokman

The Men's Section

Orthodox Jewish Men in an Egalitarian World

Brandeis University Press

Waltham, Massachusetts

Brandeis University Press
An imprint of University Press of New England
www.upne.com
© 2011 Brandeis University
All rights reserved
Manufactured in the United States of America
Designed by Katherine B. Kimball
Typeset in Minion by Integrated Publishing Solutions

University Press of New England is a member of the Green Press Initiative. The paper used in this book meets their minimum requirement for recycled paper.

For permission to reproduce any of the material in this book, contact Permissions, University Press of New England, One Court Street, Suite 250, Lebanon NH 03766; or visit www.upne.com

Library of Congress Cataloging-in-Publication Data
Sztokman, Elana Maryles.
The men's section: Orthodox Jewish men in an egalitarian world / Elana Maryles Sztokman. — 1st ed.
p.   cm. — (HBI series on Jewish women)
Includes bibliographical references and index.
ISBN 978-1-61168-078-2 (cloth : alk. paper)—ISBN 978-1-61168-079-9 (pbk. : alk. paper)—ISBN 978-1-61168-080-5 (e-book)
1. Equality—Religious aspects—Judaism.   2. Orthodox Judaism—Doctrines.   3. Women (Jewish law)   4. Shira Hadasha (Jerusalem)   I. Title.
BM645.E85S98   2011
296.081—dc23   2011030022

5 4 3 2 1

The publication of this book was generously supported by the Lucius N. Littauer Foundation.

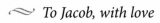 *To Jacob, with love*

Contents

Foreword

Sylvia Barack Fishman

In traditional Orthodox synagogues, worshippers are partitioned into male and female spaces. "The women's section," as it is often called, seats girls and women, who do not take vocal leadership roles in the Hebrew service, despite the fact that today many Orthodox women have excellent Judaic educations and liturgical knowledge. The women's section is a clearly defined area—a balcony, or a section of seats behind a latticework, curtain, or fencelike structure—and it is never where the holy ark containing the Torah scrolls is located. All the action of the service is conducted by the worshipping congregation of men and boys over age thirteen in the space where the Torah and the podiums to read, chant, lead the congregation, and deliver sermons are also located. By default, one may call this main congregational area, as Elana Maryles Sztokman ironically does, "the men's section."

Sztokman went from "following the rules" of Orthodox female comportment to "stepping out" of her "assigned role." For the first time in a life that had included weekly attendance at Orthodox Sabbath prayer services, she felt "truly present" when she led the congregation at the first Shira Hadasha Partnership Minyan in Jerusalem—a liberal Orthodox service that inaugurated a new approach, allowing women over age twelve to be called to the Torah, to read from the Torah scroll, and to lead parts of the service for men and women who sit separated, in the Orthodox fashion, by a *mekhitza* partition. However, unlike most other Orthodox congregations, the *mekhitza* in a Partnership Minyan allows males and females equal access to the Torah service. And, as Sztokman explains in this fascinating and lively social analysis, the innovations are far more than visual.

Some girls and women who participate in Partnership Minyanim—which now number 22 in the United States, Israel, Australia and elsewhere—regard their enfranchisement as an unexamined and welcome gift. But Sztokman has a researcher's curiosity. Who are the men frequenting Partnership Minyanim, she wondered? Are they ideological feminists? Extraordinary individuals? Why would they voluntarily relinquish the exclusive ownership that men enjoy in conventional Orthodox prayer services, while still remaining committed to the obligation of thrice-daily prayer? Unlike men in more liberal wings of Judaism, where female worshippers are sometimes the majority these days, the men in Partnership Minyanim retain their Orthodox sense of male obligation. On principle, Partnership Minyanim do not commence without a *minyan* (prayer quorum) of ten men, plus ten women. In a world where women's enfranchisement has often been accompanied by declining male interest and involvement, the men of the Partnership Minyan provide an intriguing model.

Sztokman freely admits that her research has been one expression of her advocacy within a Partnership Minyan in Modi'in, Israel, where she lives. She vividly describes the great passion for prayer among the men of her childhood in devoutly Orthodox Williamsburg, Brooklyn, where synagogue Judaism was an unchallenged men's club. She traces the process through which the first Partnership Minyanim were created, placing them in the context of simultaneously emerging Independent Congregations like Mechon Hadar in New York. With her keen eye for telling details, her wit, and her startling insights, Sztokman shows that although gender equality was a profoundly motivating goal for both Orthodox and non-Orthodox innovative congregations, women would not have been able to achieve change in either "without the compliance of men, especially powerful men." The first lesson of her study, then, is that male partnership made women's greater participation possible.

This book's subject is "men who dwell in transition"—not always a comfortable position! As the construction of femaleness changes, so does the construction of maleness. All-male environments like Orthodox synagogue leadership are often permeated by pressure to follow all the rules incumbent on men, and Sztokman brilliantly lays out the multiple ways that Orthodox societies box men into patriarchal systems: Orthodox men compete on scales of piety, earnestness, and ritual and intellectual precision. Men who don't measure up are viewed as dilettantes, and considered less manly and strong. The prayer shawl, *tallit*, which some men managed to safeguard even in Holocaust concentration camps, is symbolic of this male seriousness and strength, as are the phylacteries, *teffilin*, proudly donned by Orthodox Israeli soldiers every weekday, without exception, even on the front lines. For Israeli Jews, these ritual objects are thus super-male symbols of *gevura*, courage and prowess—words that come from the same Hebrew root as the word for male, *gever*. Along comes Orthodox feminism, with one of Sztokman's mentors being photographed in *tallit* and *tefillin* while she nurses a baby! It should not be surprising that in Israel resistance to feminist changes sometimes take more dramatic form than in the United States, and Sztokman skillfully unpacks the significances of the resistance as well as the changes.

Male on male competition demands flawless public performance skills in chanting from the Torah scroll and leading services, and sloppiness is punished by a "culture of pouncing on the flawed layner (Torah reader)"—a circumstance terrifying to neophyte Torah readers. Young men are trained not to react emotionally when veteran readers "bark" corrections at them. For many, not reacting means not feeling—and eventually feeling nothing throughout the prayer service, she argues. The swift Israeli prayer service has an ethos of "*ba'im, gomrim, holchim,*" "we come, we finish, we go." Religious emotions of excitement, affection and anticipation are much more likely to be aroused by "learning," the rigorous study of rabbinic texts than they are by prayer in conventional Orthodox settings. The study of the Talmud, particularly sections dealing with *halakha*, Jewish law, creates a "discursive framework for Jewish men" which rewards certain types of creativity and brilliance.

This multifaceted interweaving of gendered religious performance with virility provides the context for the tensions some Israel Orthodox men feel when they join quasi-egalitarian Partnership Minyanim. Involvement conveys not only diminution of male exclusivity, but even of masculinity itself. In Israeli society, a man who abrogates his own authority to a female is sometimes called a *smartut*, a rag—perhaps the best English slang equivalent is "wimp." Men often fall victim to essentialist thinking about themselves as well as about women. Essentialist thinking is also reinforced by the Orthodox habit of ostracizing those who seem to defect from socially approved behaviors, what one of Sztokman's informants calls "power wielding in the name of God."

Despite these powerful mechanisms for social conditioning, however, Partnership Minyanim continue to thrive. The final chapters of Sztokman's book describe the complex negotiations that ensue both in personal and in congregational life. The men who persist "are changing the way they do Jewish masculinity," she writes, identifying a typology of three models: (1) Those who join to think for themselves and reconceptualize halakhic obligation; (2) those who seek spirituality and emotion in prayer, and find those attributes in Partnership Minyanim; and (3) those interested in re-engineering Orthodox societies, relationships, and community. Regardless of their motivations, the ranks of Partnership Minyanim include a disproportionate number of academics, who "have an appreciation for historical impact on halakha." Many resist "GroupThink" as a phenomenon and look to these congregations as environments that encourage independent thinking. Many appreciate the aesthetic, which blends musicality and spirituality with liturgical rigor. And many say they have been influenced by the women in their lives—mothers, sisters, daughters, and wives.

The changes Sztokman analyzes are ongoing, and she conveys a palpable sense of their vulnerability and the social and religious flux that continues. Her nuanced discussions of men and women in a transitional world challenges readers' understandings of Modern Orthodoxy, along with social constructions of maleness and femaleness. She has opened a fresh new chapter in thinking about gender and Jews.

Acknowledgments

This book is a product of four years of research, writing, and conversations around the world with people who are sincerely dedicated to bringing about *tikkun olam*.

I would like to thank the men who agreed to be interviewed for this book—men who eagerly took me into their lives and communities, opened up their hearts and minds and shared with me their ideas, their doubts, their ambivalence, their vulnerability, and the narratives of their lives. This book is about them, and I hope that I accurately and effectively captured their identities and their spirits.

I would like to thank three men in particular: Rabbi Mendel Shapiro, Rabbi Professor Daniel Sperber, and Dr. Elitzur Bar-Asher Siegel, whose interviews gave the research depth, integrity, and passion. Thank you for the time and for all your efforts on behalf of partnership synagogues, and I hope the research supports your important work.

This research is the brainchild of Rabbi Aaron Frank, whose interest in gentle religious masculinity is obvious from his entire persona and being. Aaron had the idea for this research but is too busy doing the real work of education to carry it out. Thank you, Aaron, for entrusting me with your vision. I'm honored by the camaraderie as well as the friendship, and I hope I've done the issue justice.

I owe an enormous debt of gratitude to Kehillat Darchei Noam in Modi'in, where this book germinated and where the majority of the observations took place. It has been a tumultuous ride, one full of lessons and progressions, some of which were quite difficult. There are many wonderful people in this special community who have been dedicating their lives to creating a religious space that is open and inclusive. I hope this book gives them the support that they need in their divine endeavors and acts as a catalyst for healing and growth.

Many other partnership synagogues invited me in as participant, observer, and/or interviewer, including Shira Hadasha in Jerusalem, Baka Shivyoni in Jerusalem, Shira Hadasha in Melbourne, and synagogues in New York, Connecticut, Massachusetts, Chicago, and Los Angeles. I hope this book helps all these pioneering communities develop a strong framework that will fortify and expand their vital work.

I would like to thank the Hadassah-Brandeis Institute for the grant that enabled me to embark on this project. I would especially like to thank Professor Sylvia Barack Fishman and Professor Shulamit Reinharz, who believed in me from the beginning. Professor Reinharz eagerly asked me for my manuscript when it was still in its infancy, giving me the impetus to see it through. Professor Fishman provided advice, counsel, and encouragement all the way through and at times went out on a limb for me, which is an incredible gift. Thank you so much for that. Thanks also to Professor Phyllis Deutsch of University Press of New England and Lori Miller.

Dr. Ariella Zeller, my original partner in this endeavor and anthropologist par excellence, has been part editor, part confidante, part collaborator, and part sister. Her imprint is everywhere on the manuscript, and on my soul. Thank you, friend.

Professor Alice Shalvi, whom I've had the privilege of calling my mentor, took the time to read and edit the entire manuscript at an early stage. Thank you for the brilliant insights and constant support in all my work.

Hinda Hoffman, an outstanding editor, mentor, and friend, took this work and turned it into a coherent book. Hinda devoted countless hours not only to fixing my punctuation, grammar, and diction (how can I even write this paragraph without showing it to her first?), but also to being a patient and wise sounding-board for all my ideas. Hinda's work on both content and form was invaluable.

Dr. Jonathan Rynhold, friend, colleague, and scholar, always made time to help me flesh out ideas and analysis. His insights into trends in world Jewry helped sharpen many of the ideas in this book and hopefully made the research relevant and up to date with current research.

Several other people, including interviewees, read and commented on different chapters and sections and offered insights: Chaim Kram, Shlomo Quinn, Jay Engelmeyer, Aaron Frank, Fred Gorsetman, and Tsippi Kaufman. Thank you for taking the time and for taking it seriously.

Audiences that listened to me talk about this research became invaluable sources of ideas and reflection and provided new angles and perspective on a myriad of topics. I would like to thank Professor Avinoam Rosenak and the entire Van Leer seminar group that engaged in some lively discussions on the topic, and the Van Leer Institute for the opportunity to learn and speak about the research. Thank you to JOFA and Kolech for inviting me to speak about the research. Thank you to Dr. Adam Ferziger of Bar Ilan University for another lively seminar on the topic.

Thank you to my editor at *The Forward*, Gabrielle Birkner, for offering me countless opportunities to write about my work, and for the interview podcast. And special thanks to Joel Katz for all the shout-outs.

I am blessed to have some wonderful friends and relatives with whom I've discussed issues and ideas that directly and indirectly illuminated this work: Ilana Teitelbaum Reichert, Chaya Gorsetman, Jackie Bitensky, Annie Eisen, Elise Rynhold, Anna Ballin, Ariella Rand, Inbal Gal, Ilona Fischer, Helen Maryles Shankman, Mona Farkas Berdugo, Leslie Granat, Nechama Munk, and Matti Munk. I'd like to thank the following people for conversations and openness: Avi Gilboa, Eli Sacks, Moshe Ohali, Malachi Kranzler, and Ofer Glanz. Thanks also to the Facebook friends who engaged in some stimulating chats about different aspects of this work.

This research became the topic of conversation at too many Shabbat meals to count. I would like to thank all my hosts and guests and friends on different continents who have engaged with me and joined me on the journey. I would especially like to thank the men around the table for whom some of the ideas were at times quite confronting. I am inspired by the openness and flexibility of thought that I have encountered, and it gives me hope that this research may in fact facilitate change and greater communal compassion and kindness.

I would like to thank my Jewish matriarchs—my mother, mother-in-law, grandmothers, aunts, cousins, sisters, and all the Jewish women who came before me. I carry their legacy of Jewish womanhood on my shoulders, a legacy that informed this work and inspired me to try to make a difference.

A very special thank-you goes to the Jewish men who molded me. To my father, Matthew J. Maryles, who taught me love of Torah and the Jewish people, and unknowingly taught me how to layn by osmosis, and to my grandfathers, David Maryles and Louis Schmeltz, may their memory be blessed, who provided a glimpse into my Jewish heritage, and the power of being a cantor and going to *minyan* three times a day. This book is really about you, and I thank you for allowing me to explore your culture (even if I didn't exactly ask permission). Thank you for being models of strength and dedication to the Jewish people.

My children, Avigayil, Efrayim, Yonina, and Meital, have put up with a lot in the making of this book. They have had to tolerate not only the trials and tribulations of intense research and writing, but also all the questions and musings that I brought to the kitchen table, whether or not they were ready and/or interested. The truth is, I think that they have grown along with me, have ridden the waves of change and transformation throughout our journey together, and have remained balanced, joyful, and wise. I am so proud of all of you, so grateful for your understanding and for your beauty, and so blessed to be sharing life with such amazing creatures of God.

I think that my son, Efrayim, should be singled out for a special thank-you, because as the only boy in the house—learning in yeshiva, no less—he has had to deal with the particular challenge of going through adolescence while living with a feminist mother who happens to be researching Orthodox men. Effie is full of wisdom and strength and a profound commitment to goodness and compassion in this world. One of my proudest moments during this research was when an interviewee told me that the reason he decided to come to the partnership synagogue is that on his first encounter with the synagogue, an eleven-year-old boy welcomed his son and invited him to play basketball. That boy, he told me, was Effie. Effie is a beautiful boy, and his power is in his kindness.

Mostly I would like to thank Jacob, my best friend, always sticking up for me, even when he knows I'm wrong. I went sailing across the sun, made it through the Milky Way to see the lights all faded and that heaven is overrated. So I've landed (for now), and am so grateful to have the chance to fly in this life with you. Thank you for all the love and friendship, and for sharing the journey.

Finally, my deepest gratitude goes to my Creator, for enabling me to be the vehicle for the birth of this book. I hope it will be a catalyst for growth and awareness, and will bring more compassion into this world.

The Men's Section

Prologue

ONE COLD SATURDAY MORNING, I walked into a synagogue in Jerusalem and did something I had never done before: I led the prayer service. It was January 2002, and my friend Haviva Ner David had called me to let me know that a new prayer group was forming and needed a woman cantor, a *hazzanit*. This was not a Conservative community, where this is normal, but rather an Orthodox group that was trying to give women as many roles in the service as was possible within Jewish law. Haviva said women would be allowed to read from the Torah, to be called up to the Torah, and to lead certain sections of the service. This was quite a coup in a world where such roles for women were until then virtually unheard of. Haviva said that the whole project was about to become academic because no woman was willing to do it. "If you don't do it, we may have to ask a man to lead services instead. And that would just defeat the whole purpose," she said.

Despite my then thirty-three years of dwelling in Orthodox communities, despite the fact that my father is a seasoned cantor and Torah reader, and that his father was a famous cantor, and despite the fact that I had spent hundreds of hours sitting in synagogues listening to others leading the service, the thought of doing it myself was daunting—and, frankly, exhilarating.

"Okay," I said. Ignoring my complete lack of experience, and displaying either courage, blind faith, or startling irreverence, I agreed to do it. I called my friend Aaron Frank, an Orthodox feminist rabbi and Carlebach devotee, and asked for help. He taught me some tunes, made a tape recording, and guided me. I practiced for hours, suddenly making explicit what had only been passively understood, paying attention to stops and starts, memorizing melodies that I had heard since I was a child, and taking ownership, for the first time in my life, of a text that had been central to my religious identity for decades. I was ready to become a *hazzanit*.

This particular Shabbat was about to make history, not only for me, but also for the entire Orthodox world. It was the very first Shabbat service of Shira Hadasha (literally "new song"), an Orthodox-egalitarian synagogue that has since become a legendary, world-renowned focus of conversation at countless dinner tables and blogs, and a must-see tourist spot for Jews of all denominations visiting Jerusalem. That first week, Haviva, along with Tova Hartman, a Harvard-educated feminist professor who was the spirit and energy behind the initiative, were nervous that nobody would come. This was not a lecture hall where people from nondescript backgrounds were taking notes and writing academic papers on feminist theory or researching sources on women in Jewish law. This was an attempt to actually change Orthodox women's lives. To succeed, they needed ten men, a quorum, willing to place themselves, their families, and their religious identities behind a completely new idea. It was all rather unsettling.

That first Shabbat everyone watched the door in nervous anticipation. Would people come? Would anyone protest? Would some rabbi that nobody ever heard of issue an edict of excommunication? Would the participants even know what we were trying to do? To everyone's delight, that first Shabbatt, in which over fifty people participated, and which took place at the International Cultural Center for Youth on Emek Refaim Street in the funky and cosmopolitan German Colony, passed without incident. Within a year or two, it evolved into a standing-room-only service. This became the experiment that exceeded everyone's wildest dreams.

Shira Hadasha had some unexpected consequences as well. Like the proverbial pebble tossed in the pond, it sent ripples throughout the Jewish world, altering Orthodox discourse and practice. Feminist communities have been emboldened, and the model has been duplicated in various versions in at least twenty additional communities from New York to Melbourne. Shira Hadasha enabled more-public roles for women and permanently changed the rules of what is considered possible within Orthodoxy. As one journalist in Modi'in, Israel, wrote, "People are asking: If *they* are doing it, why can't *we*?" Suddenly, rather than asking "Can we allow women to lead?" Orthodox communities were asking "Why shouldn't we?"

For many women, the world impact was not nearly as significant as the personal one. That Shabbat morning in January 2002, I was not thinking about numbers or broad social change—I was feeling alive. *Liberated*. This was the moment when I stepped out of my assigned role, when I rejected that cloistered enclave that is the "woman's place" and experienced feeling truly present in synagogue for the first time.

For me, growing up in Brooklyn, New York, in the 1980s in a fairly typical modern Orthodox family of four daughters, going to synagogue on Shabbat had pretty much one meaning: *clothes*. My sisters and I would spend most of Friday planning our outfits down to the last detail, walking up Avenue J to fill in the missing pantyhose, earrings, nail polish, shoes, and any form of accessory that would enable us to stand out while following the fashion rules. Shabbat morning was full of the female family ritual of negotiating earrings and belts and deliberating over jackets and the weather until we hit the "scene"— that is, the *shul*, or synagogue. My sisters and I usually arrived toward the second half of the service. The prayer leader was like a stage performer—if you were lucky, it felt like going to a concert; but at other times the audience could be seen looking at their watches, snickering at their bench-mates' jokes, or nodding off. Reprimands to stop the constant chatter were frequent, supplemented by the occasional loud *rap rap rap* on the podium.

There was a large stage at the front of the men's section, where four seats faced the congregation. One seat was reserved for the rabbi, one for the president, and two for other communal leaders, such as the chairman or treasurer. I suppose the idea that a woman would hold one of those positions never even entered anyone's mind. As far as I know, no woman ever asked to sit in one of those chairs; leadership was indelibly etched into the men's section, and everyone seemed content. Certainly no woman ever asked to lead the services or to be president—in fact, I doubt it ever occurred to anyone to imagine such a scenario. There was no discussion, no suggestion, and no protest. That was the standard Shabbat experience of my youth.

For my father, however, Shabbat was an entirely different affair. He would wake up early and, as if getting ready for work, put on his suit and tie, make a cup of tea, read the newspaper, and head off to synagogue in time for *shaharit*, the morning service. He was a seasoned *ba'al keriya*, reader of the Torah, having mastered the complex tradition of *trop*, cantillations, at the age of thirteen. Sometimes, the sounds of my father practicing his reading on Shabbat morning spread through the house, filling my lungs and spirit with the ancient chants as my body rose to inhale the Shabbat. I loved those sounds, perhaps as an unconscious alternative to the clothes ritual, or perhaps because I also longed to take part in this time-honored Jewish heritage of words and song.

But alas, I was a girl. The idea that I would one day read from the Torah was beyond my life experience, a thought that was as likely to enter my consciousness as the possibility of one day becoming an astronaut or a Broadway dancer. These were things that religious girls simply did not do. Listening to my father practice his cantillations was the closest thing I had to a meaningful prayer experience.

As years passed, my own sense of alienation from Orthodoxy, especially Orthodox synagogue life, swelled. For a few years, I tried to come to synagogue earlier, in time for Torah reading, feeling a connection to this part of the service. Sometimes I would pay close attention to my father's chanting, trying to figure out what notes the little lines on top of the text signified. It was like a puzzle, like learning to read music by listening to someone else play the piano. It was enchanting and stimulating, but owned by someone else. Eventually, when I became a young mother and going to synagogue was more of an effort, these moments subsided, and synagogue faded from my life. When Shira Hadasha opened, I had pretty much stopped going to synagogue altogether, except to stand outside and socialize. For although the sanctuary may not be a place for young mothers, the Shabbat community experience is still a central feature of Orthodox life.

Becoming a *hazzanit* in the synagogue was one of several watershed experiences that profoundly altered me and helped me discover my own belief system and identity. It was as if it released my spirit and let me know that the sanctuary was a place where I actually belonged, where my presence mattered, where I could fully participate, where my space was a space not on the side of (passive) women, but rather in the center where prayer happened, where real connection to God was taking place. For the first time in my life, I felt like I was actually *in* synagogue. The Jewish heritage that I yearned for from behind the *mehitza*, the partition, became mine.

The establishment of Shira Hadasha was also a defining moment for my family. Shortly after it opened we moved to Melbourne, Australia, for three years. Because there was no equivalent of Shira Hadasha, I spent many Shabbat mornings at home. I eventually hooked up with the Orthodox Women's Network, a group of remarkable, feminist women who have their own prayer groups once a month at *mincha*, the Shabbat afternoon service. There, under the warm and caring guidance of Dr. Jordy Hyman, Janet Belleli, and Naomi Dessauer, I learned to read from the Torah for the first time, and became an avid reader. Though relegated to a space outside the synagogue, these women gave me the courage, inspiration, practical tools, and friendship that enabled me to take ownership of this tradition among like-minded women.

When my oldest daughter became bat mitzvah in our third year in Melbourne, we gave her all the options for celebration. At the age of eight, she had been to Shira Hadasha with me, where she led the *Yigdal* at the end of the service, a role generally given to underage boys in Orthodox synagogues. Unlike me, she knew what it felt like to lead services. She had also come with me to the women's prayer group many times, including for her friends' bat mitzvah celebrations. She had also been to disco parties, and to the Conservative synagogue, and had experienced virtually the entire range of options for a bat mitzvah celebration. She chose the Shira Hadasha model because, she said, "the women's group is unfair—why should we leave the men out?" I asked her to repeat that answer several times, because I did not comprehend what could possibly be unfair to men. *My* experiences of female exclusion were not *her* experiences. She felt that she had every opportunity to read Torah, to participate, to lead services. And in a bizarre irony, the only exclusion that she witnessed was the exclusion of *men* from the women's service! Shira Hadasha, in a matter of a few short years, had shifted my daughter's perception of justice in the world. I had to wrap my head around the fact that her reality was simply different from mine; the world had changed rapidly indeed.

So we booked a hall and created our own private synagogue for the bat mitzvah, Shira Hadasha style, and it was one of the most amazing experiences I have ever had. Listening to my daughter read her entire portion, both from the Bible and Prophet sections, in a room filled with two hundred people was moving beyond words. Women who were called up to the Torah for the first time in their lives cried. My friend Janice Broder brought her eighty-year-old mother, who also cried. "It was the first time I had ever touched a Torah," she later told me. My daughter laughs when I recount this story and finds it amusing that something so run-of-the-mill for her can be so wondrous to others. But it was an enormous event, the first of its kind in Melbourne, one that changed reality for many of those present.

A month later, a group led by Professor Mark Baker decided that it was time to make this type of service regularly available to the Melbourne Jewish community. Though these were our last few months in Australia before returning to Israel, they were in some ways the most spiritually fulfilling, because for the first time we had a Shabbat experience as a family in which we all felt like equal participants. Sometimes I would read Torah, sometimes my daughter, and we all went to synagogue together. It was wonderful, and it changed our lives and shifted our expectations irreversibly.

When we moved back to Israel in August 2005 and settled in Modi'in, we naturally joined a group of people who were experimenting with a similar synagogue model. After two months, the group, Kehillat Darchei Noam, started an Orthodox-egalitarian Friday night service in a private garden. Within two months, the group rented a space, borrowed a Torah, and initiated a Shabbat morning service as well. My family immediately became actively involved, despite a bit of a trek every Shabbat. It was uplifting to be in a comfortable place where the values that we believed in so strongly were shared. It is not surprising that within two years the community had seventy member families—not bad for a group that was not sure it would survive its first month.

My personal involvement with what has become dubbed in some places the "Ortho-egal *shul*" has taken on different roles over the past six years. I have been *hazzanit*, layner, teacher, event planner, Web-content writer, youth leader, and advocate. Between Melbourne and Modi'in, however, as I finished my doctorate and continued my professional interest in ethnographic research, my attention turned to research. Ethnography has that gripping effect: once an observer, always an observer. I could not take off my research lens.

What particularly intrigued me about places like Darchei Noam and Shira Hadasha were the *men*. It seemed to me that the motivations for coming to a synagogue like this were very different for men and women. As a woman, I could point to my own sense of disenfranchisement, the emotional and spiritual void that the synagogue was filling, and my quest for meaningful religious life. But I wondered: *Why are the men here?*

My curiosity was magnified during an otherwise innocuous conversation with a male friend, a liberal-Orthodox Jew whose bookshelves are lined with feminist literature, who has four daughters, and who I assumed would be supportive of the Shira Hadasha venture. To my surprise, he said, "I can never pray in a synagogue like Shira Hadasha—because if women are doing everything, what is left for men to do?" I considered this remark, and as much as it pained me, I understood. Clearly the men who go to a partnership *minyan*, or congregation,[1] are giving up something and getting seemingly little in return. The partnership model deprives men of absolute authority and ownership of the synagogue experience. I was intrigued at how men navigate that tension.

In 2006, therefore, after having taken part in three different Orthodox-egalitarian synagogues in three cities over two continents, I set out to find out about these men-enablers who go to partnership or Ortho-egal *shuls*. I needed to understand these men, who were willing to go against social and religious convention on behalf of women, willing to risk alienation from religious normative life, to be labeled "non-Orthodox," and to abdicate their proud roles as exclusive synagogue leaders. They actively engage in a form of social change on behalf of others, despite bombardments of messages about licentiousness, excessive sexuality, and threatening the continuity of sacred law. I wanted to speak to them, to find out what drives them, what motivates them, and what issues they have to navigate to be in this space. This book, then, is about men changing, and about changing men.

With this research, my connection to these synagogues has taken a new turn. It comes from a place of curious wonder, from the desire to open up an unexplored world. The gender navigations of Orthodox men have, indeed, led to uncharted lands in the ocean of qualitative research. It is thrilling and exhilarating to be at the edge of such discovery. Yet, ironically, I am discovering a world in which I have dwelled my entire life—that is, Orthodox Judaism. How strange for something to be so very familiar and yet completely foreign and unknown—the world of men. As Sara Delamont writes,[2] if women are changing, men ultimately have to change as well. Exploring men's inner lives within religious Jewish practice has been an amazing and eye-opening voyage.

Part I ∿ Introducing Orthodox Men

If

If you can keep your head when all about you
Are losing theirs and blaming it on you;
If you can trust yourself when all men doubt you,
But make allowance for their doubting too;
If you can wait and not be tired by waiting,
Or being lied about, don't deal in lies,
Or being hated, don't give way to hating,
And yet don't look too good, nor talk too wise;

If you can dream—and not make dreams your master;
If you can think—and not make thoughts your aim;
If you can meet with Triumph and Disaster
And treat those two impostors just the same;
If you can bear to hear the truth you've spoken
Twisted by knaves to make a trap for fools,
Or watch the things you gave your life to, broken,
And stoop and build 'em up with worn-out tools;

If you can make one heap of all your winnings
And risk it on one turn of pitch-and-toss,
And lose, and start again at your beginnings
And never breathe a word about your loss;
If you can force your heart and nerve and sinew
To serve your turn long after they are gone,
And so hold on when there is nothing in you
Except the Will which says to them: "Hold on";

If you can talk with crowds and keep your virtue,
Or walk with Kings—nor lose the common touch;
If neither foes nor loving friends can hurt you;
If all men count with you, but none too much;
If you can fill the unforgiving minute
With sixty seconds' worth of distance run,
Yours is the Earth and everything that's in it,
And—which is more—you'll be a Man, my son!

—RUDYARD KIPLING

CHAPTER 1

Jewish Men on the Borders

SEVEN FIFTY-FIVE AM, the sky is clear and there is a warm breeze. It is early enough to hear birds still chirping, but late enough to detect the first sensations of Middle Eastern heat. Unlike most mornings at this hour when the streets are filled with car-pool traffic and commuters, when honking minivans mix with the smell of bus exhaust, this morning is calm and quiet, and the streets are empty and listless. In fact, if you listen quietly enough, you may even be able to faintly hear the sounds of a weekend sleeping in. It is Saturday, the Seventh Day, Shabbat, or, for some Israelis, *Yom Shabbat*. For almost everyone in Modi'in, Israel, it is a day of rest.

Besides the hum of wheels originating from occasional clusters of skinny, spandex-clad bicyclists, the only noticeable movement at this hour comes from men in crisp white button-down shirts and dark trousers, skullcaps on their heads, holding velvet, silk, or plastic-covered pouches. Their pace is steady and forthright, their faces determined and focused, as they head toward *shul*.

The *shul* ingathering has been a signpost in a Jewish man's life for generations. For some, that ritual is a weekly one, reserved for Friday night and Shabbat morning; for others, the ritual is daily. For my maternal grandfather, Louis Schmeltz, born in White Russia in the early twentieth century and living most of his life in Williamsburg, Brooklyn, the time for *minyan* was sacrosanct, a thrice-daily event that would not be interrupted or set aside for anyone or anything. We all knew that every day at *mincha* time he went on his way, without discussion, dispute, or display. It just *was*. Everywhere there are large clusters of Jews; the *minyan* is a hub of life for men, with the pinnacle on Shabbat. More than any other regular event, Shabbat services are the supreme ingathering for Jewish men.

At least that is how it used to be. Today it's primarily an ingathering of *Orthodox* men, those who still seek out a traditional, partitioned men's section. Champions of an ancient vision of Jewish life, guardians of a tradition that molds Jewish identity and defines masculinity, these male Shabbat ingatherings are a result of years, decades, or generations of socialization. They offer a male "script," where men take on prescribed roles following an entire culture of programming. This is not a simple script. It requires an early wake-up on the weekend, defying the wider culture and arguably some physiological demands, all for the sake of attending the long recitation of ancient texts, which were written thousands of years ago and which may or may not have personal meaning. This is a script of obedience and constancy, a dutiful submission to an elaborate code of behavior that over centuries and generations defined that "Jewish man," but today has morphed into the "Orthodox man."

Although changes within Orthodoxy over the past twenty to thirty years have challenged the adaptation of the male script, the synagogue remains a men's space. In the synagogue near my home in Modi'in, for example, men occupy the women's section on weekday mornings, secure in the thus far unchallenged assumption that not a single woman will appear. When I was growing up, men used to occupy the women's section of our local synagogue even on Friday nights, causing an awkward and annoyed shuffling around on those rare occasions when my sisters and I would decide to go to *shul*. A blogger named Tamar, writing at "Blogging the *Kaddish*," recently recounted her experience of walking into the women's section only to find it filled with garbage bags, "big smelly garbage bags. . . . There is a metaphor here, and it is not even remotely subtle. Women are trash. Trash belongs where the women usually go. Wow. Thanks." In many Orthodox synagogues, the women's section is far removed from the center, up high or unseen. Despite changing trends and arguably increasing numbers of women attending synagogue, Orthodox synagogue attendance remains very much a men's thing.

It is not only the structure of the Orthodox synagogue that makes it a men's space, but also the activities conducted in the space. The service revolves around prayer and Torah reading, both of which are led by men, and for which the presence of ten men is a necessary condition. Moreover, the act of "becoming a man" in Orthodoxy, the bar mitzvah, also revolves around these same activities— prayer and Torah reading. The men's section is therefore the central location where men's identities are molded, where they learn how to stand up and take their place among men, where they enter the ranks and are brought into the fold, embraced—perhaps not literally but certainly figuratively—by generations of men before them, where they learn how Jewish men have been defining for generations what it means to be a man. Jeffrey Salkin writes about the significance of the synagogue in formulating male identity:

> In the Jewish world, macho became the art of Torah. This is why Jewish men would pray, "Blessed is God, Who has not made me a woman." If one was not a woman,

then one was a man—and a real man had access to Torah. The yeshiva and the synagogue were the places where intense Jewish male bonding happened. . . . That may have been why Jewish men did not include women in the *minyan*. The *minyan* was the ultimate male bonding. To engage in a text, hearing God speaking, and to pray—speaking to God: That was man's work.[1]

The synagogue, a Jewish version of the classic men's club, is a place where men are inducted into the rules and regulations that govern masculinity, and where men adapt to the male script and learn to master the behaviors and norms that society expects of them.

This "Be a Jewish man" script is captivating, though not entirely understood. Aviva Cantor believes that Jewish masculinity was defined by a Diaspora reality that ingrained in Jewish men a sense of powerlessness that set them apart from their Gentile counterparts. She argues that because they were unable to prevent the rape of "their" women by the powers that be, they compensated by creating power roles within their families and communities.[2] Daniel Boyarin builds on Cantor's analysis but contends that over generations, Jewish men in exile developed a nonviolent "effeminate" persona, a frail-bodied, intellectual, and almost passive masculinity that stood in opposition to non-Jewish muscular physicality, a persona that morphed into modern secular Jewish identity in figures such as Woody Allen.[3] Oz Almog similarly argues that the Zionist movement sought to deconstruct this image of frail masculinity by reinventing the large, fit, and combative Jewish man.[4]

Not all scholars accept Boyarin's analysis of Diaspora Jewish masculinity as passive and nonviolent.[5] Admiel Kosman, for example, posits that calling Jewish men "nonviolent" is disingenuous because it ignores the power wielding, control, and manipulation—especially vis-à-vis women and weak men—that has characterized many Jewish all-male settings. He demonstrates that power, hierarchy, and patriarchy constituted the very essence of yeshiva life throughout Jewish Diaspora history.[6] Similarly, Warren Rosenberg disputes the "widely held stereotype of Jewish men [as] nonviolent. Erudite, comedic, malleable, non-threatening, part nebbish, part schlemiel, Jewish men do not fight, they talk. One might imagine a cross between Clark Kent and the early Woody Allen as the quintessential Jewish American male."[7] He argues that violence, rooted in Jewish texts, surfaces in Jewish masculinities in complex and intriguing ways.

Other scholars view masculinity as a negotiation between these different pressures. Harry Brod says that Jewish violence is present, but only in the "intellectual" and nonphysical sense. He asserts that "the stereotype of the boisterous, hard-drinking, brawny brawler is not part of my culture. Yet its analogue appears when Jewish men practice their own brand of intellectual muscle-flexing, trying to destroy one another's arguments rather than armaments."[8] Michael G. Holzman, writing from the perspective of Reform Judaism, confirms these perceived tensions between images of Jewish masculinity. "When we look at these men," he writes, "with all of these options available, we still find many of them struggling, even if they are unaware of the struggle. . . . Many Jewish men still cling to the awkwardness and neuroses of a Woody Allen character in an ironic nostalgic way."[9]

Trying to understand what it *means* to be a Jewish man is arguably as complex as trying to *be* one. If generations in exile forced men to grapple with their own powerlessness and to reinvent communal structures to feed into their withering masculinity, today the situation is dramatically different. Three major transformations in the modern era have created the impetus for Jewish men to redefine masculinity: modernity and the Enlightenment have restructured hierarchies and relationships between the Jews and their surrounding cultures; the state of Israel has created a locus for Jewish masculine physicality and the creation of a Gentile-like model of man as soldier-conqueror, an image that was in complete opposition to the scrawny-rabbi-behind-the-scenes manipulator image; and the movement for women's equality, influencing the development of multiple denominations within Judaism, has created venues in which women break open the traditional Jewish men's clubs, leaving men groping for a new location for induction into Jewish masculinities. Whereas "Jewish man" once had clear contours vis-à-vis non-Jews and women, those contours are now blurred and shifting. Given these complex circumstances of contemporary Jewish masculinity, it is no wonder that Jewish men are struggling, that their identities are in flux, and that they have two millennia of socialization to reconfigure.

For Orthodox men, the current climate is even more complicated. Modern Orthodoxy, in the throes of heated debates and potentially enormous change around gender roles such as female clergy and female cantors, is arguably in the midst of a gender revolution. At the same time, there are signs of tremendous gender backlash—increased insistence on separation by gender in public spaces, accompanying violence against women, rising antiwomen rhetoric, and more. Samuel Heilman believes that Orthodoxy is on the brink of splitting into two groups, which would permanently alter the way Jewish life is conceived in the modern world.[10] Whether there will indeed be two groups remains to be seen, but what is certain is that Orthodox men are being pulled in two competing directions with full force.

Given these changes, it is hardly surprising that Orthodox men are in the midst of a maelstrom. Standing between past and present, between old and new, between tradition and change, between self and community, between individualism and commitment, and between masculinity and feminism, they are facing a Jewish world that will never be the same. They are representatives of a world that once was, hanging on to a perceived tradition while struggling to reinvent it for modern times. They may or may not be aware of it, and they may or may not be doing it consciously or purposefully, but faced with modernity, feminism, and a desire to maintain a vision of an ancient tradition, Orthodox men are forced into a process of reinventing what it means to be a man, and ultimately what it means to be a Jew.[11]

The purpose of this book, therefore, is to unravel the struggles of Orthodox men by understanding the different forces imposed on their identities, by exploring the many ways in which Orthodox men navigate these different forces, and by examining the changes that some men are going through as a result of these processes, as well as the impact of these changes not only on their own identities but also on the landscape of Orthodox Jewry. The research looks at where Orthodox men are coming from, where they are going, and what obstacles they have along the way. In short, it is a book about identity in transition, about men redefining their identities and surrounding cultures in a world that is changing at a vigorous pace.

A Condensed History of Orthodox Judaism

Orthodox Judaism should have been extinct by now, at least according to Marshall Sklare, one of the leading scholars of Jewish sociology, who announced in the 1950s that Orthodoxy was nearing its demise. (In the 1970s, he admitted that he may have been wrong.) According to Steven M. Cohen and Samuel Heilman, Orthodoxy was perceived as being "a vestige of another era, and unsuited to the circumstances of contemporary culture."[12] Although arguments remain about whether the Orthodox community is growing or shrinking,[13] for some people the fact that the community "did not fulfill the expectations of many that it would disappear in the atmosphere of modern Western civilization" is in itself a surprise.[14] Remarkably, the Orthodox community has remained a fairly constant 8–10 percent of American Jewry, although the 2002 National Jewish Population Survey (NJPS) put it at 6 percent, and Heilman put it at closer to 12 percent.[15]

The perseverance of Orthodoxy reflects the tension between tradition and modern culture and Western life. Structurally, the disappearance of the traditional *kehilla*, or community, in favor of urban life and what Cohen calls "bourgeois domesticity" involved the loss of an all-encompassing "infrastructure of fraternal, charitable, social welfare, educational, and occupational associations, all of which were permeated with religious significance."[16] Charles Liebman argues that modernity confronts Jewish life ideologically as well as structurally, imposing a value system of individualism. He claims that the transition into modernity is "a movement from destiny to choice." The modern world rejects the type of absolute authority that traditional Judaism is built on and replaces it with a world of cause and effect and observable phenomenon. Modern life, which has no need for God and tradition, leaves traditional Jews with a "discontinuity between experience and belief."[17]

While this discontinuity is beset by insecurity, it is also filled with promise. The insecurities and anxieties are "more complex and acute than the insecurities of their medieval ancestors," writes Cohen, but the individualism challenges the entire conceptualization of religion. There is an "open market of religious alternatives," which makes denominational development an instrument of personalizing one's religious experience.[18] On the other hand, denominational affiliation can also reflect a desire to maintain the old, a rejection of individualism in favor of maintaining group identification. Orthodoxy, in particular, seems to be a response to perceived overemphasis on individualism in modern society. Certainly that is how Orthodoxy began at the turn of the century. Its first signs of formal organization came in response to Reform Judaism's perceived overcommitment to individual freedom and rejection of Jewish authority.[19] A complete rejection of modern ideologies has always been an underlying theme in Orthodox Judaism.

Denominational commitment within Orthodoxy, therefore, is simultaneously a reflection of individual choice and a rejection of perceived overemphasis on individualism in favor of group-based identity and traditionalism. This dualistic identity vis-à-vis modern ideologies is reflected in competing rhetoric that characterizes the entire history of Orthodoxy. The theme of absolute rejection of modernity coexists with balance, negotiation, and integration. Liebman conceives these themes as "reduction" versus "innovation," either discounting the modern experience (such as by rejecting science) or creatively innovating and reinterpreting modern phenomena within a belief narrative.

Although modern Orthodoxy is historically characterized by a stronger emphasis on innovation and negotiation rather than reduction, the particular dynamics of this negotiation is the subject of some debate. Heilman and Cohen argue that Orthodox Jews compartmentalize their identities, using the "Jewish" part under certain circumstances and the "modern" parts under others.[20] Sylvia Barack Fishman, however, understands the process that many Orthodox Jews undergo not as "compartmentalization" but rather as "coalescing"—that is, merging identities by "incorporating American liberal values such as free choice, universalism, individualism, and pluralism into their understanding of Jewish identity."[21] Compartmentalization, she argues, is often rooted in embarrassment—a desire to "hide" one's Jewishness in certain circumstances. Today, modern Jews have less general embarrassment than they once had, and as such the compartmentalization model no longer holds. Jews are not choosing between modernity and tradition, but are rather finding creative ways to blend the two. This is particularly true in modern Orthodoxy, which she argues has a strong ideological disposition toward "Torah with *derekh eretz*," of synthesizing modernity and tradition.[22]

Fishman believes that gender is a formidable impetus for identity negotiation. Women have had a tremendous influence on promoting the coalescing model in transforming American Jewish life, and American life in general. Jewish women have profoundly influenced the feminist movement in America, Fishman argues, and in turn feminism has radically impacted all aspects of Jewish life. The locations of this feminist encounter with Orthodoxy are also often the most charged. Recent events at the Western Wall in Jerusalem, for example, where Orthodox groups violently opposed women's prayer groups— the very groups that Fishman sees as idealized sites of coalescing[23]—testify to a great tension. Similarly, Marc D. Stern views the tension between Orthodoxy and modernity as reflecting "a conflict between the fundamental commitment of American society . . . to the equal treatment of all people . . . and the different, often non-egalitarian requirements of *halakha*."[24] He adds that "there is no denying that the modern feminist movement has created many difficulties for Orthodoxy."[25] Negotiation of identity in terms of change versus tradition, therefore, has been taking place for some time, and issues of gender are at its core.

These tensions within Orthodoxy find expression in some compelling demographic shifts. According to the NJPS, Jews' denominational self-identities are often more fluid than static. Indeed, among Jews over the age of fifty-five, there was significant attrition from Orthodoxy over the past forty years. Consider this: In 1971, 11 percent of American Jews self-defined as Orthodox, 42 percent as Conservative, and 33 percent as Reform. In 1990, 6 percent self-defined as Orthodox, 40 percent as Conservative, and 39 percent as Reform. While 22 percent of the respondents were *raised* Orthodox, only 6 percent currently *remain* Orthodox. That's a fascinating trend of attrition among the older generation. Put differently, 29 percent of respondents were raised Conservative, and 40 percent currently are, and 26 percent were raised Reform, and 39 percent currently are. Furthermore, only 24 percent of respondents who were raised Orthodox currently are, as opposed to 62 percent of Conservative and 79 percent of Reform. According to this portrait, in the older generation, people left Orthodoxy in far greater numbers than in any other denomination.[26] This portrait, however, is different among twenty- and thirty-year-olds. According to Cohen, although today the Orthodox community makes up approximately 10 percent of American Jews, it makes up a larger percentage of younger Jews and 37 percent of all children affiliated with synagogues. Moreover, younger Jews have stayed in Orthodoxy in much larger numbers than their older counterparts, and among younger people, the Orthodox retention rate is actually higher than the Conservative retention rate, making Orthodoxy arguably the fastest-growing Jewish denomination in America.[27]

Denominational identification, therefore, is really only a small piece of the story of American Jewish identity; the real story is the "switching." The story of movement is actually much more interesting than the story of static identity, as American Jews have been increasingly identifying themselves with fluidity. That fluid identity does not have its own name and is thus often invisible. Often that fluidity is attributed only to non-Orthodox groups. In Orthodoxy, with higher birthrates, lower assimilation rates, and higher Jewish literacy rates than in other populations, there is less fluidity than in other groups, which keeps the culture tight.[28] Again this is only part of the story, however, because there are increasing indications of fluidity and attrition in Orthodoxy as well.

In Israel, the history of Orthodox society and culture is related but distinct. The Israeli culture that most closely parallels modern Orthodoxy is religious Zionism. Religious Zionism was born later than the nineteenth-century Germanic modern Orthodoxy, and the main tension between tradition and modernity revolves less around science and relationships to secular society and more around secular Zionism and the state of Israel.[29] Despite these differences, religious Zionism and modern Orthodoxy have had a symbiotic relationship over the years, with shared population migrations, scholarly writings, and a language of Jewish law.[30] The two groups also share some interesting trends and phenomena, such as radicalization within certain settings, and a fear of los-ing youth to non-religious lifestyles.[31] Perhaps most significantly, both religious Zionism and modern Orthodoxy have experienced feminist challenges from within their movements.[32] These parallel patterns and overlaps, coupled with migratory patterns of religious Jews between Israel and North America, have created the sense that "Orthodoxy" is not only American but also worldwide. This symbiotic relationship has increased in recent years as well, due to in-creased travel to and from Israel, the growth of gap-year programs in Israel, and technological advances that ease communication.[33]

This assumption of shared language, ideology, and culture has its limitations. If American modern Orthodoxy is in conversation with other American de-nominations, then the question is, with whom is religious Zionism in conversa-tion? As Yair Sheleg points out, Conservative and Reform Judaism are American "imports" to Israel that have not yet taken root. In fact, while the "shifts" de-scribed by American Jewish sociologists refer to shifts between denominations, the "shifts" examined by sociologists of Israeli religious life are between reli-gious and secular.[34] Why this is so and whether it will continue to be true are questions that beg exploration. Meanwhile, however, in trying to understand Orthodox sociological trends, it is fascinating to compare American and Israeli patterns and language for both similarities and differences—similarities in the struggle to maintain a tradition within a surrounding secular society, and dif-ferences in the particular characteristics of that surrounding environment. This story about fluidity between denominations, and between Israeli and American versions of religiousness, is currently being played out—and it is a story not only about relationships between modernity and tradition, but also about gender.

Invisible Movement: The Partnership Synagogue

Over the past decade, while the American Jewish community was busy talking about identity, commitment, tradition, and continuity, the facts on the ground shifted, and people began challenging existing denominational frameworks—even within Orthodoxy. In 2002, a new synagogue concept sprang up, now called a "partnership synagogue," or at times an "Ortho-egal *minyan*," and since then, over twenty-two partnership synagogues have cropped up around the world—in New York, Massachusetts, Washington, Chicago, Los Angeles, Aus-tralia, Switzerland, and several cities in Israel—all built upon a similar gender protocol. Interestingly, these synagogues began almost simultaneously in North

America and Israel, with Shira Hadasha in Jerusalem opening up within months of Darkhei Noam[35] in New York. They tweaked and tinkered with the service to maximize women's equal participation, while keeping strictly to the letter of *halakha*.[36] In practice, these are gender-segregated congregations in which the gender partition is moved or fragmented in certain places to allow women to stand at the central podium and read from the Torah, make the blessing on the Torah, chant the weekly prophetical portion of the Bible known as the *haftarah*, lead some parts of the service, teach Torah, and make speeches. Women also sit on boards and take part in decision-making, unlike in most Orthodox synagogues. Women do not, however, lead parts of the service that are thought to require a traditional quorum, or *minyan*, such as the *kaddish* and *kedusha*; although significant obstacles equality have been broken down, the service is still loyal to an Orthodox reading of Jewish law, and the gender partition, though mobile and flexible, remains inviolable. These synagogues, which follow the same broad ideology and similar practices, are perhaps loosely connected, and they all reside in that same abstruse area on communal fringes, where social definitions and identities are shifting.

The spread of partnership *minyanim* has been, in some ways, remarkable, and it reflects, to a certain degree, the increasing search for individualism within Orthodoxy. According to William Kaplowitz, there are active *minyanim* in five different countries, not evenly dispersed but rather clustered in groups, especially in New York and Jerusalem, and they are completely absent elsewhere. This reflects, he argues, the idea that this is a culture that is transferred from place to place one person at a time.[37] In at least one case, the entire *minyan* is thought to be dependent on one man's work and ideology. In other words, men have a vital role in establishing, sustaining, and transporting the culture, which is carried by individuals who have developed an unwavering commitment to the model.

The spread of this model is also a reflection of broader trends in denominational fluidity. In 2006, a group of rabbis got together and established an organization called Mechon Hadar, which runs "The *Minyan* Project," a network of fifty independent *minyanim* around the United States. The notion of "independence" is telling, as is the focus on gender. The organization boasts the "first fully egalitarian yeshiva in North America," considers women's rights and social justice a central part of its mission, and claims to represent some fourteen thousand participants.[38] Clearly this denominational fluidity, the search for independent identity—especially gender identity—within existing communal structures is a growing trend with its own energy and momentum. Something is happening, and the partnership synagogue is undoubtedly part of the phenomenon.

Initial stirrings of these shifts began in the late 1990s. Mendel Shapiro, a fifty-seven-year-old, mild-mannered Jerusalem lawyer and father of six—and closet Orthodox rabbi—wrote an article in 1999 about the *halakha* of women and Torah reading, which became the legalistic blueprint for Shira Hadasha. Shapiro's article challenged the most basic gender assumptions of Orthodox worship and paved the way for the events that followed.[39] It helped dismantle the standard Orthodox prayer service, which is replete with patriarchal symbols and practices. Indeed, the cantor, the Torah readers, the announcers, the blessers, the honorees, and the celebrants are by default men, on the men's side of the partition. Women, passive and invisible, are not only prohibited from taking an active role, but are also physically set apart from the center of activity. For a woman's voice to be heard in the service is taboo, as is the possibility of a woman's body to be visible at the podium and near the Torah. The formal rabbinic leadership is also male. Even the more benign aspects of synagogue participation—such as making the announcements or leading the lay board—are roles almost never assigned to women in Orthodox synagogues. Shapiro argues that there is no serious objection in Jewish law to having women in most of these roles and that it is time for Orthodoxy to wake up and make some changes.

Shapiro's article sent ripples in the Jewish world. Rabbi Yehuda Henkin wrote a lengthy article in opposition, which the *Edah Journal* published side by side with Shapiro's article. Henkin's argument is unabashedly sociological: "Women's *aliyot* remain outside the consensus, and a congregation that institutes them is not Orthodox in name and will not long remain Orthodox in practice. In my judgment, this is an accurate statement now and for the foreseeable future, and I see no point in arguing about it."[40] Meanwhile, rabbinic scholar Rabbi Dr. Daniel Sperber wrote a book that supports Shapiro and unravels Henkin's arguments about *halakha*, historical-social processes, and the inclusion of women. Sperber told me in an interview that opposition "is based on the underlying idea that 'your ancestors didn't do it; your parents didn't do it; and therefore your children are forbidden to do it.' But is that the way in which halakhic issues should be approached? Must we regard the halakhic dynamic as 'what was will always be'? . . . The prohibitions against offending people and the notions of dignity of the individual are so central to *halakha* that they override their many traditional practices."[41] Shapiro, like Sperber, connects these issues to the broader historical narrative and says that the reason why some rabbis are against women's participation is not *halakha* per se, "but rather a sense of ingrained conservatism, naturally suspicious of change. . . . It upsets the received religious order. . . . What I cannot abide is the prevailing attitude in the Orthodox community that refuses to tolerate innovative practices simply because they fail to conform to social convention."[42]

Meanwhile, the partnership model slowly spread in Israel and North America—in parallel processes that belie a fascinating if often unspoken synergy between the two religious communities. Michal Bar-Asher Siegal, a doctoral student in religion at Yale University, and her husband, Elitzur Bar-Asher Siegal, a doctoral student in linguistics at Harvard University, were influential in starting a partnership synagogue in New Haven, Connecticut, and the opposition was just as quick to come. Elitzur faced the threat of excommunication by local rabbis, which meant that for a while he was not allowed to be called up to the Torah in some other local synagogues. He approached one of the rabbis who called for his excommunication, and called for an open discussion about it, which led to a public discussion about *halakha*—and the opposition eventually waned. "I think he respected me because I was coming from a position of *halakha*, and knew that I am committed to *halakha*," Elitzur recalled. As a result, the New Haven partnership synagogue is now strong and growing. Since then, Michal and Elitzur have traveled around the United States as halakhic advisers for partnership *minyanim*. "Informally, we kind of function almost as rabbis for the congregations," Elitzur said. They also spoke together at the 2007 Jewish Orthodox Feminist Alliance (JOFA) conference and co-published a pamphlet, *A Guide to the Halakhic Minyanim*, in Hebrew and English, the first halakhic guidebook for partnership synagogues. "I am a feminist," Elitzur said in an interview in the summer of 2008. "It's a sexist system, bound by strict adherence to a sexist framework and resistant to change."[43]

Rereading Men

One of the most interesting aspects of these trends is the role of the men. While the role of women in challenging patriarchal norms is rather intuitive—it is easy to understand why women would take a firm stand in undoing practices that render them powerless and invisible—the role of men, which is remarkably strong within these synagogues, is less readily apparent. In fact, the changes involved in challenging patriarchy are likely difficult for men. In partnership synagogues, where women have taken visible, central roles in leading the services, standing on the podium that was once reserved for men only, singing out in their soprano voices the liturgies that were specially designed to accommodate bass, baritone, or tenor, reading from the Torah and making blessings after which the entire congregation answers "amen," thus formally acknowledging women at the hub rather than the periphery, it is not just the worship that has been transformed, but also the whole notion of "masculine" and "feminine." This must be startling for Orthodox men. Like women entering a men's locker room, women presiding in the synagogue are confronting, awkward, and unsettling. Certainly the men who come out supporting women's participation publicly are taking obvious risks in order to empower women, as well as abdicating their own positions of power within the sanctuary and elsewhere. More than that, though, the changing roles of women break down the entire male script that takes place in the *shul*. If a woman reads Torah, takes public roles and leads the services, what will men be left with as they try to hold on to the process of *becoming* a man? How does one become a man when what was once man is now man *or* woman?

As difficult as it seems to be for men to abdicate both control and identity, it is fascinating to note that much of the public discourse and leadership of this phenomenon is dominated by men. The *Edah Journal* printed only men's articles, as did the *Jerusalem Post*. Similarly, when Shira Hadasha opened in Melbourne, the *Australian Jewish News* published a series of "pro" and "con" op-ed pieces about the new *minyan*—pieces written almost exclusively by men. The only woman writer was a twenty-year-old recent yeshiva graduate arguing *against* women's participation in services. Michal Bar-Asher Siegal, a learned Talmudist, is one of a small handful of women participating in the formal discourse as an expert. Tova Hartman's book offers a feminist-halakhic rationale for the partnership *minyan*, though she is considered a feminist scholar and not necessarily a halakhic one.[44] At the JOFA conference, Alanna Cooper also spoke alongside the Bar-Asher Siegals about this trend. These three women—Bar-Asher Siegal, Hartman, and Cooper—notwithstanding, the movement is so male-dominated that rarely if ever do women stand alone as authorities. When Shira Hadasha in Melbourne wanted to hear an "Israeli" perspective on the subject, they brought in a man from Jerusalem, not a woman. Despite Hartman's book, men are clearly perceived as being in charge of the discussion. On an extensive source sheet compiled by one of the men in the Modi'in community that has been widely circulated in partnership synagogues, of the thirty-one sources listed, only two were written by women. Tellingly, William Kaplowitz's master's thesis on partnership *minyanim* has a majority of male informants—and obviously is written by a man. And incidentally, Mechon Hadar was also started by all men.[45] The partnership synagogue, which on the surface seems to be about changing women's roles, is owned in large part by men.

The men promoting women's involvement also highlight the many ways in which gender is entrenched in that culture. While women may act and demand change, they cannot achieve change without the compliance of men, especially powerful men. Until this generation, any discussion of Orthodox identity was by definition about men. This is reflected in writings on Orthodoxy, which until very recently were entirely by men.[46] The subjects of study are also often men-only, by virtue of the fact that any discussion of life in the sanctuary or in the rabbinate or in the yeshiva is by definition about men. It's not surprising, therefore, that as Orthodoxy changes, men are taking the reins on the process. Not only do men still need to give the formal, halakhic legitimation for anything that will call itself "Orthodox," but men's physical presence in the sanctuary is also necessary for the event of women's empowerment to take place. Even in places where the community waits for ten women to begin, there will ultimately be no *minyan* without ten men. In other places, the community does not wait for women at all. All of the *minyanim* represented in this study have men in leadership positions—in some cases, to the exclusion of women. In other words, the collaboration of the men, both literally and figuratively, remains critical to the existence of this movement.

Yet, paradoxically, within these existing power structures, men are advocating for women's entry into formerly all-men's spaces, enabling women and abdicating their own control in favor of women.

The men who go to partnership synagogues are a fascinating group. They are men on the boundaries of Orthodox society and on the cusp of broad historical change, dwelling in transition. They have willingly abandoned the "men's club" version of synagogue and communal life, placed themselves on the tumultuous border between social groups, and risked living with ill-defined social-religious identities. They stand nameless between movements, between identities, between past and present, between stagnation and change, on the brink of an unknown future full of possibility and insecurity. They hold on to a heritage with new visions, part of an Orthodoxy that was once eulogized, holding on to that label but brazenly seeking change. They grapple, both holding on to *halakha* and breaking conventions. They are scattered around the world, and exist in a barely noticeable virtual community, visibly and sometimes invisibly engaged in dialogue with one another. They travel between communities and take their values with them as they build. These men, who act on feminist ideology, are both changing and sustaining, doing something a bit new and different while supporting the structures of one of the most patriarchal systems in existence. They are men who are stepping aside from some of the most cherished roles in their culture in order to let women take ownership of what was once exclusively theirs. That is a remarkable and extraordinarily captivating act.

We need to hear their stories. After all, for men to be such enablers, they must be undergoing a significant shift in their own conceptions of what it means to be a Jewish man—even if they are not yet talking about it or even conscious of it. Men are actively changing women's lives, but maybe they are really changing their own lives. This is their story. The struggle over Orthodox identity is actually a story about changing men, even when we think it's about women. The topic of men's identities, however, usually remains a silent, ignored subtext.

Clearly, the active role of men in deconstructing patriarchy suggests that these patriarchal roles are as difficult for men as they are for women. This reflects trends beyond Orthodoxy in Western society in general. "To be a man" often means to be counted on to fulfill a whole range of expectations: to be the all-knowing fixer of things in the house and under the car's hood; to make a lot of money in order to provide for a family; to have a full head of hair and smooth skin, with biceps and an abdominal six-pack to match; to have business cards that read "director" or "president" of something; to love and follow all sports, and to enjoy these sports even more with beer and pictures of naked women, but also to know how to wine and dine the wife in grand romantic style; and mostly to be in control of life and the environment, unflustered, the rock that everyone relies on. That's quite a bit of patriarchal pressure on men. Add to this the new-age-man expectations of being able to change diapers, brush girls' hair, and cook dinner, and the demands are tremendous.

These expectations leave many men with a constant sense of inadequacy. A man who is not particularly handy, who is short and stocky, who does not aspire to be a successful entrepreneur, who does not enjoy sports, or who is earning a working-class wage, can easily feel deficient. But unlike women who have earned certain freedoms to break from traditional femininity, men are stuck in a world in which these images of masculinity continue to dominate the public consciousness. A man cannot easily say "I don't want to be a man" without risking some major repercussions.

In the world of Orthodox Judaism, in which gender roles are even more starkly laid out, being a man likely includes all these images plus. In modern Orthodoxy in particular, a society that simultaneously dwells in both contemporary Western culture and ancient Jewish culture, the pressures to be a man emanate from multiple sources. While the "Western" components of that masculine identity have been studied to some extent, however, the Jewish components have been studied less, and the particularly Orthodox components virtually not at all.

These are the issues that informed this research. The first goal of this research, then, is to unpack the characteristics of Orthodox manhood by answering the question "What does it mean to be an 'Orthodox man'?" What messages do Orthodox men receive from society about being a man? When Orthodox men tell thirteen-year-old boys at their bar mitzvahs, "Now you are a man," what do they mean? The second goal of the research is to explore how these particular men grapple with those messages, and how they have changed these definitions of masculinity within their own identities. After all, the ideals that surround us do not entirely define us. We internalize some aspects of the ideal while rejecting others. We accept and comply in some ways but assert our independence in others. Those processes, in which we push and pull, negotiate and navigate, conform and stand out, are more accurate descriptions of dynamic identity than the portrait of the ideal. It's about how Orthodox men are challenging expectations and redefining masculinity. The third goal of this book is to examine the impact of these individual changes on broader Jewish culture and society. The transitions and navigations that men are experiencing are bringing about significant shifts in Judaism, especially Orthodox Judaism. Although Orthodox men often do not have a language to describe their own dissatisfaction with the masculinities that they were socialized into, this dissatisfaction is at the heart of many of the changes and tensions that are occurring today in Orthodoxy. The third section of the book frames those trends within shifting gender identities among men.

The Men of Partnership Synagogues

This book is based on fifty-four in-depth interviews with men age eighteen to age sixty-nine, from around the world, who belong to partnership synagogues.[47] The interviews, conducted between November 2006 and June 2008, explore men's relationship with religion, community, women, and self.

The men interviewed are by definition border dwellers. They live in Orthodoxy but are challenging norms and hold a complex worldview of insiders and outsiders. Most of the men have emerged from Orthodoxy, and the rest have chosen Orthodoxy. What they all have in common is that they are shifting vis-à-vis Orthodox culture, manipulating issues of *halakha*, *mehitza* (partition), and synagogue practice all within the development of gender identity. They have insights about normative Orthodoxy and a conglomerate of impressions and experiences from their movement toward the edges. The interviews explore where the men came from—that is, where they were until 2002—how they arrived at this place, and what navigations it took in their own gender identity along the way. I was perhaps looking at a two-for-one-sale: I wanted to get a portrait of what Orthodox men grapple with in their identities, and how this particular group, the border dwellers, are negotiating these identities in the new spaces, looking in and looking out, or looking forward while looking back.

It is important to note that the men interviewed here are not "representative" in the positivistic sense of a representative sample. This is not quantitative research, and it does not offer statistical analysis. Rather, this study offers perspectives on social changes, culture, and identity in transition. It is a compilation of stories about men in transition within a shifting religious culture—stories that illuminate broad processes of sociological change. It is a series of snapshots from that position on the border, snapshots with their own unique angles and views that can help the men on the inside better understand some of the processes that they are undergoing as well.

This is undoubtedly an overwhelmingly Ashkenazi portrait, not only because of the near absence of Sephardic informants, but also because the Sephardic synagogue contains its own cultural forms and practices that are not represented in these texts. In addition, the role of the young boy in the Sephardic synagogue is different from that of the boy in the Ashkenazi synagogue. Even Orthodoxy, which is a movement with German origins, is by definition a reflection of Ashkenazi society and culture.[48] It is quite possible that this entire book is entirely about Ashkenazi culture. Its relevance to Sephardic men is something that later research will have to explore. This is also clearly a class-driven portrait, with an interview pool representing zero unemployment at the time of the interviews,[49] and 30 percent of informants have doctorates. The entire culture is one with bourgeois assumptions and language.

The largest cluster of the research—twenty-eight interviews as well as the overwhelming majority of observations—takes place around Darchei Noam, the partnership synagogue established in 2005 by a group of families in Modi'in, Israel, a suburban town between Jerusalem and Tel Aviv, with a strong middle-class, family-centered dynamic. Most of the founding families are homeowners, few work in Modi'in because there is no real business center, and all have children. The synagogue is a mix of native Israelis and native English speakers (born in the United States, England, Australia, and South Africa). All the Israeli informants and most of the English-speaking informants are from the religious Zionist world, and the rest are from Conservative, Reform, or nonreligious backgrounds. There are no converts, and no ultra-Orthodox informants. The research follows the evolution of the synagogue and the ways in which informants wrestle with issues of identity and community development. I took part in meetings, encounters, services, and informal gatherings, sat on the board for one year, led regular services and children's services, organized events for Darfur refugees and Ethiopian children, led the Education Committee for a while, officially sat on the *halakha* committee (though the committee, significantly, never met), and actively participated in the development of the synagogue. I took an active and vested interest in the advancement of the synagogue, blending the research and the activism in a perhaps unusual way, such that the research became an avenue of my activism, and my activism became an integral part of the research. My relationships with informants were similarly intermingled, as colleagues and interviewees, and many conversations around the Shabbat lunch table or the coffee table bounced between synagogue planning and updates about the research. I also elicited feedback on different findings from key informants who read sections along the way—a tricky but important part of the process that kept the research reliable and valid.[50]

Approximately another third of the interviewees belong to Shira Hadasha in Jerusalem, which has a very different dynamic from that of Darchei Noam. Shira Hadasha has a small core group of middle- and upper-class families who live in Jerusalem. The rest of the community is composed of singles, the overwhelming majority of whom come from English-speaking origins and the majority of whom are Orthodox, including one formerly ultra-Orthodox informant. Shira Hadasha can have several hundred congregants on a given Shabbat, but the overwhelming majority of them are often in transit, including those visiting Jerusalem for a few hours to those living in Israel for a year or two. While Darchei Noam is small, static, quiet, and in some ways predictable, Shira Hadasha is massive, commanding, dynamic, and unpredictable. Darchei Noam is also much more Israeli and middle Israel, while Shira Hadasha is almost international, located as it is in the heart of the incredibly diverse German Colony. Darchei Noam is suburbia, and Shira Hadasha is in one of the main cosmopolitan and academic centers of Israel. These dynamics undoubtedly influence the characters of the communities and the issues facing the informants.

The rest of the interviewees come from elsewhere in the world: New York, Connecticut, Massachusetts, New Jersey, Chicago, Los Angeles, Zichron Yakov in Israel, a second partnership synagogue in Jerusalem called Baka Shivyoni, and Melbourne, Australia. The interviewees collectively were born in nine different countries, have a range of native languages—English, Hebrew, Russian, French, and German—and all speak Hebrew and the language of *halakha*. As a group, they are in conversation with one another, speaking about similar issues of concern, of politics, religion, and feminism from both global and local perspectives. They are a strikingly mobile group—born in one city and landing elsewhere. Some have been to more than one partnership *minyan*, and some are serial *minyan* organizers. Interestingly, Modi'in is a twelve-year-old city and by definition represents geographic mobility—people who started elsewhere. A number of Modi'in respondents came from Jerusalem, and the rest from around the world.

Despite the spread, the men interviewed are strikingly interconnected, influenced by the activities of others like them in other parts of the world, and speak in remarkably similar terms about religion and life. I ended up interviewing several sets of brothers and brothers-in-law—not necessarily in the same *minyan* or even in the same city—as well as a father and son, several cousins, and many who described decades of connections with other men in their own or other partnership *minyanim*, either in schools, youth groups, summer camps, or work. I also had my own connections with some of the men. There are men whom I've worked with, studied with, and grown up with. At least two of the men were childhood friends of my sisters, and I shared an alma mater and city of birth with a handful of others. There are also men who socialize with my spouse, or whose wives are friends of mine, or whose children play with my children, or who know my spouse from childhood in Australia—all of which added layers of intimacy to the conversation and gave me a certain legitimacy as an "insider," as someone who is a known quantity and can be allowed in the door. While I would not claim that this is any kind of representative sample—that is, "I am not representative" narrative is an integral part of the research—it nonetheless includes a rich array of Jewish religious experience. Moreover, what is certain is that the Orthodox cultural world is very intertwined, even if international. As one informant said, "Orthodoxy is like that eighties game, six degrees of separation from Kevin Bacon."

In this ethnographic/participant observation research, I was part insider and part outsider. Certainly I attended Orthodox institutions and have been a member of Orthodox communities in different cities and countries, and I therefore know the codes, the lingo, the body language, the movements and the nuances, and in that sense I'm the quintessential insider. Nevertheless, I have never been a man. I was in some ways part of the research, but in other ways forever the outsider. As a woman researching men—in fact, as a feminist researcher interviewing men in a traditionally patriarchal society—my position was complex.

The research, too, is complex, and concurrently explores several issues. While the research is about men, it is also about Orthodoxy, about shifting trends in Jewish life, and about the relationship between identity and social change. The partnership synagogue has within it the potential to reconfigure the Jewish world and to offer a new solution to the eternal question of balancing tradition and modernity. These men are committed to this solution, and this research sets out to understand why and how. I wanted to find out about the men who have dwelled in this Jewish world for so many generations, men who, in the twenty-first century, are suddenly setting aside a perceived two-thousand-year-old traditional male script in order to make room for women. I wanted to understand where they come from, who they are today, and if their definitions of manhood have changed since women began to break down the doors. Finally, I wanted to know what all this means for Orthodoxy, for women, and for the future of Jewish life.

CHAPTER 2

The "BOMB": The "Be an Orthodox Man" Box

〰 WHEN MY HUSBAND and I visited New Zealand in December 2002, we spent Shabbat in Auckland when it happened to be the weekend of the bar mitzvah of the son of David Nathan: not the original David Nathan—who was one of the first Jews in New Zealand in the 1840s, a pioneering real estate and department store tycoon, and eventually the mayor of Auckland—but his direct descendant. The lobby of the building, adorned with nineteenth-century photos and museum-like signage pointing out the impressive role of New Zealand Jewry over nearly two centuries, displayed many prominent artifacts from the Nathan family. The massive sanctuary could probably hold two thousand people—nearly half the entire Jewish population of Auckland—though at this particular event there were approximately 100–150 people scattered around this vast space, most of whom came especially for the celebration. The rabbi stood next to the bar mitzvah boy performing the laying and *haftarah*, announced page numbers across the sanctuary, gave an English synopsis of each of the seven Torah portions before the boy began, and kept the service lively with impromptu jokes. He was master of ceremonies, trainer, theologian, and comedian all rolled into one, and conveyed an awkward blend of optimism and desperation in encouraging visitors to return next week. Meanwhile, the boy read his portion with flawless precision and apparent ease, and the rabbi declared that this was the most meticulous reading of a bar mitzvah boy he had ever heard in his life. "I hope you will keep coming back," he told the lad, patting his shoulder while smiling up at the crowd, as if the boy's skill and performance would provide just the right motivation that Auckland Jews needed to renew their commitment to synagogue life and bring back the hordes. *No pressure.*

This synagogue experience was a vivid illustration of the way Orthodox practice socializes its youth into preserving identity through a vision of the past. This boy's initiation into Jewish culture was a moment of induction into an entire religious tradition and heritage, with all its expectations and appendages—and it suddenly all rested on his shoulders, the onus to keep the Jewish culture and a Jewish genealogy of this dwindling community thriving. Charged with carry-ing past and future in his little being, the boy looked up at the nearly empty Auckland synagogue hall as if the fate of New Zealand Jewry—or perhaps Jewry in general—depended on his proficiency in mastering the *trop. Really, no pressure.*

Wherever Jews have traveled throughout their sojourns, Jewish men have received the same message: *be a man.* It is a message that saturates the bar mitz-vah ritual and trickles down into the rest of the subject's life. *We are counting on you. You are responsible not only for yourself but for those around you, your fam-ily, the community, and the Jewish people of past, present, and future.*

While much feminist literature focuses on what patriarchal structures do to women, masculinities studies focus on what patriarchy does to *men.* R. W. Con-nell, in describing the many ways in which societal notions of "hegemonic man" disempower men, explores many of the social, economic, and political attributes of masculinities, such as competition, aggression, emotionlessness, sexual conquest, "bread-winning," and power.[1] "Hegemony," Connell and James Messerschmidt write, "meant ascendancy achieved through culture, institu-tions, and persuasion."[2] Michael Kimmel writes about a variant of hegemonic masculinity, "marketplace man," a white-collar image in which men are ex-pected to exist in a competitive, all-male, aggressive, and performance-oriented culture and to vehemently avoid home life.[3] Kimmel argues that "marketplace man" has limited access to behaviors and social processes—for example, friend-ship, compassion, and care—processes that are seen as female and therefore out of bounds.

In many ways, masculinity is less about relationships between men and women and more about relationships among men. By overemphasizing men's roles as dominators, patriarchal structures have created a world in which men often live in fear of domination by other men. Kimmel writes that "many fem-inist analyses failed to resonate with men's own experiences. Not a surprise, since women theorized about masculinity from their point of view, from the way women experienced masculinity. . . . But the historical record has re-vealed a somewhat different picture. Manhood is less about the drive for dom-ination and more about the fear of others dominating us, having power or control over us."[4]

One of the most powerful locations of this intimidating man-on-man in-duction into masculinity is the "men's club," an institution to which only males are permitted entry, and where men define and act out masculinity for other men. From Little League to the gentlemen's club, the all-male sphere is arguably a site in which "hegemonic man" is acculturated, where the components of these masculinities are most explicit. Michael Messner, for example, researching boys and sports, describes the ways in which organized sports reinforce emotional distance by enabling boys to become "winners" in a rule-bound, competitive, hierarchical, and violent world.[5] Gary Fine similarly describes the many ways in which Little League baseball in America turns young boys into "men."[6] The socialization into masculinity that takes places in the all-male sphere seems to be an important window into male gender identity.

Susan Faludi's extensive studies of all-male institutions investigated some colorful American settings (including professional football, the army, a shipyard construction company, the McDonnell Douglas aerospace company, drag queens, Spur Posse, astronauts, Christian "Promise Keepers," and a male fashion magazine) and exposed what she called the culture of "ornamental masculinity," in which men are valued for their symbolism, gazed upon for looks over substance, and measured by superficial scales of popular culture for "success" and "manliness." Faludi argues that there is a troubling overlap between the genders in the way one's worth is increasingly measured societally through external beauty, youthfulness, and thinness. She poignantly documents the pain that many men experience, and how enormous man-on-man pressure in the all-male sphere can be. In intensely male places, men can become trapped in their own cultures, destined for a life of always trying to measure up, and often failing. Faludi understood not only the intensity of masculine identity, but also the very real difficulty men have in challenging their own gender norms.[7] Ultimately, what these and many other studies indicate is that patriarchy is damaging not only to women, but also to men.

With these insights, I turned inward to look at Orthodoxy, the patriarchal world that I come from and know best, to conduct "ethnography at home" and explore Orthodox masculinity.

A Condensed Portrait

The following is a list of the men I interviewed, and some basic data. I removed their names after discovering that readers tend to comb the details to try to identify themselves or men that they know. I decided that in order to protect the informants, I could not connect even their pseudonyms to their real names. Nonetheless, basic data on informants is helpful. The data is further analyzed in Appendix B.

Table 2.1

City of residence	Country of birth	Age	Marital status	Children	Religious upbringing	Profession	Degrees	Shul
Jerusalem	US	48	M	4	Orthodox	Non-profit	Lawyer and rabbi	SHJ[a]
Boston	US	28	S	0	Orthodox	Writer	MA	Tehilla MA
Modi'in	Israel	41	M	2	Orthodox	Academic	MA	DNM[b]
Evanston, IL	US	55	M	3	Orthodox	Hillel Rabbi	Rabbi+BA	Kol Sasson
Modi'in	Israel	42	M	4	Orthodox	Academic	PhD	DNM
Modi'in	Israel	40	M	4	Orthodox	Computers	MA	DNM
Yale	Israel	31	M	0	Orthodox	Academic	PhD	Urim
Jerusalem	UK	65	M	*	Orthodox	Academic	Rabbi PhD	SHJ
LA	US	29	M	1	Chabad	Teacher	BA and rabbi	10+10
Modi'in	Israel	40	M	1	Secular	Teacher	BA	DNM
*	US	32	M	2	Traditional	*	BA and rabbi	*
Modi'in	UK	39	M	2	Orthodox	Academic	PhD	DNM
Modi'in	Australia	43	M	3	Orthodox	Hi tech	BA	DNM
Jerusalem	Israel	29	M	0	Orthodox	Grad student	MA	BS[c]
Modi'in	US	42	M	2	Conservative	Sales	HS+	DNM
Modi'in	US	37	M	3	Conservative	Academic	PhD	DNM
Modi'in	US	68	D	2	Conservative	Retired	HS+	DNM
Modi'in	Israel	44	M	4	Orthodox	Sales	MA	DNM
Modi'in	UK	65	M	4	Orthodox	Retired	MA	DNM
Modi'in	US	34	D-M	2	Orthodox	Psychology	MA	DNM
LA	US	27	S	0	Conservative	Academic	MA	10+10
Modi'in	Australia	36	M	4	Orthodox	Marketing	BA-BSc	DNM
Forest Hills	US	34	M	0	Conservative	Teacher	MA	Tehilla FH
NYC	Europe*	61	M	2	Orthodox	Computers	BA	Migdal Or
Melbourne	Australia	50	M	7	Orthodox	Academic	PhD	SH Aus[d]
Modi'in	Canada	34	M	3	Orthodox	Lawyer	BA and law	DNM
Jerusalem	Israel	31	S	0	Orthodox	*	BA	BS
Modi'in	US	37	M-D	4	Orthodox	*	BA	DNM

Jerusalem	US	57	M	6	Orthodox	Lawyer	Lawyer and Rabbi	PhD	SHJ
Jerusalem	US	39	S	0	Orthodox	Hi tech		PhD	SHJ + DNNY[e]
Modi'in	Israel	35	M	3	Orthodox	Psychology		PhD	DNM
Jerusalem	Europe*	42	M	3	Orthodox	Academic		PhD	SHJ
Jerusalem	FSU	32	S	0	Secular	Hi tech		PhD	SHJ
Jerusalem	Israel	39	M	4	Orthodox	Academic		PhD	BS
Modi'in	Israel	42	D	3	Orthodox	Computers		BA	DNM
Jerusalem	Israel	40	S	0	Orthodox	Teacher		BA	SHJ
Modi'in	Israel	40	M	3	Traditional	Consultant		MA	DNM
Modi'in	Israel	50	M	2	Orthodox	*		BA	DNM
Jerusalem	Europe*	38	M	5	Orthodox	Academic		PhD	SHJ
New Haven	US	31	M	1	Orthodox	Academic		PhD	Urim
Modi'in	US/Israel	48	M	6	Orthodox	Hi tech		BA	DNM
Modi'in	US	42	M	4	Conservative	Computers		BSc	DNM
New Rochelle	US	55	M	2	Orthodox	Non-profit		BA	Kol Echad
Modi'in	US	46	M	2	Conservative	Marketing		MA	DNM
Modi'in	Israel	52	M	4	Orthodox	Computers		BSc	DNM
Jerusalem	Israel	41	M	2	Orthodox	Academic		PhD	SHJ
Modi'in	US	69	M	2	Conservative	Retired		MA	DNM
Modi'in	Israel	36	M	3	Orthodox	Computers		PhD	DNM
Modi'in	US	38	M	4	Orthodox	Non-profit		BA	DNM
New Rochelle	US	54	M	3	Orthodox	Doctor		Dr	Kol Echad
Zichron Yaakov	US	41	M	5	Orthodox	Psychologist		MA	Zichron
Modi'in	Israel	38	M	3	Conservative	Computers		BSc	DNM

Notes: * indicates a detail left out because it would reveal the person's identity to those in his community. All names were omitted to protect the identity of the persons in the table.

a Shira Hadasha Jerusalem
b Darchei Noam Modi'in
c Baka Shivyoni
d Shira Hadasha Australia
e Darkhei Noam New York

VERBAL ABUSE:	Tough		Have money	PHYSICAL ABUSE:
	Aggressive		Never ask for help	
Wimp =>	Competitive	*Anger*	Angry	<= Hit/beat up
		Sadness		
Girl =>	In control	*Love*	Yell	<= Teased
Sissy =>	No feelings	*Connection*	Intimidate	<= Isolated
		Confusion		
Mama's boy =>	Don't cry	*Low self-*	Responsible	<= Rejected
	Take charge	*worth*	Take it	
Nerd =>		*Resentment*		<= Forced to
	Don't make	*Curiosity*	Don't back down	play sports
Fag =>	mistakes	*Excitement*		
		Isolation	Have sex with	
Punk =>	Succeed		women	<= Sexual assault
Mark =>				
Bitch =>				

FIGURE 2.1 Paul Kivel, the "'Act Like a Man' Box," in *Masculinities*, ed. Mark Hussey (Englewood Cliffs, N.J.: Prentice Hall, 2003), pages 69–72.

The "Be a Man" Box

The conceptual framework of this research is based on an article by Paul Kivel, "The 'Act Like a Man' Box," which lays out the many components of masculinity among many Western, English-speaking, middle- and upper-middle-class men.[8] Kivel's "box" has three components: the attributes of a "man"; the physical and verbal tools of abuse that keep boys and men in the box; and the emotions trapped in the middle of the box that are unable to emerge.

I asked myself what the "'be an Orthodox man' box" would look like. That is, if men were to describe their experiences of socialization in the all-male sphere of Orthodox synagogue life (the men's side of the partition, as it were), what would they come up with? Before I set out to understand what brought men to the partnership synagogue and how they were able to set aside their "masculinity," I had to unravel what that masculinity is to begin with. It is clear that whatever is in the box, the men in the partnership synagogues are choosing to set it aside, to resist and to reject it. In order to understand that process, I first had to open up the box and look inside. Or rather, I had to ask the men to open up *their* box and show me what was inside.

Some of the components of the box are more obvious than others, and certainly they all interact in one form or another. Unpacking the box is like taking a knot out of a ball of yarn that has been sitting in dust for a long time. It takes untangling and patience, and one hopes not to make any damaging ruptures in the process.

"Be Serious": The Many Pressures to Perform

At the Mini-Israel tourist site in Latrun, Israel, which features a collection of miniature sculptures that depict microcosms of Israeli life, there is a very telling model of the Western Wall. The artist constructed dozens if not hundreds of miniature statues of men with prayer shawls over their heads and *tefillin* phylacteries wrapped around their arms,[9] all of them mechanically rocking, or "*shokeling*"—executing a rapid succession of bows. It's a powerful depiction, because it captures perhaps one of the most vivid components of the Orthodox man. He has his ritual objects enveloping his body, he and those around him perform with unyielding commitment, and he is very serious. These impressions of Orthodox men are very similar to those that flooded the interviews.

One of the first words to jump out from the interviews is "commitment." One informant, Shalom, said he feels good "because I am davening [praying] with a group of people who have committed themselves to being committed faithful, committed Jews." "Orthodox" and "committed" in some ways go hand in hand and are often stated in the same breath. Tom, for example, said that the men in his synagogue are "very committed, learned, Orthodox men." Another informant, Zachary, described the process of becoming religious as "I just said, okay, this is a commitment I want to make, but I don't remember for what." Similarly, another informant said, simply, that being an Orthodox man means "to obligate yourself to something, like the davening, three times a day." That is, the Orthodox man is distinguished by a commitment to "something"—it does not even necessarily matter what, though in the latter case, significantly, the example is prayer. But the point of the statement is less about prayer and more about being a committed person, someone who does not fly through the world aimlessly and thoughtlessly but rather someone who has taken upon himself a personal responsibility. Zachary, who became Orthodox twenty years ago, even had trouble understanding what his specific commitment was for. "Commitment for what?" he asked. "I mean for myself? For God? For the Jewish people? What am I doing this for?"

A telling metaphor that often accompanies this language of commitment is a "scale." This scale metaphor, like the metaphor of "strengthening,"[10] is a form of measurement, pitting men against one another using external barometers. Eitan, for example, regularly looks around and places the men he sees on a continuum of serious commitment. "In every synagogue you will clearly find some men who lead more and others who are pulled," he explained. "It finds expression in commitment to prayers, between those who try harder to come [on time] and others who don't. This scale exists in every synagogue."[11] A scale reflects something visible, tangible, and measurable, and makes an abstract concept like "commitment" more identifiable. This is important for people trying to define their identities. Ehud, for example, looks at "people sitting outside and talking, not because they are really watching their children, which is legitimate because somebody really has to look after the children, but just because. That really bothers me." The sense of men watching and measuring one another on the scale of observance, performance, or seriousness seems to help them define their religious identities through visible and identified markers.

This scale of commitment also helps distinguish men from "not" Orthodox men. Mark, for example, said that Reform services "skimmed the surface of our texts and our traditions. They don't plumb the depths because they're not sufficiently committed, and so I just don't find it intellectually or spiritually satisfying or appealing." Similarly, Brian describes Orthodoxy as attracting men who want an "authentic commitment," as opposed to synagogues that "have trouble getting ten men to be there on time." The sort of condescending tone that Brian takes toward men who are deemed not "committed" enough reflects not only the man-on-man gaze and accompanying scale, but also the rhetorical inter-denominational competition that characterizes American Jewry.

The language of commitment and authenticity is often closely connected to the language of "seriousness."[12] According to many men, just as the Orthodox man cannot be fly-by-night, he also cannot be haphazard, hedonistic, whimsical, or unreliable. For some men, even young boys, commitment entails seriousness, almost to the point of severity. Binyamin, for example, spent much of his early life in the Tel Aviv party scene and lived in an apartment with non-religious girls. He said that it was "a lot of fun, but at a certain stage we made the decision that it was time to meet religious girls, to be serious." That is, religious equals serious. Binyamin described the ways in which he imparts this seriousness and absolute commitment to his three sons, especially around prayer. "Always [me'az u'metamid],[13] my sons sat with me in shul on Shabbat. There was never a situation when they would play outside. . . . Today, there is no chance my older sons would say a word during the service or anything like that, or would come late to the service. They are very, very strong." For Binyamin, the "strength" of the Orthodox man is defined as sitting quiet and still in the service, being punctual, not playing and not chatting. He does not express any interest in what his sons feel, love, enjoy, or experience, but rather only what they *do*. For Orthodox men, the language of strength, seriousness, and commitment translates into an obedient, unbending performance enforced by a man-on-man gaze that for some starts in childhood. This is the residual rhetoric from the centuries-old narrative among Orthodox men, that the fate of the Jewish people rests on their shoulders.

The Triad: *Tallit*, *Tefillin*, and *Kippa*

On a recent visit to the Yad Vashem Holocaust museum in Jerusalem, I was particularly taken by a section of the museum that shows a *tallit*, a prayer shawl, that some men had somehow kept with them through the concentration camps. When I saw this prayer shawl in the Holocaust museum while conducting this research, the image evoked something new for me: a startling impression of masculinity. That is, when a Jewish man's entire life is threatened with extinction, he chose, of all things, this shawl to demonstrate his survival. Something about this object screams out, "*I am alive.*" The *tallit* keeps the Jewish man alive.

The *tallit*, the ritual shawl that for generations Jewish men have worn during prayer—along with *kippa* (skullcap) and *tefillin*—is a central part of how men demonstrate Jewish identity. When men begin to flesh out the meanings of "commitment," their descriptions are almost invariably related to prayer—not any prayer, but a very public, visible, group prayer, the prayer of the *minyan*, with all the accoutrements of Torah, *tefillin*, *tallit*, and *kippa*. When men talk about *tallit*, it often comes out as "*tallitandtefillin.*" From all the interviews this point is undeniably central: ritual prayer is the dominant focal point of Orthodox men's very physical, demanding, and identity-forming demonstrations of commitment. The tangible, ritualistic, symbolic triad of *tallit-tefillin-kippa* is like a collection of Jewish male prayer accessories that are intricately woven into men's practice of Orthodoxy.

Tallit is not only the largest of the three symbols, but is perhaps the only one that has an intuitive spiritual expression, perhaps more understandable and explainable that *tefillin*. "There is this certain sense of transformation," Michael says, when he drapes the garment around his shoulders. In his prayers, he says, *tallit* "provides me with an additional level of spiritual meaning or of spiritual grounding."

There is another element to *tallit*, however, in that it forms a social hierarchy. As a thirty-nine-year-old unmarried Ashkenazi man, Michael is not expected to wear a *tallit*. His family's custom, like that of many other Ashkenazi families, is for men not to wear a *tallit* until marriage. But Michael decided to wear a *tallit* during his prayers at home because "*tallit* created a certain environment that I found to be meaningful." In many Orthodox settings, *tallit* marks not only "man" but also "married man"—a reality that has relegated Michael to wear *tallit* only at home. For Oded, a forty-year-old single man, the pressure not to stand out among men as "the single one" led to the opposite conclusion—he wears a *tallit* in public but not in private. "The women in the synagogue can see who is without a *tallit*, who is single, who can we set him up with," he explained painfully. *Tallit* creates a gender-reversal in sexual gaze, with women examining the male body. The *tallit* offers him protection, literally and figuratively, from that gaze. Oded and Michael have similar experiences—grappling with being single men and searching for meaningful spirituality amid complex, visible social expectations that find expression around the *tallit*.

This *tallit*-based social hierarchy is painful for some Orthodox men who do not always have a language to describe their struggles. Following one of the focus groups, Avi approached me to thank me for the discussion. "It opened something up in me that I have been keeping inside for so long," he said, his eyes welling up, "and explained something that I had not understood previously. So many years I was single, I never really internalized why I always felt so put down, almost like a second-class citizen. But now I understand." It must be tough to be a single man in the Orthodox community. *Tallit*, then, is a symbolic representation of the internal hierarchies among men, and the different ways in which men are watching, measuring, and judging one another.

For some men, *tefillin* is at the core of their religious identity. Aaron, for example, said simply that being religious is about "going to *shul*, davening on a daily basis, putting on *tefillin*." He said that *tefillin* is "a central symbol for me of my religious identity, of my story . . . an important, valuable piece of who we are." Harold similarly said that *tefillin* is "seminal" for his definition as an Orthodox man. "Putting on *tefillin* is so central to being Jewish, to being a Jewish Orthodox man. It's one of the seminal things that you do to be identified amongst the Orthodox camp. I think *tefillin* goes to the very core, to me, of being an Orthodox male." Zachary, from the opposite perspective, said that because he does not "do everything that Orthodox people do, like put on *tefil-lin*," he has difficulty calling himself Orthodox. For many men, wearing *tefillin* is the quintessential definition of male Orthodox identity, of being part of the group—what "Orthodox people do," or being part of the "camp." Even when *tefillin* is done privately, it gives a man an identification with a particular group.

The daily ritual of laying *tefillin* is strongly connected to notions of commitment and loyalty. Oded, for example, said that since his bar mitzvah, he has not skipped one day. "I laid *tefillin* when I was in the army, in a cubicle in a tank, and I had a little corner in my cubicle where I kept my *tefillin*," he said. "I had a bad car accident when I spent a week in the hospital, and the first thing I asked my father to bring me was my *tefillin*. I've been to Uganda, Iceland, Mexico, India; everywhere the *tefillin* was with me." There is pride in this perfect commitment—it is international, timeless, and unequivocal. For men like Oded, regardless of the physical challenges, *tefillin* is an absolute, a physical routine that challenges and demands of the man to forgo all else in order to do what he must do. "Not skipping a day" is a source of pride at the core of Oded's identity. As he tells his bar mitzvah students, "This is a reminder of who you are and what you are."

For several men, wearing *tefillin* has a spiritual component as well as a sociological-identity component. For Ilan, one of a handful of interviewees to talk about God, *tefillin* is "about as close to a physical connection with God [as] I can get. So, for me that's kind of just—my moment of bonding with God in the morning." Moshe also said that putting on *tefillin* is "his time" in the morning for "connecting with God." For Ilan and Moshe, *tefillin* has a spiritual component strikingly absent from many other accounts. Netanel calls it "part of my personal relationship with God. It's part of an unwritten contract between us." Netanel quickly replaces the God language with the language of unfaltering commitment. "I am committed," he said. "You have to wear *tefillin* every day." Seen differently, perhaps the issues are connected. For Netanel, "commitment" is about commitment to God, which finds expression through an uncompromising practice of wearing *tefillin*. "Once in my life I ended up wearing *tefillin* at 5:30 PM because I was in battle all morning. In battle you don't wear *tefillin*. But there is no other circumstance [when I wouldn't lay *tefillin*]."

For some men, like Netanel, *tefillin* is a basic expression of commitment, expressed in the powerful metaphor of a contract with God. There is no backing out, there is no deterring, there is no "I don't feel like it," there is no flexibility or even skipping a day because you're at war. *Tefillin* is in some ways about

God, but more than that, it is an expression of absolute loyalty. The way men go to the army, the commitment to serve one's duty as a man, reinforces the way they put on *tefillin*. It's about men doing what they have to do on behalf of their people, their God. To be a good man, you have to be committed, unrelenting, reliable, and responsible. You fight the battle, you protect your country, and you wear *tefillin*. It's a very powerful image.

There may be a significant difference between Israeli and non-Israeli Orthodox masculinity, in that the former revolves to a large extent around serving in the army. In Israel, religious masculinity is compounded by elements of Israeli male culture, the Zionist narrative and war, and of course the army, where being a man is defined by emotional detachment, control, and physical strength.[14] In Hebrew, connotations of *"gever"* are related linguistically to *"l'hitgaber"* (to overcome, or get over), *"gvura"* (heroism or strength), and *"l'gvor"* (to overpower or conquer), all of which connect masculinity to war.[15] The army culture creates a lifelong theme that saturates Israeli masculinities with defining rituals and symbols for masculine identities.[16] The "sabra," the prototypical image of the heroic "new Jew," perhaps best mythologized by Oz Almog,[17] is by definition male. As Yael Ben-Zvi notes[18] in her critique of Almog's narrative, the "sexism that is so rooted in sabra culture" is embedded in masculinities that saturate Israeli society.[19] The connection between the culture of sabra, patriarchy, and war is so powerful that Israeli sociologist Edna Lomsky-Feder, as a woman researching Israeli male army cultures, calls herself a "stranger" in the culture she researched. "My situation as a woman interviewing soldiers," she poignantly reflects, is complicated by "the deep-seated perception found in Israeli society that war is male-owned territory in which women have no claim."[20] In other words, the primary axis of Israeli masculinity is through the patriarchy of war and army as all-male spheres where women are strangers. Modern Orthodox masculinity in Israel, therefore, as described by Netanel and Oded in which they put on their *tefillin* while they are in the tank, conflates these masculinities. The Orthodox male soldier is committed, active, physical, responsible, and dependable. The fate of the entire Jewish people rests on his shoulders, both in the synagogue and in battle.

Moreover, just as war is a physical performance in which emotion is shunned, *tefillin* is something you *do* more than something you *feel*. The many men who described aspects of commitment—wearing *tefillin* during war, during travel, and without ever skipping a day—did not necessarily describe how it *felt* to wear *tefillin*. Commitment is something you perform, not something you think about or feel too much. There were, however, exceptions. Moshe, a therapist by profession, who wears *tefillin* every day, talked about *tefillin* in terms of relationship. "Wearing *tefillin* is a private moment, the one time of day when I work on my relationship with my creator." Similarly, Larry, who, significantly, wears *tefillin* every few days but not every day—making him an anomaly among the men, who either wore *tefillin* every day or not at all—says, "I'm very thankful for everything I have, and when I put on my *tefillin*, that's when I express my thanks." Larry is quite unusual in this description in that he is emotional, and describes a vulnerability expressed through conversation with God. But there is an important difference between Larry and Moshe: Moshe wears *tefillin* unfailingly, giving *tefillin* the meaning of commitment and loyalty in addition to the meaning of emotional expression, whereas that unyielding commitment is not part of Larry's experience.

If the overwhelming majority of men who wear *tefillin* regularly frame the experience as a fundamental expression of Orthodoxy, then it is hardly surprising that the men who do not wear *tefillin* have trouble with their Orthodox identities. Yossi, whose two sons are in their thirties, initially did not want to discuss *tefillin*, because, as he eventually explained, he stopped the practice as his sons became adults. "When the children were growing up, I would put on *tefillin* every day," he said. "But the minute they finished school, the children weren't putting on *tefillin*." Watching his sons abandon the practice made him question his own commitment. If the boys were not committed, why should he continue to be? "I said, you know, I put it on every day, and I taught them that they should do it, and then none of them are doing it, and I kind of started letting it go." Without the element of absolute commitment, the practice lost meaning for him—and he discovered that it had been burdensome. "I'd done it all these years because I wanted them to follow in my footsteps and keep the tradition, and there they weren't doing it. So I kind of loosened up on that too. Maybe that was becoming a burden." For Yossi, *tefillin* is clearly a central part of the transmission of Orthodox masculinity, and once he realized that he had "failed" to socialize his sons, he stopped feeling obligated himself. The entire purpose was in that socialization.

Yossi's story actually begins a generation earlier, with his grandfather, an immigrant to the United States from Europe in the early part of the twentieth century, who was stubborn and strong-willed and didn't work on Shabbat. He gave Yossi his *tefillin*, and they became a heritage laden with emotional baggage and pressure around the process of formulating a Jewish-American identity, one that marks the difference between retaining the Jewish heritage versus abandoning it—or staying inside versus being outside. His grandfather had been socialized into Jewish masculinity through *tefillin*, and he took *tefillin* on as the socializing tool for his sons.

This connection between *tefillin* and Orthodox masculinity is so powerful for Yossi that as soon as he stopped wearing *tefillin*, he felt he had to stop calling himself Orthodox. Because the transmission of *tefillin* is equivalent to the transmission of Orthodoxy, and he quit the practice, he disqualifies himself entirely from Orthodox masculinity. Significantly, this Orthodoxy is an absolute definer with no room for nuances, flexibility, or partials. Even though he is in the Orthodox community and maintains other aspects of "membership," he feels he cannot call himself Orthodox because his private practice is not perfect. Moreover, he will not accept partials or modifications such as "Orthodox lite" because of the absolutism or essentialism of Orthodoxy. Orthodoxy either is or isn't—and to him, it hinges on *tefillin*. There is an interesting interplay here between the private and the public, almost a tension between these two issues. He may publicly "look" Orthodox by going to an Orthodox synagogue on Shabbat, but there is a private performance of *tefillin* that is also important to the definition.

Yossi's story revealed a striking element of his upbringing: *shame*. He did not want to talk about *tefillin* because "people don't talk about it. People won't talk about things that they feel they should be doing, or they don't want other people to know that they are not doing it," he explained. "It's shaming." For some Orthodox men, then, there is a penetrating man-on-man gaze that digs into the private sphere and builds obedience through shame. "Somebody who says he doesn't like talking about *tefillin* seems to me that he feels he has something to hide," Harold said. "I, for example, do put on *tefillin* every day, and I have no problem talking about it." The subtext here, that a man who does not wear *tefillin* "has something to hide," is striking, as if men are indeed watching one another, and as if a person's private practice, if not done like everyone else's, would be a source of shame.

After my conversation with Yossi, I found myself hesitant to ask interviewees the question "Do you wear *tefillin*?" I certainly did not want to be in a position of causing shame, though at the same time I wanted to know how they approached this key issue. I adopted a policy, perhaps like a defense attorney, to discuss *tefillin* only if the interviewee brought it up first. Overall, in the interview process, four men told me distinctly that they do not wear *tefillin*, and another twenty-one men told me that they do, and the rest did not mention it.

The descriptions that emerged from men who do not wear *tefillin* are telling. Tom described the self-discipline of daily prayer as "challenging," even though he has been Orthodox for nearly twenty years. Paradoxically, he considers praying every day the centerpiece of religiousness, yet he personally finds it a "struggle." So while Tom chooses not to pray daily, he hopes that others in the congregation are "better" than he. He has no outlet for exploring his struggle, and his struggle is by its very existence illegitimate in his own eyes. He looks at himself as if the other men in the synagogue are looking at him, a glaring man-on-man version of the judging gaze. Absolute commitment to practice that defines Orthodox masculinity leaves no room for debate, ambivalence, emotion, or personal struggle.

The centrality of *tefillin* in forming Orthodox male identity may come as a surprise—after all, when the rest of the world thinks about the Orthodox man, a different visual symbol is usually first to come up: the *kippa*. I would say that in common parlance, certainly in Hebrew but arguably in English as well, there is no single word that means "Orthodox" as clearly as the word *kippa*—or its synonyms, yarmulke and skullcap. The *kippa* clearly signifies "religious," verbally and visually. The largest religious Internet portal in Israel is kipa.org.il; there is a popular blog called "Kippa Sruga" (knitted skullcap), with the tagline "The Blog of a Good Guy"; and most recently, a popular new television series in Israel about the lives of modern Orthodox singles is titled *Srugim*—literally, "the crocheted." One of the original banners of Zav Piyus, an organization dedicated to bridging ideological rifts in Israel, has a photo of two men seen from the back of their heads, one wearing a knitted skullcap and one bareheaded. A book by Shraga Fisherman looking at the phenomenon of youth abandoning Orthodoxy in Israel is titled *Noar Hakippot Hazerukot* (Youth of the Strewn Skullcaps), as if the act of tossing the skullcap is akin to abandoning religion. In these and so many other situations, the *kippa* is a symbol for an entire community.

Whether a *kippa* is a religious-spiritual symbol, an ideological one, a moral "good guy" one, or simply a sign of identification akin to wearing a university sweatshirt is a subject of great discussion within and without the Orthodox communities around the world. Urban legend has it that when Natan Sharansky arrived in Israel the first time following a decade of incarceration, he told reporters that he does not wear a *kippa* because in Israel it is a political, not a religious symbol. On the other end of the spectrum of Israeli culture, the transsexual Israeli pop singer Dana International, in her provocative music video "Love Boy," uses the *kippa* to comment on male sexuality. The video shows a string of men from all different walks of life (each with a different "costume," such as sailor, builder, or police officer) coming into her bedroom to "serve" her—and the last one to appear at her door is a young metro-sexual wearing a tilted, knitted skullcap, as if to say the *kippa* is just another costume, another symbol of belonging to a niche in Israeli society. But beneath the costumes, all men are the same. It seems that the *kippa* is perhaps less about spirituality and religiousness and more about social identification—though what that identification is remains to be unraveled.

The symbolic significance of the *kippa* contains layers of identity and multiple meanings. For some, Orthodoxy equals *kippa*, period. Reuven, for example, describing his experience as the only religious person in his school, said, "I was the only *kippa*." Similarly, when Amitai described what it means to be a religious man, he said, "first and foremost, that he goes with a *kippa*." Tom alluded to his experience becoming Orthodox in straightforward terms of "since I put my *kippa* on." Danny always wears a *kippa* because it is "just what you do. It wasn't like a decision to choose it; it was just like putting on shoes in the morning." For Orthodox men, the *kippa* is almost a bodily fact, like getting dressed. As Koby says, "It is part of my identity. It's who I am. I don't go without a *kippa*. Just because [*kacha*]." For some men, the *kippa* is the sine qua non of their identities.

It is worth pointing out that in all of these descriptions that imply "religious means *kippa*" (as in the title of Fisherman's book), there was no attention to the gender component—that is, only *men* are wearing the *kippa*, not women. This seems to be true for informants as well as for the broader Orthodox community. For example, Fisherman interviews only men for his study on "Orthodox youth," Zav Piyus presents only men in its title imagery, and Reuven only looks at the men with a *kippa* to see if the people in his school are religious. (That there may be religious *girls* in his school was not part of the equation because he couldn't tell anything from their heads about their identity.) In fact, religious couples are often commonly referred to a "*kippa sruga* couple." Women are completely swallowed up in this male definition of Orthodoxy, but the usage is so widespread that nobody seems to notice.

Unlike the *tallit* and *tefillin*, the *kippa* is something that many men wear all day long, so it carries a more consistent and external message. Many men described wearing a *kippa* as the most immediate marker of Orthodox identification. "Society defines me as a religious man because I go with a *kippa*. It's like a tag on me," Haggai said. "I am marked as a religious man."

Outside of Israel, the *kippa* has the added external significance of separating

Orthodox men from general society—for better and for worse. Efraim described a friend whom he called "bona fide Orthodox—he grew up Orthodox, he went to day school, he always kept Shabbat, and he was really straight Orthodox," but he did not wear a *kippa* in college. "He said it made him feel uncomfortable being separate from other people and having people pointing it out," Efraim explained. "So he had his *kippa* with him, he would put it on when he ate and when he davened, and then when he said *birkat hamazon* ["Grace after Meals"], and then he would take it off. When he left the Hillel [Jewish community house on campus] he took it off." *Kippa*, then, is a marker of separation, and even "bona fide Orthodox" men do not always like that.

Efraim's description of the "bona fide Orthodox" friend who does not wear a *kippa* provides several compelling insights. In addition to the fundamental assumption that the *kippa* is a primary expectation of Orthodoxy, there is also an understanding here of a "pure" type of Orthodoxy, what he calls "bona fide." It makes one wonder what the opposite of "bona fide" would be—fake? partial? insincere? The underlying implication is that Orthodoxy is an essentialist, clear, and uninhibited form of identity. Efraim offers an enlightening description of what this "bona fide" Orthodoxy is: family life, day school, Shabbat, and something he vaguely calls "straight" Orthodox. The first two descriptions are social—family and schooling. That is, what makes one Orthodox to a certain extent is having these *credentials*. Brian, an Orthodox rabbi who grew up Conservative, echoed the "Orthodoxy as credentials" argument when he said, about his own struggles within Orthodoxy, "If you didn't grow up with that socialization, and I didn't go to B'nei Akiva and I didn't go to Camp Moshava and I didn't go to day school and I didn't go to Orthodox *yeshivot*—if you don't have that socialization, then it becomes much more raw and I think much more untenable for a lot of us." The difference between Efraim and his "Orthodox friend" ultimately comes down to socialization—who has been groomed to be "inside." Yet Efraim makes a very telling argument in his assumption that for someone who is "inside," wearing a *kippa* is automatic, and he was surprised to find this wasn't the case. What surprised Efraim is that even for a "bona fide," there can be external pressure, and perhaps even ambivalence about automatic identification as part of that group. "If I take off my *kippa*," Haggai said, "it will mess up some other aspects of life, such as belonging to a community, my children belonging to a religious school, etcetera." *Kippa* is the mark of a member.

Although several men echoed that same sentiment, other men took off their *kippa* in order to avoid that external identification. Interestingly, several men were actually *not* wearing a *kippa* during the interview. Larry, for example, one of the men who did not wear a *kippa*, described the tension between what he perceives as the external "tag" and internal religious expression—or between belonging to a group and seeking one's own spirituality. Growing up, he said, "I never walked around with a yarmulke except on Shabbat, where I put the *kippa* on before I went to *shul* and I'd keep it on with the suit and tie all day long and that'll be that. But after Shabbos, I'd take it off. It was more out of respect for everybody else, about respect for the community, than anything else." The *kippa*, he said, was more important to other people—especially his parents—than to him. "When I was twenty-two, my mom once said, 'Can't you wear a yarmulke?' I said, 'Why?' And she goes, 'Because I don't want the neighbors, you know.' And I looked at my mom and I said, 'You know what? I am who I am and I'm not wearing a *kippa*." For Larry, the act of not wearing a *kippa* enabled him to separate the personal, internal, religious component of Orthodoxy from the external, sociological, symbolic components. For him, Jewish identity is private and personal, and the *kippa* is not a necessary part of it—but this is a position that many Orthodox people, including his mother, find difficult. "What makes you Jewish is what's in the heart and what's in your head and how you treat other people," Larry said, "and that's really what it comes down to." The *kippa* is ultimately an external marker of religious identification, and Larry isn't interested.

On the flip side, for some men, taking off the *kippa* is an active, visible symbol of leaving Orthodoxy. Tom, for example, said that until fairly recently he did not wear a *kippa* because "I didn't feel I was Orthodox." Similarly, Noam, who while I was conducting this research went through significant life changes and ideological-religious changes, including getting divorced and leaving Orthodoxy, also described his shift as "since I took off the *kippa*." He said that the *kippa* "does not represent anything that I want to be part of. Not sociologically—I am not part of religious society, I don't feel part of it." Like Larry, he takes issue with the excessive emphasis on following social norms at the expense of internal beliefs and interpersonal behavior. Wearing a *kippa*, he said, "is supposed to be about taking upon oneself the yoke of heaven in the classic way of keeping commandments, but it doesn't really matter if a person does or doesn't." For Noam, the sociological marking of *kippa* represents everything that he wants to walk away from. He is rejecting the very definition of religiousness that is based on appearances, rather than a moral code. He is rejecting an entire system of what he calls "stuck" moral codes.

Leading the Prayers: Layning and *Hazzanut*

In the 2006 film *Keeping Up with the Steins*, about an American bar mitzvah, the opening scene shows the young boy watching a coming-of-age ritual in a Native American tribe, in which the tribe teaches him an elaborate ritual involving killing game. The film continues to weave a narrative around anxieties of the Jewish coming-of-age ritual (i.e., the bar mitzvah) and culminates with the boy's success in the Jewish version of the hunt: mastering the cantillations.

There is no singular moment in the life of a young man that does more to initiate him into the mores of Orthodox society than the first time he goes up to the Torah. Although wearing a *kippa* or *tefillin* provides a boy/man with the knowledge that he is Orthodox, there is enormous pressure not just to be seen as a passive member of the society, but to acquire the skills and knowledge to lead synagogue services. In this world, the man who leads services is an iconic man.

The sounds of Torah chanting, the *trop*, are unlike any other sounds, a beautiful, sui generis cultural heritage. Mastering this musical heritage requires careful learning, precision, and skill. In the movie, the star actually masters the *trop* of the *haftarah*, the weekly portion of Prophets, rather than the *parsha*, the weekly Torah portion. *Haftarah trop* is a different tune from Torah *trop* and is significantly easier—the *haftarah* portion is a fraction of the length of the Torah portion, and the reader has the notes and punctuation in front of him. The Torah portion, on the other hand, is read with no vowels, punctuation, or notes, and there are seven sections each Shabbat, sometimes eight. Mastering Torah *trop*, I suppose, is akin to learning to kill the deer instead of the rabbit.

Layning—or more precisely, *correct* layning—is one of the central characteristics of Orthodox masculinity. It is arguably the experience in which male-to-male gazing and measuring takes place most rigorously, a performance submerged in angst and anxiety—both of the performer and the observers. Many men described their experiences of being in the synagogue pews as another man performed less than correctly. Efraim described incorrect layning as "very distracting" and "grating." Gary added, "If you are going to take on responsibility, you should prepare and pronounce it right." Layning, therefore, is a performance of masculinity that combines elements of communal responsibility, precision, and a man-on-man gaze. "If they haven't taken the time to learn the thing properly, it's dissing the whole congregation," Efraim said. In fact, this insistence on precision in layning, combined with the unabashed willingness to openly and publicly correct one another, is possibly one of the most distinctive features of Orthodox culture.

Men recalled being inducted into this precise, meticulous, perfectionist layning from a young age. Isaac described being "terrified" at his bar mitzvah. "All these old men stood around the podium waiting to pounce on me, waiting for me to make a mistake," he said. "It was just terrifying." He has not layned since his bar mitzvah. Moreover, the culture of pouncing on the flawed layner is a classic initiation into masculinity—the "suck it up" and "get it right, boy" culture as it is translated in the Orthodox synagogue. "When you're corrected," Moshe said, "when they pounce on you for saying a word or even a syllable incorrectly, you're supposed to get used to it. It's very hurtful. Like, you're in the middle of reading and everyone jumps on you." According to Moshe, the expectation of precision combined with the loud, public criticism, socializes men into emotional repression. "The message to the bar mitzvah boy is—don't get upset. Don't feel it, even. So from this you learn not to feel things too much."

The common practice of publicly correcting layners seems to have an element of "sport" to it. The sport of "barking" at the layner when he makes mistakes, according to Moshe, is "connected to the issue of masculinity and femininity in synagogue, because the known masculine way is to bark. That's what's accepted. Every boy learns that because it's part of his socialization into synagogue. The girl is not familiar with it, because she doesn't encounter it." Being barked at, and sucking it up, fits in with all the other socializations into masculinity that the Orthodox boy experiences in his life. Still, while this is standard practice in Orthodoxy, and while men appear to be okay with it, some men wish it were different. "*Tefillah* itself should be a nurturing thing for the people that are doing it," Zeev explained, "as opposed to a spectator sport. [But] I don't know how you accomplish that."

What begins to emerge from this portrait is the role of meticulous, perfectionist performance in the life and identity of the Orthodox man. Orthodoxy is very outward-facing, measurable and visceral, often focused on actions that are definable and judged by others. If layning is in fact a quintessential element of Orthodox male socialization, the messages that it transmits are quite telling. There is an element of following the community, doing what you are told, not thinking too much and not feeling too much. The correction of layners combines aspects of masculinity such as perfectionism, performance, emotionlessness, and sporty competitiveness, and revolves around a verbal-cerebral performance. There is also a strong musical component to this performance. This musical mastery, however, is not one of spontaneous, passionate, improvised musical expression, but rather a strict system of precise ups and downs linked to mini-syllables. Emotion, when it comes, is in the form of contented or discontented judgment within the man-on-man gaze. If the Native American hunt inducts men into a skilled hunt for food, Orthodox culture inducts men into a skilled search for correct *trop*.

It is hardly surprising, therefore, that some men emerge from this process with a profound, inescapable sense of inadequacy. Michael, Oren, Isaac, and Hagai all admitted that they do not layn because they do not feel up to the "standard." "If you don't know everything then you're a failure," Judah said. "There is this sense of, like, well, you're not living up, you're not there, and therefore you're inadequate in some way. That's how I feel." Like Kimmel's marketplace man who is fraught with inadequacy by comparing himself to the "real" men, here, too, Orthodox men are fraught with the inadequacy around layning and knowledge. Layning is the Orthodox induction into the emotionless, competitive performance that characterizes correct masculinity—marketplace man serving God. "Ironically," Larry reflected, "layning should really invoke emotion." Yet a competitive, emotionless performance of reading from the Torah seems to be a vital component of Orthodox masculinity, which fills some men with tensions and anxieties, and they do not necessarily have a language or framework to unravel that tension.

In addition to mastering layning, Orthodox men are expected to master the leading of the prayer services. The *hazzan*, or cantor, is in some ways the Orthodox man par excellence, representing the people before God, evoking expectations of "high standards." The language that men used to describe good *hazzanut*, however, reveals a very interesting distinction between layning and *hazzanut*: unlike layning, *hazzanut* evokes emotions.

"I love *hazzanut*," Larry said. "I think it's great. It's opera. It's opera with prayers." This particular description is very Ashkenazi, based on German-style opera singing. Amitai agreed. "I love classic *hazzanut*, real *hazzanim*, like in the German synagogues of old. I love that, and if I had time and money, I would go hear them in concerts." Koby said, "It's a theater performance. I come from theater, and I love it, I love to perform." The *hazzanut* here is clearly about performance and theatrical and musical skills for the purpose of moving the congregation emotionally. Moreover, there are clear emotional expressions—"I love"—which are reserved almost exclusively for listening experiences in *shul*. A good *hazzan* makes the prayer experience pleasurable and provides men with an opportunity to explore dramatic turns of emotion—perhaps like really good theater, or perhaps like a deep spiritual experience.

Underlying this description is an important subtext of controlling the congregation's experiences. "It's also to try and bring the crowd and the situation to a new place, a new experience, a joint experience of the congregation," Koby continued. "Whether it's joy or sadness, or excitement, the goal is to bring about that communal experience. A good *hazzan* can do that." Perhaps more than anything else, then, the cultural dynamics around *hazzanut* are about *control*. As with layning, being a cantor implies expectations of performance, skill, and perfectionism that require control and mastery. These qualities imply an internal social hierarchy between those who are the masters, in control, and those who are not. Oren, for example, said he would not be a cantor because "I am not one of those who knows how to do it properly." *Hazzanut*, like layning, requires mastery, study, and learned skill, which distinguish the cans from the cannots.

As in layning, the expectation of mastery in *hazzanut* leaves some men in a class of "those who do not lead," a class which is subtly inferior. "I have never been a *hazzan*," Haggai said, almost apologetically. "I am not musical, and I never had the confidence to sing. I have never sung in any forum." While this may sound like an innocuous description, the implications are huge. "The issue of whether or not you're a *hazzan* is written on your forehead. If you're not a *hazzan* you're not a *hazzan*, and never will be, because they will never ask you to be," he said. "In the religious community, the culture does not let someone come and say, 'I want to be a *hazzan*,' especially if he hasn't learned and doesn't know." There is an absolute "written on your forehead" hierarchy between those who can lead and those who cannot. "If someone not musical would come and insist, I do not know what they would do," Koby said. "It doesn't happen." In other words, the hierarchies within the synagogue around who is and who is not *hazzan* are part of an unwritten code.

Unlike layning, *hazzanut* does not have a written set of notes to be read and learned by heart. However, there is a prevailing narrative in Orthodox synagogue life that there are "correct" and "incorrect" renderings of the liturgy, and *nusach* (literally, "version") has come to mean the quality of correctness or incorrectness of melodies for the prayers. "In the prayer of *Hallel*, for example," Gvir wrote in an e-mail to the entire congregation, "there is an obligatory *nusach* for the opening and closing blessings. . . . I am always willing to guide those who are interested in learning it." He added that in another synagogue, "there is a committee that decides that only certain songs and melodies can be sung, and it is forbidden to veer from them. Considering the importance of correct transmission of the tradition to the young generation, I would not want to hear melodies that are detached from the heritage." For Gvir, there is a very clear correct, inflexible, and immutable *nusach*, which must be perfectly transmitted to members of the community who wish to lead, as well as to the "next generation." He extends the notion of mastery and control beyond the cantor, to other potential cantors whom he generously offers to "guide." This is socialization and control in concentric circles. Gvir effectively expresses a vision of the *hazzan* as absolute master not only of the prayer services, but also of the entire community.

Robby was similarly adamant about the *nusach*. He has a vision of *hazzanut* that revolves around *nusach* and which is about controlling the emotional behaviors and reactions of the congregation. He wants precise control of the ups and downs of people's spirituality, which should be experienced uniformly, while Gvir's notion of *nusach* is received and further transmitted. In a way, Gvir remains controlled by the men who socialized him, not veering at all from what he received, while Robby takes some liberty to create his own ideas—but then expects those who come after him to follow his way. For both men, *nusach* is ultimately a fixed, authoritative, almost sacrosanct aspect of the service, and the control of *nusach* is paramount.

For some men, the impression of the *hazzan's* superiority relates not only to skill, knowledge, and leadership, but also to a supposedly superior moral code. For Nachum, there are strict hierarchies between *hazzan* and non-*hazzan* in the most absolute terms, so that not "just anyone" or "all sorts of people" can "know" how to lead. The *hazzan* must possess the proper combination of "musical style," an esoteric "theological sensitivity," and moral elitism that Nachum implies very few people have. Like in the elitist philosophies of Plato, Aristotle, and Maimonides, Nachum believes that there are different classes of men in the world and that only a few possess the intellectual and moral character that renders them suited to lead. Nachum's adaptation of these philosophies into synagogue life have created a class of cantors who are deemed superior and worthy not only for their vocal abilities but for the assumed accompanying moral superiority to the "masses." The elitism is thus clear and unequivocal, and Nachum, like Gvir, has readily established himself as the judge and jury in this hierarchical system, the one who determines membership in the closed inner circle.

Against this backdrop, it is clear why some men, like Haggai and Michael, feel inadequate leading the service. It's worth pointing out (even though this research is about men and not women) that if men are made to feel inadequate, one can only imagine how *women* feel. In the partnership *minyanim*, where women are new to leading services, and where layning and *hazzanut* are the main areas in which gender change is taking place, it is worth taking a moment to examine how men view women in these roles. In fact, some men expressed an even greater anxiety about women leading services incorrectly than men. Gvir expressed this in his desire to "teach the women of the congregation proper *nusach*," in order to ensure that they do not mess it up. His basic assumption is that women in general do it incorrectly, and he expresses a strong impulse to control the women's incorrect *nusach*. Robby says explicitly that "none of [the women in the community] have really got a *nusach*. They've kind of made up a *nusach* which has become the women's *nusach*. . . . But there is something about that *nusach* that I feel uncomfortable with, and that I don't like." He admitted that "there are a lot of women who are intimidated and scared about leading the prayers" but added, "we are not trying to just hand it out to anybody who wants."

This gender hierarchy built on correct *nusach* seemingly reflects more than just musical talent and includes some essential component of one's identity. "We have an ethos in the community which is to see the *shlichei tzibur* [cantors, literally "public messengers"] as leaders in the community," Robby said. "If you are taking on the responsibility of being a *shaliach tzibur*, then you have got to be a *shaliach* [messenger] of the *tzibur* [congregation]. As opposed to any visitor who comes, we don't allow nonmembers, for example, to be *shlichei tzibur* [leaders of the prayer service]. . . . We have got an ethos of seeing the *shlichei tzibur* as people who are taking responsibility of the prayers of the congregation on their shoulders, and that is part of the leadership of the community, and that's not something that you can give to people who are coming for the first time." For Robby, the hierarchy of *hazzanut* wrapped up in the language of perfectionism and *nusach* overlaps with gender to form hierarchies of masculinities. *Nusach* here is all about controlling societal hierarchies with a parallel gaze on incorrect men and incorrect (effectively all) women. Men who do not know *nusach* are pretty much in the same category as women—the non-knowers, the ones outside the circle of correct Orthodox masculinity, the ones who are out of the inner circle. Put differently, it's possible to interpret this to mean that a man who does not perform his *nusach* correctly is considered to be a bit like a woman.

Some men feed on these clear lines of masculinity. "If masculinity would dominate," Binyamin said, "the congregation would have a rule that someone who does not know the prayers may not go up to the podium. Someone would decide who is allowed and who is forbidden, and then the service would begin to show excellence." Exclusion of those lesser qualified is a welcome change. "Let's just say I've heard many voices, mostly women, who have said 'It's not so friendly to be a *shaliach tzibur* in Shira Hadasha," he added. "I said to myself, 'Thank God, it's about time, it's about time.'" The strict adherence to notions of masculinity through correct *nusach*, it seems, give some men a sense of security and certainty that all is right in the world.

It is worth noting, however, that the appearance of moral and intellectual superiority of the correct-*nusach hazzan* may be an illusion. "I always found that the *hazzanim* were not the most 'pious' people in my community," Larry said. "In fact, they were treated as sages even though everyone knew they were far from saints—gambling, alcoholism, and larger-than-life personalities were synonymous with the *hazzan*." Indeed, a pre–Rosh Hashana exposé in the Hebrew-language *Modi'in News* in 2008 explored the escapades of local high-paid cantors. The connection between *hazzanut* and moral superiority may in reality be suspect, but that does not alter the narrative that to be *hazzan* is to a certain extent to be the ultimate religious Jewish man.

Overall, laying and *hazzanut* are central components of Orthodox masculinity that include an entire array of expected behaviors, such as meticulous performance, perfectionism, emotionlessness, and verbal-cerebral spirituality. There is no room for spontaneous expression or for creative music. It is not hip-hop or even instrumental, and it is certainly not made up on the spot. It centers on a soloist, with an expectation that this cantor-soloist has properly received the correct *nusach* and developed the ability to transmit that *nusach* further. It is a special type of music, one carefully learned and practiced, without a single flaw in articulation. More than anything, the masculinity of laying and *hazzanut* is all about control and perfectionism—over self, over knowledge, and over congregation.

"People, come on time!"

One Shabbat morning as I lay in bed enjoying the one day during the week that the alarm clock does not go off, my then nine-year-old daughter came into the room and started nudging me. "Come on! Come on! We have to get to *shul*!" It was 6:30 AM. Services started at 8:45.

"Plenty of time," I mumbled, even accounting for the forty-minute walk ahead of us. I tried to roll over, but she was relentless. "We have to get there on time!" she insisted. "We have to be one of the first people there." Why was this so important to her? "I want to get the gold sticker!" she eventually explained. "I'll get a prize."

Apparently, the previous week, one of the men in the synagogue had announced a new plan for getting parents—both men and women, since this was, after all, a partnership synagogue—to arrive at synagogue on time. He appealed to the children: those who successfully brought their parents on time to synagogue would receive a gold sticker, and when a child accumulated ten stickers, he or she would get a prize. This, apparently, made my daughter's day.

The "please come on time" announcement had not only become commonplace at the Modi'in synagogue that I belonged to at the time, but was remarkably present in almost all the synagogues whose members I interviewed. It is quite astounding, in fact, how common, and how pressing, this line is. Men far and wide describe the tensions around getting men to synagogue on time, from the practice of offering candies to constant reprimands and meetings dedicated to the issue. This is clearly a major component of masculinity, one that blends with the pressure on meticulous performance, commitment, and perfectionism.

For men who have worked hard to live up to expectations of precision and punctuality, it can be very frustrating to be with men who are less exacting. For some, this was a real sticking point. "It is the responsibility of the community to form a *minyan* on time," Gary said. "You need people who are serious." Eitan is disappointed when synagogue is not "full of rows of people." When Nachum saw empty rows one Shabbat, "I said to [my wife] I'm packing up, I'm going to live in [the ultra-Orthodox neighborhood of] Geula." Nachum's idealizing of Geula, like his idealizing of yeshiva, is based on his need to be surrounded by correct Orthodox masculinity, even though he knows that "yeshiva is not the real world."

Punctuality is an ideal in the world of the Orthodox man. Three times a day a man is expected to pray in a quorum of ten, at prescribed times, with little flexibility. The morning prayers have to be recited by a certain time every day. The very precise hours in which these prayers are permitted are based on a fixed formula laid out two thousand years ago based on algebraic computations and the position of the sun. It's easier for men to adhere to the stringencies today because modern conveniences like the Internet, cell phones, and Blackberries make the correct prayer times easily accessible. A Hebrew Google search for "prayer times" yields eighty-seven thousand results. Clearly, praying on time is not a trivial thing.

This ideal of punctual, packed, and uninterrupted prayer can put tremendous strains on a man's life. The notion that a person can set aside this time three times a day at precise moments without any sidetracks or human needs is a reflection of the idealized, male "sterile individualism," the man who is unencumbered by life, whether child care, house duties, socializing, or sleep. The pressure on men to fill up the group, to make sure that the spaces are filled, that men are not left alone, and that there is no empty air, ensures that men are always conscious of their responsibility toward other men. Men have to be on time so that the male community can exist. Poor attendance calls into question the entire raison d'être of the community. This pressure, however, is a particular man-on-man pressure. Nachshon tellingly invoked images of both the father and the rabbi, male figures whose job it is to ensure that their sons show up when they are supposed to. Becoming a man means being educated into attendance; failure signifies an absence of spirituality and the ultimate failure of the father/rabbi as educator or socializer of young men into correct roles.

The question of punctuality and gender—that is, whether this is an Orthodox thing or an Orthodox *man* thing—begs exploration. For some men, lack of punctuality is even worse among women. The problem of women coming late, according to Eitan, for example, is "very, very apparent." Some men expect the "partnership" aspect of partnership *minyan* to mean that women should relieve them of some of the pressure. "It would be much easier if women just wouldn't come," Eitan says, admitting his willingness to abandon the entire partnership model. "This is something that really, really bothers me. Women have not internalized their commitment." In other words, women have not entered the man's box, with all its expectations. "Four o'clock in the afternoon comes, she should go pray *mincha* [afternoon prayers]," Yehiel concurs, transferring the man-on-man gaze to women. "What can you do? You have to pray *mincha*! Do *I* feel that obligation? She should also feel that obligation." To be an Orthodox man means to "feel that obligation" to come on time. Commitment is the penultimate expression of women becoming equals to men.

"It's not about how I feel"

One of the most startling moments in the interviews was when I asked Eitan how he felt when women lead the services. I asked this question to many interviewees, seeking to understand men's experience of bringing women into their space. For Eitan, however, the question was a non sequitur. "It's not in my nature to 'experience.' I don't experience emotions that way [*l'hitragesh*]," he explained.

Eitan's response confounded me. I did not know what it means to "not experience." In Hebrew, his follow-up answer added significance. The verb *l'hitragesh*—based on the root R-G-SH, which means "feeling"—is an almost generic word for all emotions. It can be used to express getting excited, being touched, becoming upset, anxiety, or just feeling emotional. It has the effect of flattening an entire array of emotional experiences. One cannot say precisely in Hebrew, "I'm excited." Listeners have to independently deduce whether the speaker is excited, angry, or anxious. While this says an enormous amount about Israeli society, it is even more telling that even this generic, unnuanced emotional expression was beyond Eitan's way of life. He rejected all of it. He called it "experience." He leaves the emotions, he told me, to his wife.

It took me some time to fully digest this answer, but when I did, it put the entire research into perspective. The perfect layning, the punctuality, the expectation of sterile individualism—all of this entails a rejection of the emotional experience of the world. Men go off and pray whether or not they feel like it; they keep on reading even when they feel like crying; they walk through the synagogue with a humiliating "non-layner" on their foreheads, and they just keep going. If they were to stop and examine the experience, it might prove just too painful.

So many men expressed Orthodoxy as a set of actions that are disconnected from emotional experiences. This emotionless practice was reflected in many different aspects of Orthodox masculinity. "I do not enjoy *tefillah*," Ehud said simply. Then with an afterthought, "Well, there was once a *minyan* I liked. . . . They start at 6 AM and finish at 6:30." Over and done with fast—that's the way to go for a man who doesn't like doing it. Shalom, for example, who wears *tefillin* every day, said that it is "a drag—I don't relish it. It's something that I do as something that—I feel it is important to do even though I don't feel like I get much out of it." One English-speaking respondent said that *shul* is usually "Wham, bam, thank you ma'am," creating a garish interplay of gender constructs. The man comes in, conquers or perhaps rapes, and politely leaves. The Hebrew version of this concept, with similar sexual overtones that possibly originated in the army culture, was "*Ba'im, gomrim, holchim*"—we come, we finish, we go.

Religious practice is something that men have to get through. It's like going to the dentist—it's painful, so do it fast and don't think too much. "I don't see anyone come out of those *minyanim* with any sort of spiritual uplift," Jonathan said. "It's grumbling and mumbling." Ehud said, "My dream is an egalitarian *minyan* that on Shabbat will not go more than an hour and a half. No singing, no dancing, nothing extra, just straight *tefillah*. That's what I like most, a Shabbat *tefillah* that does not go past the ninety-minute mark." Reuven said almost the same thing. "My father used to say to me, 'What? You pray for more than an hour and a half on Shabbat? Are you crazy? You have to move fast [*l'taktek*]. There are a lot of things to do!' My father would only pray in a synagogue that did not go over the ninety-minute mark." "Even the rabbi looks like he's going through the motions and he's bored," Jonathan added.

It is worth noting that there is a well-known cultural difference between Israel and Diaspora Orthodoxy in terms of length of Shabbat services, where Israeli *shuls* tend to start earlier and finish services faster. Nonetheless, the narratives of getting past the boredom of the experience significantly crossed boundaries and cultures.

Learning, Knowledge, and *Halakha*

The flip side of emotionless experience is an emphasis on the analytic or cerebral components of human existence. For most men, this cerebral component is referred to as "learning"—shorthand for learning Torah or learning Talmud—a language that is often immediately linked to seriousness and/or commitment. Learning is undoubtedly a central aspect of being socialized as an Orthodox man, what Larry calls "a rite of passage."

For many men in Modi'in, Eitan stood out as an example of a particularly learned man, one whose presence gave the synagogue weight and legitimacy in Orthodoxy. Moshe, for example, described Eitan as the "leader" of the synagogue because of his knowledge. Others called him the unofficial rabbi. Tom said he is glad that "men like Eitan, who have learned and have the knowledge," are in the synagogue. Eitan revels in these accolades. "I enjoy the thinking, being open to new ideas, true grappling with reality," he said. "I love the text."

It's fascinating how Eitan describes his love for learning, while elsewhere he "does not experience" and does not feel emotion. Gary, also considered a learned figure in his community, described a similar "love" for the text. The Orthodox man, it seems, is meant to reserve his emotional, sensual experiences for encounters with text. The uncompromising, unambiguous way in which Eitan models this masculinity perhaps explains his reverence among men. He succeeds in living out an ideal that many other men struggle with.

Men seek out intellectual stimulation not only out of love but also as an escape. "There is at least one big difference between the men's section and the women's section," Asher explained to me. "In the men's section, people are reading during the services. Women read much less. They come to pray." Men read "because the service is unsatisfying," he said, making learning during prayer both a reflection of cerebral masculinity and an expression of silent alienation from the service. This is men's way of saying, *I'm bored, and my only escape is intellectual.*

The intellectual escape in the synagogue finds a particularly intriguing expression in the *dvar Torah,* the sermon. Men look to the *dvar Torah* for stimulation and for relieving boredom, as well as for stretching the mind. "Learning Torah should be interesting and engaging, not a kitschy little chewed-up bite of Torah," Avi said. So men are seeking out intellectual stimulation in synagogue, but that's not always easy in a society that values conformity. "I particularly like the *divrei Torah* that are a little bit different to the—if you'll excuse the expression—'*b'mhera b'yameinu amen*' type,"[21] Jonathan said. "It always ends '*b'mhera b'yameinu amen.*'" Intellectual pursuit is a relief from the simple, cookie-cutter moralistic message that lacks independent thought and creativity. The Orthodox man seems to be seeking cerebral relief from his spiritual boredom.

Finding that intellectual freedom within the confines of Orthodoxy can be a tricky thing. Binyamin related a story about his twenty-one-year-old son who had given a *dvar Torah* in his yeshiva. "One of the older students went up to him and said, 'Where did you get those ideas from? What are your sources? What did you base on?' So my son said, 'Look, I said my opinion. It's my opinion.' They had a very difficult and bitter argument." There is a very real tension in Orthodoxy between seeming "learned" but not seeming too independent in thought—stimulating but not too creative, smart but not out of line.

Although masculinity that expects obedience and conformity without emotional exploration has elements in common with hegemonic masculinities in wider Western culture, this cerebral component, the centrality of intellectualism—as an expression of both conformity and escape—is particular to Jewish or Orthodox masculinity. According to Michael L. Satlow, rabbinic masculinity rests on two non-Jewish prerabbinic concepts of masculinity: that "self-mastery" is a prerequisite for a life of the mind, and that the life of the mind is a "characteristically masculine" activity.[22] Moreover, although there are deep historical roots to this masculinity, there are also particular expressions of identity formation that are unique to Orthodoxy in the modern era. Haym Soloveitchik describes the unique role of printed texts in the development of many of the patterns that characterize contemporary Orthodoxy.[23] Modern society has transformed a traditional religious society and culture into a subculture in which what was once an orally transmitted corpus of customs is now a set of ritualistic beliefs, objects, and practices that demand precision, meticulousness, and attention to minutiae.[24] This supercerebral Orthodox masculinity, therefore, is a particularly twentieth-century Jewish version of Western masculinity.

At the core of the entire process of intellectualizing the human experience is the mainstay of Orthodox identity: *halakha*, Jewish law. *Halakha*, a social system, a language, a code of laws, a compilation of two thousand years of cultural history, is a world unto itself, not easily defined yet ever-present in Orthodox life. *Halakha* gives rational description and definition to every element of the human condition. What is eating? *Halakha* will answer not with senses, smells, and tastes but with the systematic measuring of foods. Prayer and spirituality become the fixed recitation of words written by others. As one informant said, "I was very much into the [Yeshayahu] Leibowitz notion that says that *halakha* is like a computer. Meaning, you have a system of concepts, a system with functions, which says that you pour data into and it gives you output about what you have to do." *Halakha* is like a computer—rational, analytical, and clear, with no uncertainties. *Halakha* defines Orthodoxy, not only by providing a clear, computerized "rule book" to follow, but also by making the whole concept of following a rule book and not thinking the central feature of the Orthodox script.

This entire conversation about Orthodox identity could have begun here. Men often say that Orthodox means *halakha*. Certainly halakhic rhetoric also stands at the core of the public discourse about the partnership *minyanim*. But it's not the internal halakhic analysis that is of interest here—not the technicalities of *halakha*, the philosophy of *halakha*, the nature of *halakha*, or what *halakha* actually *says*—but rather what *halakha represents* within male identity. *Halakha* is a symbolic language that socializes men. It is volumes upon volumes of instructions for men's behavior, an invisible guiding hand as men live life. I am looking at *halakha* as a system of knowledge constructed by society, a discourse that constitutes a network of rules and events that form power hierarchies in society. For centuries *halakha* has formed an all-encompassing discursive framework for Jewish men, a language that offers men a formalized system with which to make sense out of the chaos that is human existence, and the objective here is to understand how *halakha* comprises men's identities.

The reason this is so interesting is that, as Satlow says, *halakha* is culturally *male*. Even though both Orthodox men and Orthodox women are supposed to lead their lives according to *halakha*, it is a system that addresses men, that is written by men, that sees men's lives as the primary focus and women's lives as incidental, and that functions to give men a sense of what it means to be a man. *Halakha* presumably tells people—but really men—what to do, and occasionally as an afterthought debates how these issues affect women. "A woman's voice is sinful," for example—for a *man*, obviously. "It is forbidden to touch a woman"— for a *man*. "One must pray three times a day in a *minyan*"—a *man*, that is. The often unspoken character of *halakha* is that it is language spoken between men, guiding men about every aspect of their lives, a social rule book for men, by men, and about men. Moreover, given the way Orthodox men live their lives, the *halakha* is not simply a technical rule book, but also a cultural guide. *Halakha* dictates while discounting individual emotional experience, and the Orthodox man acts. *Halakha* offers a rational, linear analysis that leads to the bottom line, and the men study and perform. *Halakha* is exemplified masculinity.

The men debated and analyzed the internal workings of *halakha* while setting forth their own individual though confined worldviews. "*Halakha* is very clear," Eitan said, describing how he was raised to understand Judaism. "*Halakha* comes and says, the Bible in front of you is the Bible, and if we want to change even one word, we have to base it on the fact that most of the books allow it." The idea of a clearly defined, absolute, and perhaps unbending *halakha* is a major feature of Orthodox male socialization. "There's a great quote by Abraham Lincoln: If you call a tail a leg, how many legs does a dog have?" Gad said, using a telling metaphor. "The answer's four, because calling a tail a leg doesn't make it a leg." In other words, *halakha* here has an absolute correctness and rightness to it, a black and white, either/or, a name that cannot be shifted or changed—and has nothing to do with human experience.

Halakha as a component of men's identities makes it hard for Orthodox men to legitimize emotional experiences. What a man feels is outside the permitted realm, simply irrelevant. When a man has a direct conflict between his emotions and his perception of *halakha*, there is no question that *halakha* is meant to come first. Doing what "feels" right is not part of Orthodox masculinity. Noam told a story about going to a rabbi for his opinion on a particular question. The rabbi replied, "'I am not giving opinions. I am giving *psak* [a halakhic ruling]." I told him I would be the one to decide," Noam reported. "He said, 'Unless you tell me you're definitely going to do it, I'm not going to answer you.'" *Halakha* is not an option, subject to feelings and whims. It is an instruction, demanding flawless, unambivalent commitment and performance. An Orthodox man does not think on his own, does not decide on his own, and does not legitimize feelings vis-à-vis *halakha*—only the rabbi, the only valid owner of halakhic knowledge, does that.

Halakha, therefore, has a huge impact on men's identities and creates a very moderate or conservative (small "c") personality—a man who deliberates at length, who doesn't move too fast, who sees a generation as a tiny unit of time, and who doesn't change easily. "*Halakha* is going to develop very slowly," Gad said. "Twenty or thirty years ago, how many [Orthodox] rabbis would have allowed women to say *kaddish*? And now there are a lot more who do it," he argued, asserting that a change that happens in thirty years is radical. "Twenty years ago, how many rabbis do you think were supporting women's prayer groups?" Here, commitment to *halakha* entails both an acceptance of the "slow change" narrative, as well as the authority of the rabbis who determine when change is "allowed." There is also a narrative of not being too "radical." *Halakha* is seen as creating a moderate persona and a moderate community, making *moderation* part of the box.

Significantly, the sociological practice that is *halakha* is about men deliberating about women. Within this framework, women are seen as less "halakhic" when they give expression to their emotions. Eitan described a "principled disagreement" with a woman named Miri who said that she is unmotivated to come to *shul* on time because "there are not more moving prayers." For Eitan, this is not halakhic and not Orthodox, but rather feminine and wrong. "Prayer is prayer, first and foremost," he argued. "What, you think everyone can decide for himself? Raise doubt? Give his own interpretations? *Halakha* does not establish that prayer is prayer only when it 'does it' for you. Commitment is commitment." Issues of commitment and *halakha* are locked into the masculine emotionlessness, punctuality, and restraint on individual freedom, desire, and thought. There is an entire dichotomy between male-female, emotion-intellect, action-inaction, commitment-apathy, community-individual, proper prayer–improper prayer. The Orthodox man does not think for himself, decide for himself, or act for himself, but rather demonstrates unwavering commitment by doing what the collective expects of him—like coming to synagogue, on time, consistently, whether he likes it or not.

Family Man

When Yohanan, a forty-two-year-old American man, was thinking about leaving his job, packing up his family, and moving to Israel, he was petrified. "I can't move until I have a job lined up," he told me. "How can I walk into *shul* and face everyone when I don't have a job?" As if to say, the first thing that happens to a man in the synagogue is that other men look at him and want to know what he does for a living. This version of Orthodox man can perhaps be construed as "marketplace man goes to *shul*."

Many men echoed this sentiment. When an Orthodox man walks into synagogue on Shabbat, he feels all eyes on him, not only wondering whether he put on *tefillin* that week or whether he went to a Talmud class that morning but also whether or not he has a secure job. Like marketplace man, Orthodox man has to be the provider, but he also has to walk into synagogue every week and face other men. Certainly any Western man without a job has his masculinity challenged, but most can stay out of the spotlight to escape this man-on-man gaze. Orthodox man, however, goes to synagogue, where the masculine competition, pressure, and gaze hit him in the face every week.

There is arguably no set of male conventions as widespread and as powerful as the expectation to get married, have children, and, most important, adequately provide for them, and Orthodox man is no exception. There is a prescribed life path set out for the Orthodox man, a set of conventions as rigidly directed as *halakha* itself. As Oded said rather succinctly, "The regular path means someone who finishes high school, say yeshiva, goes to yeshiva and army, goes to university, does a second degree, finishes it, goes to work in a respectable place and does not leave for at least five years, establishes a family, looks after his children, and what interests him first and foremost is his family and children and the house he is building in Modi'in and not some trip he's going to take to Greece or Turkey." It is the socialization of man into provider and stable, unchanging, dependable, responsible white-collar worker. The main additions here are yeshiva and army (the latter obviously unique to the Israeli man), implying that the Orthodox man is perhaps a more burdened version of marketplace man. The glaring class component of masculinity within Orthodoxy has not only ethnic implications but also implications about sexual orientation around being a straight, married man. More than one informant said that in "a typical *shul*, the men talk about soccer and the stock exchange." Noam added, "When we told our son that we were getting divorced, he said, 'Our family is not normal.'" Even today, with increasing divorce rates and the preponderance of mixed and blended families, "normal" as married remains a powerful socializing force for the Orthodox man. In other words, Orthodox masculinity contains strong elements of normative Western masculinity.

The Orthodox man that emerges from this research group is definitively bourgeois. "We are members of a bourgeois, materialistic society," Reuven said. "We are slaves to money. We all go out early in the morning to work. There is no time. . . . We're all slaves to time. You have to take care of the children, think about whether you put the food in the oven or did you forget a million things." The pressure to "provide" is vital to identity. The life of the Orthodox man is one of pressure, tension, and an absence of space for the self. Many men pointed to the moment in their lives when they had to "get serious" and "work to be able to provide."

The provider pressure is another element of socially prescribed behavior, almost like an economic mirror to *halakha*. The Orthodox man does what is expected of him. "When a man defines himself as religious nationalist," Asher says, "you already know about him a thousand things: what he believes in and what he does not believe in, what he does and what he does not do, what he thinks and what he does not think. And the tragedy is that it's true. There are too many times when this sectarianism determines his social, political, economic, religious, and bourgeois opinions." The bourgeois component of the Orthodox man "box" intertwines with all the other socially prescribed elements—political, religious, and behavioral conventions. "The economic bourgeois, the search for 'quality of life,'" Asher argues, is part of "an entire set of beliefs that are more or less accepted. It's an absolute acceptance of a truth. . . . What are the professions that yeshiva graduates go to? They will go to what's called the 'professions' that have a definite economic status." The bourgeois Orthodox man has a predetermined socioeconomic class, a choice of professions, a set of political opinions, and an overall status that derives from fulfilling societal expectations around Orthodox masculinities. There is also an implied status of "provider," of seeking out "quality of life," which means economic and social status "stability."

It is worth noting that this aspect of the Orthodox man box is unique to modern Orthodoxy and does not represent ultra-Orthodox, or *haredi*, men. Yochai Hakak, in his extensive study on ultra-Orthodox men,[25] analyzes the ways in which pressure *not* to work informs ultra–Orthodox masculinity. This particular difference, a striking issue considering the prevalence of the provider image within masculinity across cultures, raises important issues about what defines Orthodoxy and whether modern Orthodox and ultra-Orthodox can even be grouped in one social category. Given the extensive research on the role of the "breadwinner" image in masculinities across cultures, countries, and classes, however, I submit that ultra-Orthodox masculinity is an exceptional case that demands its own research.[26] Moreover, there are indications, in Hakak's research and elsewhere,[27] that ultra-Orthodox masculinity is currently in the midst of a transition vis-à-vis breadwinning, so this whole topic may demand a new analysis in the near future.[28]

The breadwinning aspect of masculinity is inextricably linked to the image of the "family man," the strong, dependable, virile husband and father. One interviewee described an experience when he was an eighteen-year-old yeshiva student. "The rabbi, the head of the yeshiva, looked at the *beit midrash* [house of study] full of dozens of guys and said, in all earnestness, 'Just remember: *shiksas* [non-Jewish women, derogatorily] are for practice.'" Sure, the Orthodox man is dedicated to his family, but his sexuality—as long as it's hetero— is legitimate. Another example of this strange tension between monogamous commitment and sexual activity is the infamous "*tefillin* date," which Larry explained as follows: "You're going to go on a date, you bring your *tefillin*— okay, great, so you're not supposed to be sleeping with women before you're married, but we know it happens anyway, so bring your *tefillin* to put on . . . in the morning." Larry laughed as he described the rabbi's wink-wink approach to Orthodox men's sexuality. "If you're going to go on a date and you're going to sleep over, please bring your *tefillin*." Active heterosexuality—even being unmarried—fits more easily into Orthodox male expectations than not wearing *tefillin*. This story sets up a hierarchy of identity in which *tefillin* is the highest priority, then heterosexuality, and only then marriage. Only among Orthodox men could such a bizarre amalgam of masculinities as the "*tefillin* date" exist.

The expected though understated heterosexual virility of the Orthodox man took expression in indirect and sometimes surprising ways during the course of this research. When I asked to interview men about "masculinities," some men chuckled. One man said he had to think about it, because "It sounds so intimate," as if he assumed we were going to be talking about sex. After the interview that he eventually agreed to, he said, "That wasn't so bad at all," because it was not what he expected. Indeed, two other informants told me that when I mentioned research on "masculinity," they assumed I was going to ask them about sex. "You say masculinity, and we think of the locker room, of measuring up," one informant said, laughing. One informant stopped me as we reached the end of the interview and said, "When are we going to start talking about masculinity?" He, too, assumed that the interview would be about sex. For some Orthodox men, it seems, "masculinity" means most clearly heterosexual virility.

The Orthodox synagogue itself, with the curtain as a partition between the sexes, actually feeds into that sense of virility, or what Tom calls a "healthy libido." When a man commented that he gets "distracted" when he sees a woman during prayer, Tom became defensive about his own sexuality. "I think I have a healthy libido and I love looking at pretty women, but it's not to such an extent that it's hard for me to focus." The curtained partition, a reminder to men that they are meant to get aroused around women, is part of the pressure on men to live active heterosexual lives.

Revisiting the Box

Orthodox men are socialized into an identity that resembles the box in figure 2.2:

Committed	Mastery
Serious	Emotional detachment
Tefillin	
Kippa	Punctuality
Tallit	Learning
Public performance	Knowing
	Halakha
Layning	Cerebral
Hazzanut	Sporty
Standards	Provider
Perfectionism	Bourgeois
Control	Married/straight

FIGURE 2.2 The "be an Orthodox man" box

Aspects of this box resemble Kivel's box—for example, performance, straight, emotional detachment, and the ability to provide. Other aspects are unique to Orthodox men—most obviously *tallit* and *tefillin*, but perhaps less obviously, the emphasis on the intellectual. Other components borrow from gender, ethnicity, and class, such as the Germanic emphasis on punctuality and perfectionism. The Orthodox man, therefore, is a complex amalgam of cultural, ethnic, and economic forces and inputs, not all of which are unique to Orthodoxy. The processes by which men navigate these forces and inputs and the particular dynamics at work in keeping men inside are the subjects of the following chapter.

CHAPTER 3

On Hippies, Heretics, and Hafifniks
Keeping Orthodox Men inside the Box

〰 SOLOMON E. ASCH, a Polish-born social psychologist at Columbia University in the first half of the twentieth century, wanted to know what makes human beings conform to group behavior. He discovered that people are more likely to go with the group, even when the group is obviously wrong, rather than stand against the group and tell the obvious truth.[1] His experiments shocked people. We do not want to believe that people are such conformists that they are willing to forgo common sense in order to fit in. Apparently, however, this is part of the human condition. Asch's work led to decades of research into what makes people conform, and established categories and rationalizations that have been further analyzed and nuanced. The basic fact of human conformity has remained indisputable.

The fact that Orthodox men also have a "box" that they more or less adhere to should not come as a surprise. Everyone has a box. We all follow rules from a multitude of sources in our lives in order to fit in, because the alternative is frankly a lot less attractive. Actually, what makes people *not* conform can be more intriguing, but this chapter is about the social forces that Orthodox men confront that keep them conforming, or in the box. This chapter looks at two dynamics: male typecasts or caricatures of men "outside" the box, and social pressures particular to the Orthodox community.

Who Is outside the Box?

Hafifnik

If I had to choose one word that foils "Orthodox man" it would not be "secular" or even "Reform" but first and foremost *hafifnik*, a Hebrew slang word that lacks an easy English equivalent. It's something like a slacker, someone who isn't serious, who doesn't try too hard, who is a little lazy, perhaps hedonistic, and who jokes around and takes life just a little too calmly and selfishly. He's not aggressive, he's not ambitious, and he doesn't care much about anyone or anything. He is not the kind of guy to stand up and lead the charge, and ultimately he just cannot be relied on for much. In short, he's not really much of a man. And even though the word is a Hebrew/Israeli usage, the caricature reflects much of what Orthodox men around the world described as the personality that they most emphatically avoid and reject.

If Orthodox man is all about serious and meticulous public performance, clearly the polar opposite of this identity is a nonperformer, or someone who does not take himself seriously in doing Orthodoxy.[2] "A *hafifnik* is measured by what time he comes to *shul*," Haggai explained. "It's like someone is taking a stopwatch and measuring what time people come, making like a graph according to the time people walk into *shul*." There is a remarkable use of the sports metaphor here. As if in a race with a stopwatch, men are expected to complete the race of getting to synagogue, in competition with every other man in the congregation. Elements of precision combine with performance to create a culture of watching, measuring, and evaluating one another's religiousness. The *hafifnik* is not punctual, tight, precise, or meticulous in his ritual performance, and other men are watching him.

Although the word is not easily translated, the concept is remarkably cross-cultural. Brian, for example, complains about the lack of punctuality in his American *minyan*, something he says he has "seen across the board in partnership synagogues." He says that there are many "people who don't wash before they eat, and they don't necessarily *bentsch* [recite "Grace after Meals"], and I'm not sure how many of them are necessarily putting on *tefillin* every morning," and are thus outside of what he calls "normative Orthodox Judaism. . . . They would fall short." I think that "falling short" is an English-language version of *hafifnik*. It is all about measuring masculinity. When Brian says "people," he means "men"; he is watching and measuring men and their masculinity.

Men, in turn, internalize the gaze[3]—for better and for worse. Tom, in a difficult admission, said, "I am a *hafifnik*. I am not meticulous about every little thing." Some men sense being watched and labeled, and internalize the judgments. "I don't want people to say that just because we are an egalitarian *minyan* that we are *hafifnikim*," Moshe said, "but I can understand it." Like women who stare at the mirror and call themselves ugly, some men look at themselves through the eyes of others and say, "*hafifnik*."

To a certain extent, though, the *hafifnik* reflects values of flexibility and ambivalence. "It's not negative," Avi says. "It's a fact that people come here who are more open, who really need a different kind of framework because they are ambivalent. This is an integral part of being open. It means being open to all sorts of different things." This is a powerful statement about Orthodox masculinity: ambivalence and uncertainty are outside the box. Tom concurs. "I wouldn't call myself a *hafifnik*," he reflects. "I would say I am wrestling with my davening—a sort of *hafifnik*." Tom internalizes the gaze but remains unsure. "Who is a *hafifnik*?" Reuven challenges. "Nobody keeps all the commandments. . . . We are all striving to keep more. . . . How do you know? Nobody has the right to judge. Nobody." The *hafifnik* is feeling, wondering, and wrestling, all of which are not part of what it means to be an Orthodox man. The *hafifnik* is the antithesis of the Orthodox man because rather than meticulously, emotionlessly perform, he gives credence to his own ambivalence.

Reform

Another major fear among Orthodox men is being labeled "Reform." Orthodox men in Israel can frequently be heard defending themselves as "not Reform."[4] "When someone new walks into the synagogue," Oren said, "the question is, 'Wait a second, am I with the Reform? What's going on here?' You have to say to him, 'Look, it's Orthodox.'" Orthodox stands in a dichotomous tension with Reform, most notably over women's participation. As soon as a woman's voice is heard, the immediate reaction is to label "Reform." That reaction is followed by another quick reaction, which is that it's not "me." There is an aversion to Reform that forms a clear marker, like a red line drawn as a contour around the identities of Orthodox men. "I place a very clear line on the framework in which I live, which is an absolutely halakhic framework," Binyamin said unequivocally. "I do not see the Conservative horizon and certainly not the Reform horizon." "Reform is outside of the fence," Noam concurred. "It is worse than not kosher—it is absolute *treif*, like eating pig." Efraim added, "The term *Reformim* is used as a slur."

Some informants argued that the "*Reformim*" threat is more Israeli than American. "In Israel, people do not know the difference between Reform and Conservative," Shlomo said, maintaining that "not Orthodox" is all lumped together outside the box. Although the Reform-Orthodox delineation may be more stinging in Israel than elsewhere, the entire denominational discussion is arguably an American import. The fear of becoming Reform goes back to the nineteenth-century rhetorical battles that formed the underpinnings of Orthodoxy. Today, for Orthodox men, Reform and Conservative converge into one identity that is effectively "anything but Orthodox." That said, the particular location of non-Orthodox denominational identity within Orthodox culture and the difference between how these identities are constructed in Israel versus North America demand their own analyses and are the subject of a more-detailed discussion in a later chapter.

Secular/Nonreligious/*Hiloni*

Another threat around the box, perhaps the most intuitive one, is the threat of being labeled as nonreligious, secular, or, in Hebrew, "*hiloni.*" In American parlance, it is described as "OTD"—"off the *derekh*," or off the path. The dividing line between religious and nonreligious is possibly just as strong as the line between Orthodox and Reform, but maybe not. In Israel, *hiloni* has a certain legitimacy that Conservative and Reform do not have. Avi continues to say that it is possible to be *hiloni* and still feel part of the Orthodox community. "My wife has a niece like that," he said. "She doesn't keep mitzvoth, but she feels connected in many ways to the Orthodox community." Why "secular" is less threatening to the Orthodox man's identity than "Conservative" is a vital issue, one that will be explored later on.

Weird/"Hippy"

Growing up in Orthodox New York in the 1970s and 1980s, I have very specific memories of how "hippies" were regarded. The long hair, the unmatched clothes, the impertinence, the slow pace, the irreverence toward convention, and mostly the dwelling on the fringes of normalcy—all this came together into one image of "not us."

All these images returned to me the first time I heard an informant describe Shira Hadasha as not "hippyish," as opposed to other synagogues where he did not feel comfortable and walked out. "It's kind of a gut feeling," Judah said, trying to explain why he walked out of the other "hippyish" synagogue. "It is just something in my heart. . . . It just didn't seem right to me. . . . It felt a little weird and a little different." Similarly, Yehiel described his discomfort with what he called "new age," which is possibly related to *hafifnik*. It's about not being a powerful, ambitious, go-getter kind of man, the kind of man who moves and shakes, whom others can rely on to be steady, strong willed, and firm. Hippy implies that same wishy-washiness, those who take time to sing instead of getting the job done. I think it implies a nonserious, nondedicated, not-really-Orthodox, and not-really-a-man's-man type of man. Even worse—being a hippy means being weird. It's not just about slacking off. It's about a complete and utter failure to conform to the codes and conventions of Orthodox societal expectations, the straight and narrow.

Wimp

When I originally asked Tom for an interview, he replied, "I get it. You want to know if all the men at our *shul* are wimps." I said no, but he insisted. "I'm not a wimp. I lift weights and I play basketball. Really!" The fear of being labeled a "wimp" is clearly a powerful dynamic in the identities of Orthodox men.

Several years ago, I taught a class to a group of Orthodox women on Judges chapter four about Barak, the commander-in-chief in the army of Deborah the prophetess, who insists that he will not go to war against the Canaanite chief Sisera without Deborah. She tells him to go without her because "All of Israel will say that Sisera fell to a woman." Barak, unmoved, insisted that she lead the way. She led, he followed, and they won the war and brought peace to Israel for forty years, in an event that signaled arguably the only biblical record of an army of men being led by a woman. "Wimp!" one of the women in the class said. "Barak was weak!" "Woos," an Australian woman added. Poor Barak, I thought. Finally a man is willing to support a strong woman, and he is put down—by, of all people, *women.* So this wimp paranoia is real, and for good reason. Men are afraid that if they are not aggressive, decisive, alpha males, they will be categorized as "wimp" or weak, by both men and women.

I used the Judges text in some of my interviews to elicit responses from men about Barak's character. Tom responded, "You want to know if I think he's a wimp?" Gary said directly, "Barak is not a wimp" and then accused me of trying to manipulate him into showing that he is an antifeminist. Actually, I think I was stepping into a world that automatically perceives my question as, "You think that kind of guy is a wimp?"

Clearly "wimp" is more than just a man who does not lift weights. Being led by a woman, rejecting the position of first in command, and expressing uncertainty are all part of the caricature that is placed outside Orthodox masculinity.

Tom, who explored his own self-perception of "wimp," described this caricature at length:

> I am a sensitive guy, and the flip side of that is that I don't make much money. The
> stereotypical nonsensitive guy may be a little bit more successful at work, and
> successful in terms of money. . . . I am a good listener. I think I am compassionate,
> and that would be my definition of what a sensitive man is. But again the flip side is
> that I don't have as much drive, as much push. . . . Maybe that killer instinct would
> have benefited me more. . . . I always tried to avoid conflicts, I never felt comfort-
> able with conflict. I maybe wish that I was maybe a little bit more aggressive, a lit
> bit more assertive. And I was shy.

Tom has internalized the idea that a compassionate, nonaggressive, sensitive, nonambitious working-class man is by definition more of a "wimp." He
cannot see himself as both sensitive and manly. Moreover, he adds that he is
glad that other men in the synagogue are not like him, completing the internalized hierarchy according to which correct Orthodox masculinity requires non-
wimps, or men not like him.

A Hebrew slang variation on wimp is *smartut*, or rag, or perhaps a doormat.
The implication of these metaphors is weakness, frailty, and lack of personal
power. In a discussion about this research in one of my classes on qualitative
research methods, an Orthodox female student reacted very strongly to this
research.

> "Tell me," she said, "is it true about the men of Shira Hadasha?"
> "Is what true?" I asked in response.
> "You know," she said, hesitating, "that they're different from regular Orthodox
> men?"
> "What do you mean?" I said.
> "Look," she explained, "I went in there once, just to see, out of curiosity. The
> women's section is so loud. All you hear are the women. You can barely even hear
> the men. I mean, it was nice for me, but my husband would never be able to go
> there. It's not for a man like him. You have to be a certain kind of man to let the
> women be louder than you like that."
> "What kind of man?" I asked.
> "You know," she said, "a rag [*smartut*]."

Again there is this cruelty of women toward men who are not aggressive,
dominating alpha males. A man who is not power wielding is less of a man.

Wimp also relates to men's relationship to women, in that, for example, Barak was a wimp for being led by a woman. For Reuven, a man is a wimp if he allows himself to be pushed around, especially by women. "Most of the men in the synagogue are floor rags [*smartut*]. It means that they clean with him, they use him. . . . If you look in the Talmud, a man would spend his Fridays washing and cleaning himself, and studying Torah." Reuven's ideal is to be a man of leisure whose wife does all the cleaning and preparation for Shabbat, and he bemoans the fact that he does most of those chores himself. To be a rag is to be doing women's work and to be pushed around.

The wimpiness of men being led by a woman was frequently expressed in the context of the partnership synagogue. "On the men's side, there is a sense that, like the joke, 'I'm here for my wife,'" Binyamin said. "It's transferring responsibility. The women are strong and praying and doing the work, so we [the men] can sit and nap." A wimp, then, is a man who is weaker than a woman, who is led by women, and whose voice is softer than women's. That is, losing for women is wimpy.

Gay

The marginalization of gay men within Orthodoxy has recently entered the public discourse in full force. Some notable events on the subject include the publication of Stephen Greenberg's book about being a homosexual Orthodox rabbi; the production of the film *Trembling before God*; the screening of a documentary film in Israel interviewing Orthodox rabbis on homosexuality; a conference at Yeshiva University on homosexuality; the development of a gay character on the popular Israeli television drama about Orthodoxy, *Srugim*; and the publication of a letter signed by Orthodox leaders urging compassion and inclusion vis-à-vis homosexual members of the community. All of these events have brought to the fore the tense reality of being a gay man in Orthodox culture. "Young gay people seeking help from rabbis have been given an array of advice and reproof," Greenberg writes. "Some have been told to fast and roll in the snow, to recite certain psalms, or to eat figs. . . . Many, until recently, were encouraged to marry, with the promise that it would all work out."[5]

Several years ago, a Brooklyn yeshiva drew headlines when the school principal left after coming out of the closet. Adin, a graduate and later employee of the school who had a close relationship with the principal, was deeply affected by the entire incident and called it "very disheartening. The fact that he couldn't be comfortable with himself within the community, that he needed to leave and that the pressure that he internally felt to withdraw, it totally turned him off to the Jewish community. And he was a tremendous asset, and it's a terrible shame." The principal's sexual identity overshadowed all else, all his other achievements and accomplishments, and even his relationships with his students. Gay men are often not given *aliyot* in *shul*, and according to Adin, "if they know he's gay, then he's not [even] *allowed* in the *shul*. It's just that extreme homophobia."

Single

Just as "gay" stands outside the Orthodox man box that demands heterosexual marriage, so does bachelorhood. Single men and formerly single men described their sense of not having a place in the community, meaning not having a proper masculine identity. Single men are socially and sociologically outsiders. Several interviewees who are single decried their experiences of being ignored and unseen in their communities. "Couples flock together," Ilan said. "Orthodoxy does not have a place for single people," Adin added. The entire social network of Orthodox life is designed around heterosexual pairing up, and single men are simply odd ones out. With that, there is still a communal ambivalence toward single sexual activity. Adin described sexual activity among his single Orthodox friends that is both accepted de facto and hidden from public view so as not to offend religious conventions. Orthodoxy does not have a space for single men, especially not sexually active ones.

It is worth noting that this issue is probably harder on women than on men. Society is perhaps more focused on the woman's predicament than the man's. The man has more options and still has more freedom than women. Nevertheless, Orthodox singlehood is not without some painful moments of exclusion for men as well.

Keeping Men inside the Box

In Modi'in, there is a synagogue basketball league for men, and while announcements were regularly made about games, inviting community members to "cheer on our guys," no announcement was ever made about the formation of the team. Some men were even surprised when the first game was announced. "When did they decide who is on the team?" Tom asked. "I guess they didn't want me." Indeed, team members were handpicked. "Anyone who wasn't part of the inner circle of guys didn't get to play," agreed Larry, who despite being six feet, six inches, mostly sat on the bench before quitting the team. "There are certain guys who are allowed to play and there are certain guys who aren't. That's it."

The way the team is managed reflects an important aspect of Orthodox men's culture, in which collegiality and equality are set aside for the sake of elitism or excellence. The competitiveness and unspoken internal hierarchies, reinforced by a man-on-man gaze, leave men to navigate their own emotional experiences, sense of exclusion, and hurt. This basketball story sheds light on some of the most powerful forces at work within Orthodox male culture.

Hierarchies

Hierarchies are a regular fixture among Orthodox men, and the men who are on the "outs" in one respect or another know it. Some of these hierarchies have already been explored—who can lead services, who can layn, or who gives a better speech. There are also classic male hierarchies around more universally male measures such as who is better at sports or who has a better job. The "scale" metaphor seems to be deeply embedded, and these scales are not mere abstractions. They are the basis for networks and groups within the Orthodox world in which, as Noam said, "It's like Orwell's *Animal Farm.* All men are equal, but some men are more equal than others."

Many men described hierarchies, cliques, and snobbery among men in synagogue, like in an exclusive social club. "There is an internal hierarchy in the synagogue," Moshe, for example, told me. "There are veterans and newcomers, there are stricter and more lenient. . . . You can tell by who is dominant. There are people who are among the founders, so they like have more say. . . . Until fairly recently, I was still feeling like an outsider." Avi concurred. "When I first came, I had the feeling that people were very closed in, they would not open up. . . . But I think it's better than other *minyanim* where people really fight over their place. Here people are a little nicer." These descriptions can be superimposed on many other social clubs. "Religious Zionist people are like—they're born together, they grew up together, they do their bar mitzvah together, they go to the army together, they marry each other afterward, and they move to a place together," Zachary described. "They keep a very, very tight mesh around themselves and go like that in groups . . . in their own like cliques. Like high school. It's a little bizarre." The groupings in the synagogue seem to fulfill an almost identical purpose of creating social markers that enable men to know if they are correct or incorrect, inside or outside.

Perhaps the most extreme example of cliquishness was Reuven's story about his son's bar mitzvah in his previous synagogue, which Reuven "hated to death" because of elitism:

> When my son became bar mitzvah, he had long hair. He came to *shul* for the whole year before his bar mitzvah, on Friday night and Shabbat morning. He wore a *kippa*, but they looked at him strangely. I am sure that these boys are so sensitive that they fully understand people's looks. A place that invites them, they know invites them, and a place that doesn't invite them, they know doesn't. The Shabbat of the bar mitzvah, he read two *aliyot* and the *haftarah*. In the middle—and I was praying in that synagogue from the moment we came to Modi'in—one of the *gabbaim* came up to me about the *kiddush* we were making. "What *kashruth* supervision does your food have?" *Kiddush* is in half an hour, maybe fifteen minutes, but because I was not in the clique, nobody helped me do anything to prepare the *kiddush*.[6] Never mind. Anyway, that's just one story, but it's typical. Just like that. The intolerance, the inability to accept the other.

A boy who has long hair is assumed to be not religious and not keeping kosher—a hippy, perhaps. It did not matter that Reuven did all he thought he was meant to do in order to be a proper Orthodox man—showing up regularly and punctually, socializing his son into bar mitzvah, leading the service, making a *kiddush*. In the end, however, he was outside the clique and made to feel suspect, even at his son's bar mitzvah.

Groupthink

The descriptions of Orthodoxy are at times reminiscent of what George Orwell in *1984* called "groupthink." Men described different ways in which men are pressured to follow a party line in the way they think and act. The groupthink takes the form of how a *dvar Torah* is written (without nontraditional sources, and in some cases without offering one's own opinion) or of what is considered a legitimate political viewpoint (right wing in Israel), or of what professions men should enter (white collar, well paid). Sometimes the groupthink enters personal decisions as well, like an invisible "they" guiding what everyone "thinks" and does.

Many men describe "the framework" or "the camp" as the assumed boundary for decisions and behaviors. Even something as seemingly personal as choosing a school is subject to the pressure to stay "inside the group." But more than that, it's about acting and thinking the way "mainstream" Orthodoxy expects, whatever mainstream is. Steve calls it "narrow-mindedness"—people who feel they "have to bow down to the people who are more to the right," meaning ultra-Orthodox Jews, and "accommodate others." It's about accommodating the group. Efraim called it "the attitude"—pressure to follow Orthodox convention, not necessarily *halakha*, but more societal norms. It is about not causing waves, veering from norms, or upsetting the pack, a type of conformity based on thinking and behaving like everyone else.

Fear

Yitzhak, a religious Israeli man who lives in a settlement near Modi'in, whose son was kidnapped and murdered by Hamas terrorists, is an activist for Palestinian rights, an act that his coreligionists find unacceptable. When he walked into synagogue on the anniversary, or *yahrzheit*, of his son's death in order to say the customary mourner's *kaddish* for his son, the men of the synagogue walked out in order to ensure that he did not have a *minyan*, a proper ten-man quorum to say "*amen*." This sinister group act—publicly and physically declaring him a pariah for his leftist political views by depriving him of the ability to mourn his son in synagogue—could only be done in a setting of Orthodox men. "Imagine being the person who expresses a leftist opinion in an Orthodox synagogue," Yizhak's friend Noam said. "You will encounter verbal abuse. In some places they won't let you come in. The moment you act a little differently, you're removed from the community."

Although this story is extreme, it reflects the nonphysical forms of intimidation and ostracism that Orthodox men at times use. It is Jewish male power wielding in which men exert complete power over other men's lives and experiences—without having to actually raise a fist. Jerry, for example, was once ostracized by his community for carrying on Shabbat.[7] "The people I had known all my life didn't say 'Good Shabbos' to me when I would see them in the street," he recalled painfully. Ostracizing, a tool for effectively removing a person with independent ideas from the social group, is one of the most powerful instruments for keeping men in the box through intimidation. The message is that there is no deviation from Orthodox group norms.

When groupthink is followed by ostracism, the implications for men can be severe. In Australia, for example, Jonathan reported that the rabbi of a synagogue two blocks from Shira Hadasha "actually instructed his congregants that if they happened to be walking home along Balaclava Road, they should not walk on the footpath in front of Shira Hadasha. So, believe it or not, they would actually either cross the road, or much more dangerously and ominously, they would actually walk in the gutter so as to not walk past the *minyan*." In Chicago, there have been similar incidents of ostracism. One informant explained that because he studied for the rabbinate in an institution not considered "mainstream" enough, the local Orthodox rabbinic umbrella organization, the Rabbinical Council of America, will not accept him for membership. Although he shrugs it off, saying sardonically that "the only thing joining enables you to do is to be thrown out," there are other implications. "It means if there are conversion cases I want to do, do people accept those conversions?" He is worried about the ostracism less for himself and more for his congregants. Ostracism makes good fodder for jokes, but it is not only symbolic; it can have real implications for people's lives.

Making ideas absolute this way has an obvious power dynamic. The one doing the ostracizing or making determinations of right and wrong has the power—power to give and take status, power to set the agenda, power to make the rules on how Judaism is done. Sometimes it doesn't even take ostracism, only flexing some muscle, as when Noam asked to discuss the partition at the next synagogue meeting but Eitan rejected it, saying, "There are some things that we don't discuss." When forces of power preempt discussions, there is a control of ideas before they are even publicly aired. Moreover, the language of absolute authority, coupled with the divine implications of halakhic language, create social hierarchies that determine whose ideas are worthy of being heard and whose ideas are not, what Michael refers to as the social hierarchy of moral superiority. "It is power wielding in the name of God," Noam added. The boundaries of the box are therefore glued in place by absolutist language and social defiance spewed out in an often inflexible language of authority. This works because, as Zeev said, "people are afraid of what God is thinking."

To be an ideal Orthodox man means to be separated out from the rest of the world and to be guided entirely by the group. Since the group is following God's moral code, once a man is in, there is no reason to look elsewhere, or to look inward. As Noam summarized, to be an Orthodox man means "to have a straight path, and if you veer from it, you are not part of the group. It's the way, and the margins get narrower and narrower as you go."

Don't be a:	Committed	Mastery	Social pressures:
Hafifnik =>	Serious	Emotional detachment	<= *Hierarchies*
Falling Short =>	*Tefillin*		
Reform =>	*Kippa*	Punctuality	<= *Cliques*
Hiloni =>	*Tallit*	Learning	
Wimp =>	Public performance	Knowing	<= *Elitism*
Smartut =>	*Layning*	*Halakha*	<= *Groupthink*
Weird =>	*Hazzanut*	Cerebral	<= *Ostracism*
Hippy =>	Standards	Sporty	
Single =>	Perfectionism	Provider	<= *Fear*
Gay =>	Control	Bourgeois	
		Married/straight	

FIGURE 3.1 Quick view of the "be an Orthodox man" box, with pressures to keep men inside. Using Paul Kivel's analysis, the box begs the question: What emotions do men press deep inside in order to be able to remain in the box?

Conclusions

In trying to understand what it means to be an Orthodox man, I found a remarkably interwoven collection of narratives by men who are engaged in similar wrestlings of identity. I found men talking to each other from across continents, speaking the same language and grappling with many of the same issues. They are also in conversation with men outside their communities, with other "marketplace men," struggling to be themselves in a world full of expectations.

In many ways, however, they are in their own world. The emphasis on ritual performance around prayer is in some ways an extension of marketplace man, but in others it is distinct. The cultures of layning, learning, and *hazzanut*, combined with the language of *kippa, tefillin,* and *tallit,* form a unique and vivid cultural portrait of masculinity, one that revolves around meticulousness, punctuality, and performance, as well as an emotionless practice of spirituality. Some of the forces used to implement conformity, a type of cerebral, religious, nonviolent bullying, such as ostracism, however, are unique to Orthodoxy.

Although many of these components are inarguably male—such as layning, *kippa, tefillin,* and *tallit*—other components, such as family-centeredness, meticulousness, and absolute commitment, may arguably have a cross-gender application. What may be more similar between the genders is the impact of groupthink, the pressure to be like everyone else and follow the "herd." While this has different implications for men and women—with women being pressured more strongly into marriage and child care, for example—there are certain parallels. What follows after groupthink, however, the threat of ostracism, is most definitively male. Only a man can be threatened with being left out of a *minyan*.

What makes the Orthodox man box unique, therefore, is the interplay between marketplace man and Orthodox culture, which cements an extreme form of gender differences with no room for flexibility. Orthodox masculinity is distinct in the way that synagogue is the location for enforcing a man-on-man gaze, for the way male competition revolves around being the most learned, the best layner, or the most punctual, for the taboo of emotionality during the service (dancing, meditation, or unstructured musical expression), for the restrictions against independent halakhic thought, and for churning out bar mitzvah boys with the message of "You're a man—don't get upset—so the entire community is relying on you." Finally, the tactics for keeping the Orthodox man in line are uniquely Orthodox. The forces of social pressure through ostracizing and threats backed up by rabbis speaking on behalf of "God" create some very powerful socializing forces.

Part II ⁓ Changing Men, Changing Society

Masculinity is not something given to you, but
something you gain. And you gain it by winning
small battles with honor.

—NORMAN MAILER

CHAPTER 4

Orthodox Men Creating Partnership

How Men Challenge Masculinity by Joining a Partnership *Minyan*

~ IN THE WINTER of 2005, a group in Modi'in decided to create a new synagogue. Motivated by a seeming dearth of inspiring local synagogues in a city that was eight years young, moved by the innovation of Shira Hadasha, and intrigued by the variety of accumulated experiences among group members, these people set on a path to build a new, alternative place of worship. They held meetings, invited speakers, consulted texts, deliberated, and discussed. It was quite an exciting time, when people met like-minded neighbors whom they did not know existed, and when friendships were molded and formed, energized by the passions of collaboratively building something that one deeply believes in. It was the birth of a community that filled a hole in the lives and spirits of many religious Jews in Modi'in.

After nearly a year of meetings, group members narrowed down their decisions to two synagogue models: Yedidya and Shira Hadasha. Yedidya is an Orthodox synagogue community in Jerusalem established in 1980 that is dedicated to issues of social justice and equality. Before Shira Hadasha came along, Yedidya was considered the most pro-women Orthodox synagogue in Jerusalem and possibly in Israel, even radical, for practices such as having all-women's Torah reading services, having women presidents and board members, and having women give sermons and make announcements. Yedidya does not go so far as to have women lead the services or layn in front of men, although the idea that they will one day is not beyond possibility. For the Modi'in group, a Yedidya model would have been a mostly "normal" Orthodox synagogue that enabled women to create alternative rituals outside the main sanctuary. By contrast, the Shira Hadasha model was "radical," and would allow women to take leadership roles within the main service, as they do in Shira Hadasha.

For some, Yedidya went far enough. The rationale for going with the Yedidya model was mainly pragmatic and political; some people were afraid that a Shira Hadasha–style service would not attract enough members. By contrast, some people were excited about the Shira Hadasha model, were not all that concerned about whether numbers of attendees would swell, and were mostly unwilling to compromise on the issue of women's participation. And for some who had regularly attended Shira Hadasha, the full partnership model was completely doable and not radical at all. The group took a vote: Shira Hadasha won by one vote, and Darchei Noam was born.

Orthodox men are changing—slowly, in fits and starts, and with more than a few obstacles. They are standing at an intersection of religion and modernity, of past and present, of men and women, of individual and community. They are in this place and are navigating, pushing and pulling and redefining their identities, making "Orthodox man" their own.

We all do this. We all confront social expectations and demands on our identities and negotiate with them in different ways. So much of who we are is a product of our societal influences—family, friends, community, Hollywood culture, and more—but that is only half the story. For as much as we conform, we also resist and change, picking and choosing, internalizing and resisting, redefining and adjusting, submitting in some ways and subverting in others. This, here, is the interesting part of identity—those places where we grapple with the tension between what society tells us to do and what we choose for ourselves. We wrestle, we challenge, we rebel, and we ultimately construct our own identities. Who we are is effectively a great big jumbled array of forces, some from society and some from our own internal force of independence and resistance.

Sometimes change is purposeful, and sometimes it just happens, but what is certain is that our identities are formed through these moments of negotiation. They are the moments when we take what we were taught and then choose. Our identities are formed from a rather indiscriminate and largely unsystematic collection of those moments. We are all complex tangles of pressures and resistances, of processes in which we go through life figuring out one way or another who the "I" is within the expectation of the "we" that is our society. We set our boundaries as we try to adjust them. We want to be accepted by others, and also to feel that we are living freely. It is this tension between social construction and agency that gives us each a unique definition of who we are.

This is the stuff of identity. It is dynamic and vibrant. And for the men of this Modi'in synagogue, located at a volatile intersection of social processes, it is potent. These are men who are in the midst of a maelstrom in which Jewish masculinity is being redefined.

Changing Synagogues / Changing Men

Every man who makes a decision to join a partnership synagogue is by definition changing. Attending a service that has existed for less than a decade requires an act of abandoning previous ritualistic norms and actively stepping into something new, different, and in some ways unknown. Whatever his motivations, and whether his choices are active or passive, conscious or subconscious, the act of joining this *minyan* is an act of challenging the religious identity into which he was socialized. Moreover, he is changing his gender identity, because the partnership is most obviously challenging accepted gender scripts. Yet the public discussions of the partnership format focus on changing *women's* roles, not changing *men's* roles. The idea that men have to adjust their own gender script in order for women to change theirs is not part of the formal discourse on the subject. And yet that is precisely what is happening.

Interestingly, these unspoken adjustments that Orthodox men make in the partnership synagogue are taking place elsewhere in the Jewish community at large, with Orthodox men as the latest arrivals. Sylvia Barack Fishman, in a comprehensive study of men's and women's communal participation, found that as women in the liberal Jewish community become empowered, the men of the community seem to lose interest in their own Jewishness.[1] Steven Cohen and Arnold Eisen wrote that among the "moderately affiliated," women are taking the lead, sometimes to the exclusion of men.[2] In the Reform movement, increased women's roles have supposedly led to a decline in men's participation rates, what some are calling the "boy crisis."[3] "Jewish boys are on center stage now," wrote *Lilith* editor Susan Weidman Schneider. "They're the source of the latest demographic panic. . . . Who ever thought we'd be keeping boys and men interested in Jewish life?"[4] In fact, *Lilith* dedicated an entire issue to Jewish boys, with a cover blaring, "Boys are the new girls." "There has never been a better time to be a Jewish woman in America," lamented *Lilith* associate editor Melanie Weiss, "but to be a Jewish *man* in America, you can expect not much more than the same old, same old."[5] Actually, Weiss's point is not entirely true, because when women enter synagogue life, it's not the "same old, same old" for men, but more like "less and less" for men.

The idea that women's increased participation leads to decreased men's par-

ticipation is only understandable if we look at the connection between the synagogue and masculine gender identity. It is tempting to look at this issue in
terms of a zero-sum game, that there is limited social capital and power in communal life, and the more women take over power and leadership, the less there
is for men. But I think it's more than that. Men are not just losing out, they are
retreating. When women enter the perceived "men's space," men walk away.
This is what my friend was telling me when he said that he cannot go to a partnership *minyan* where women are doing what men are meant to be doing. As
soon as women start taking on these roles, men are at a loss about how to define
what it means to be a Jewish man. They are left confused, unsure, and no longer
interested. Put differently, if all that hard work of going to synagogue and practicing layning and being a *gabbai* and making a speech no longer gives them the
satisfaction of knowing "I am a man," then men are lacking a reason to put in
all that effort. It just doesn't seem to hold their interest anymore. It doesn't give
them anything.

If for so many generations men's *shul*-going was tied to masculinity, and
today, for many men, women's empowerment means men's disempowerment,
then the men who *are* going to partnership *minyanim* must be doing masculinity differently. They must have somehow stepped out of that Jewish masculinity
narrative. Men coming to the partnership *minyan* may not describe the process
precisely this way, but at some point in the decision to stand in a place where
women are doing what was always meant to be men's jobs, they have edited the
Jewish man script. They may not always have the language to describe it, and
they may not even be aware of what they are doing. In fact, when I described
this very idea to a 2009 conference at the Van Leer Institute—"Men in the partnership *minyan* are changing, making adjustments in their minds to accommodate women's participation" is how I put it—one of my copanelists, who
spoke on a different topic but happens to participate in a partnership *minyan*,
took the microphone, looked at me, and said, "Thank you. Now I understand
what I've been going through." There is little if any conversation about the adjustments men have to make in order to grapple with women's taking on roles
that once defined masculinity. But what is clear is that men who come to the
partnership synagogue, who have left "standard" Orthodoxy and entered this
space, are changing the way they do Jewish masculinity. They are challenging
the "be an Orthodox man" box.

For some men this process is conscious, while for others it is incidental;
some men can elegantly articulate the process, while others cannot. Yet every

man I interviewed had a narrative around "my previous *shul*" or "my previous community" or "the way I grew up." There was not a single man who did not have some story, some experience, which brought him to the place where he was coming to a partnership synagogue. Whether the transition was active or passive, conscious or subconscious, family-centered or individual, for every man, coming to a partnership *minyan* constituted an act of resistance vis-à-vis previous synagogue experiences.

There are three different paradigms of men changing through the partnership synagogue. One paradigm is about men joining partnership synagogues to change the way *halakha* is construed in their identities. The second paradigm is about joining the partnership synagogue in order to challenge notions of spirituality and emotion. The third paradigm is about joining the partnership synagogues to change the way men are socialized into relationships and community.

Paradigm 1: A Battle to Think for Himself

Halakha is the preferred discourse of Orthodox men. It is the discourse that commands Orthodox life, molds decision-making, and dictates thinking and behavior. *Halakha* is safe, structured, secure, and knowable. It is a vast system of rules, regulations, and routines that enables its adherents to stay busy in the details of daily existence—eating, dressing, talking, and of course praying—without necessarily thinking too much about why. Everything a man needs to know about what to do, when, and how is found in *halakha*.

The partnership *minyan* movement emerged from a halakhic conversation. Women may have talked about how they felt in *shul*, but until Mendel Shapiro wrote his halakhic treatise, nothing was going to happen. Changing gender roles in the synagogue was made socially possible only through intense and intricate readings and interpretations of ancient texts. It is a movement that is, at its core, built on verbiage and textual analysis.

Perhaps this is reflected in the large number of academics and PhDs in my research-sample population. The doctorate, especially in the social sciences, where all but three of the academics I interviewed specialize, reflects a creative though ultimately analytical approach to social issues. As Mendel Shapiro explained to me, "Those who have an academic Jewish background, even if they are Orthodox, have an appreciation for historical impact on *halakha*. They're capable of contextualizing *halakha* and understanding it in maybe certain forms that existed in one period and can be revived today." In other words, Jewish academics are exemplary thinkers. If they want to make a change, they will likely do it with the backing of textual analysis.

Actually, Mendel Shapiro made a second interesting point about Jewish Orthodox academics. "It's a group that also has a certain amount of anticlericalism," he said. That is, men who come to the partnership synagogue are often motivated by a desire to cerebrally reconstruct and redefine *halakha*. The "anticlericalism" is a reflection of the sense that an individual man can take ownership of the legal code and independently analyze and interpret it. Of course, this very process is exactly what raises the ire of the partnership synagogue's detractors. As one of the essays in the *Jerusalem Post* against the partnership *minyan*, titled "Egalitarian *minyanim*? Not authentic, not Orthodox," argued,

> The problem is that, for all it may be accomplishing, Shira Hadasha is not a halakhic congregation. . . . I make this claim not because of the fact that the Bar-Ashers and Shira Hadasha allow women's participation in many parts of the service traditionally off-limits to them. It may very well be that there are halakhically acceptable ways to do much of what they advocate. However, the process by which they arrived at these conclusions is not a legitimate halakhic process. . . .
>
> The relative weight assigned to a particular opinion is dependent on the scholar expressing it. Although there is no established procedure for determining exactly who has the power to render binding rulings, *halakha* does insist that each generation has certain leaders whose authority derives from their widespread acceptance. Particularly when attempting to break with established practice, the approval of recognized authorities is essential. . . .
>
> An environment in which everyone ultimately makes his [*sic*] own decisions and nobody has the power to say "no" may be democratic and tolerant. People may find it inclusive, welcoming and spiritually uplifting. But it is not halakhic.[6]

The partnership *minyan* is by definition an expression of resistance to *halakha* simply because of the way *halakha* has been previously constructed. This author describes *halakha* as an elitist, authoritarian, monolithic set of rules that is antithetical to values of democracy and tolerance. It is precisely this construction that the partnership *minyan*—with its many academic participants—is seeking to undo.

For many men, the decision to make a change in their synagogue practice indicates a resistance to the role of this monolithic *halakha* in their lives. "Orthodoxy sees religion as being very frozen in time. It's ahistorical," Michael mused. "There were cultural influences going on in the shaping of *halakha*, and it's important to recognize those things that are historical influence in the shaping of *halakha*. Not everything from the Talmud is pure." Michael, who was brought up in a very Orthodox community in Chicago, is unpacking the *halakha* that he was raised on. He is taking ownership of his identity in a process of cerebral analysis of community. "As I was maturing, [I realized] that the world was a lot larger and had a lot more to offer than the narrow world that I was educated in and that the community was sort of still keeping me in," he said. "So I think there was a large degree of, I wouldn't say rebellion, but a degree of dissatisfaction." Efraim also had trouble with Orthodoxy because of the way *halakha* is presented. "This is my struggle in Orthodoxy today, in general," he reflected. "On the one hand, I have respect for the halakhic system and I have respect for rules, as they have been handed down over the generations, the centuries, or whatever. On the other hand, some of them seem completely arbitrary and ridiculous, so I think they are pathetic. So I have very strong ambivalence about the whole Orthodox world and Orthodoxy and *halakha* and what have you." It seems that the way *halakha* is transmitted in many places, as frozen and fixed, invites resistance from certain men.

Many men have difficulty with how they are socialized into *halakha*, but sometimes it takes time—years or even decades—to unravel it all. For thirty-one-year-old Koby, the process of unpacking *halakha* has been going on since high school graduation and culminated in the partnership synagogue. After a brief and unsuccessful post–high school period learning in a yeshiva, where, he said, "I always felt like an outsider," he switched to what he said is called a "postmodern yeshiva . . . but I don't know what that means. All I know is, it's very different. Something about the yeshiva leads you to think in every direction and doesn't obligate you to think religiously. The questions and dialogue are completely open. There is more space to ask questions, to check things." Freethinking placed Koby as an "outsider" in the standard Orthodox world; his outsiderness was not about his practices or behavior, but all about his ideas.

His theological journey began with gender issues. "My mother does not cover her hair, and I came to realize that this was seen as not legitimate and not okay, problematic," he said. "Maybe my questions came from a place where I wanted to just say, 'This is legitimate, too.' Maybe I needed to protect that place. So I started to ask questions, all kinds of religious questions on religious identity and why and God and Torah and written law. Slowly things began to move, to change, to break apart and be rebuilt." Koby found himself struggling to legitimize freethinking in a world that creates strict barriers of right and wrong, in and out. He began his transition by asking questions about these definitions of Orthodoxy, religion, and the meaning of life. "It's not that I was a social outcast, but I had different opinions," he said. "I had a hard time with rabbis who educated us to just go and do what you're told . . . and you'll understand at the end. I came out against that. I don't accept that." Koby's problem in the yeshiva was theological and abstract. It wasn't that he was actually learning in a co-ed group, but he was discussing such a group's validity. It wasn't that he himself was a woman uncovering hair, but was debating its legitimacy. The shift that Koby describes is one in thinking, in which open discussion is encouraged. This was resistance because it was different from all the other Orthodox environments he had been to. He was struggling against a society that intended to mold him as a person who should not think independently and who must follow *halakha* blindly and unquestioningly, as interpreted by his teachers.

In rejecting the blind following, Koby was branded as an outsider—at least until he entered the new yeshiva with a different cultural setting:

> We all joked that it was a place for yeshiva refugees. We were all outsiders, and suddenly we had a place where others were grappling with the same questions. . . . And now, in the synagogue, it's very comfortable, totally different. You don't have to define yourself according to what you are not, but you can be what you are. Today I'm not an outsider anymore in that sense. I'm whole.

Perceptions of "outsider" are a function of the cultural setting that a person dwells in. For most of Koby's life in Orthodoxy, freethinking practice constructed him as outsider. Today, however, the synagogue fulfills a vital function in not making him an outsider for thinking differently. In other words, the synagogue has created a new cultural setting that reconstructs religion as a place where freethinking is acceptable, even welcome. It is perhaps a rebuilding of Orthodox intellectual culture.

Many men described feelings of being an "outsider" for the way they thought about *halakha*. Almost all the men I interviewed said, "I am not typical." For an Orthodox man to think for himself places him outside the norm. But if he comes to a place like Shira Hadasha, the man who thinks for himself is among peers, like-minded fellows who do not marginalize him but welcome his intellectual curiosity and creativity. Yehiel explained that he is involved in his synagogue because "to continue living in a world that does not take into account feminist insights is a *moral* injustice and a *halakhic* injustice [*avel musari v'avel hilkhati*]." Yehiel is battling for *halakha*, for the moral correctness of how *hala-*

kha is done, which is reflected in women's status. It is almost as if *halakha* is an entity of its own with a life of its own, like a wounded animal that needs care. Similarly, Eitan's motivation for being in the synagogue is about changing *halakha*, almost to the point of "healing" *halakha*. "I believe that *halakha* has to change," he said. "I think that this is good for *halakha*, or correct halakhically. What motivates me most here is the conception of *halakha* that I think it's correct that it be this way." For Eitan, *halakha* is almost alive, an entity that grapples with reality, that can be broken and fixed, that needs looking after. Eitan is on duty, on guard, looking after that which is very dear to him and is being distorted and harmed by the rest of Orthodox society. He is a man on a cerebral mission.

Other men are motivated by a desire to change the notion of absolute authority and *halakha* and to promote a more personal and personalized *halakha*. Michael decries "an overreliance on rabbinic authority and rabbinic opinion for almost every aspect of life, an emphasis on stringency when there need not be one, especially on finding minority opinions to establish stringent practices . . . and along with that comes a sense of moral superiority." Some men would like to form their own religious identities beyond the controlling gaze of rabbis, in what Mendel Shapiro calls "anticlericalism," a major challenge to Orthodox masculinity. "That's the way it is today," Noam said. "Rabbis want this absolute authority, to take away people's ability to make their own decisions, to think for themselves." "I have a great disregard for rabbis in general," Michael added. "They usurped greater authority than was intended for them, and the community has also allowed them to do that, and even in some ways sought for them to do it, and I have a high disregard for that." Some men would like to focus less on mindless, rote performance and more on religion as a source of meaning in life. "The way that Orthodoxy has now evolved," Michael said, "is detached from what religion is really supposed to do. What's it meant to do in your life? What kind of meaning is it meant to give in your life? What kind of outlook is it meant to provide you with toward the world?" Michael is challenging *halakha* as a restrictive code and working to reinvent it as a guide for meaningful life.

To some men, the partnership *minyan* offers an outlet for their anticlerical, independent-minded halakhic grapplings. Eitan finds himself "going through a change" vis-à-vis *halakha* since joining the partnership synagogue. "The dichotomy between those who follow *halakha* and those who don't was too absolute— either you keep *halakha* or you don't. The gray wasn't there. Today, I have more thoughts about that. . . . The spectrum is broader and less clear-cut." He finds himself thinking not just about *halakha* but also about humanity. "I wonder if *halakha* is more of a social *halakha* in which, whatever societal custom is, that becomes its halakhic design. It's hard to compare one *halakha* and the next. That's how I tend to think these days." So Eitan is moving from an analytical, cerebral conception of *halakha* to one that is more human and humane. Still, Eitan, while struggling, is not entirely certain about how far he is willing to take his resistance. His bottom line remains "commitment." "It's difficult for me," he admitted, "because in every society that has customs, it's important to have the commitment to what you call *halakha*, to what you define as halakhic commitment." Therefore, while the philosophical struggle in his mind may reflect a certain resistance to norms of Orthodox masculinity, he is still stuck in a strong male gaze.

So men are thinking and writing about *halakha*, and a real, palpable disillusionment and anger about *halakha* drive many men to be part of the partnership *minyan*. At the same time, the language of *halakha* is an omnipresent force, maintaining hierarchies of knowers and nonknowers, those committed and those not committed. And even among those fighting to change halakhic norms, the emotional, spiritual, and social aspects of life sometimes remain unchecked.

Paradigm 2: Bringing Prayer to Life

Men like Koby and Eitan, whose resistance to Orthodox masculinity revolves around cerebral processes, independent thought, and *halakha*, often see themselves as exceptional or atypical. After all, they are not blindly accepting the ideas that they were taught but formulating new ones. In fact, however, they are in many ways quintessentially Orthodox, not only because they are working as insiders within the system that they know in order to make change, but also because the process of challenging *halakha* is largely an intellectual, cerebral process. In that way, they are still entirely in the box, still using only the tools that have been given the most legitimacy for men, the tools of rhetorical analysis. They have not unpacked at all the social, emotional, or even spiritual components of Orthodox masculinity. They may have joined or even helped build a new synagogue, but they would like the synagogue to be just like every other Orthodox synagogue in every way except for women's participation. The men who want halakhic flexibility in an intellectual sphere still expect a prayer experience that is based on meticulous, perfectionist, punctual performance. They have not challenged the male persona. They are merely changing in their heads.

Other men, however, take issue specifically with the emotionlessness, the rigidity, the inflexibility, the perfunctory performance, the cold academicness, and the continued man-on-man gaze about perfection and exemplary performance. They are seeking out a synagogue practice that not only challenges women's roles, but also challenges legalistic, compartmentalized, emotionless religious practice.

The Orthodox synagogue service is full of words, all of which, except for the Torah and *haftarah* readings, are repeated almost precisely word for word each week, for years and decades, generations and centuries. That may be awe-inspiring, a startling testament to the power of tradition, or really boring. It is hardly surprising that some people have trouble finding God in the rote repetition—no matter how skillfully the *hazzan* sings the repetition of the *amidah*. Some men, the ones who are brave enough to break out of the cerebral, analytical mode, are seeking a form of spiritual expression that is absent from the typical Orthodox synagogue experience, and this is their motivation for being involved in the partnership synagogue.

Tom, for example, has trouble with all the verbiage. "I don't really connect to so much talking," he says, and adds that this may not reflect the way Judaism was practiced in Temple times. "Anyone who finds *shul* to be less than a spiritual experience should mourn the destruction of the Temple, because for whatever you want to say about the Temple, I bet it was a very sensuous experience, smells and movements and visceral, and I think that you felt something different." Tom is searching for an experience that will ignite not only his brain but also his physical senses—but he does not find that in Orthodoxy. "For me, going to *shul*, at the very best it is an intellectual kind of pursuit, not very much an emotional one. . . . It's not so fulfilling spiritually." Unlike prayer in perhaps some other religions, Orthodox prayer is not spontaneous, passionate, or particularly visceral but is a prefab recitation of a whole book of words. It is also not individualistic but group formatted.

It's not just the verbiage that some men find difficult, but also the overemphasis on minutiae. "I can't bear sitting in *shul* with loads of Pope Piuses running around, getting worried about whether you opened the ark with your left hand or your right hand," Danny said. Because of all this minutiae and meticulousness, Danny cannot "relate to God" in *shul* and does not like the prayer, although he continues to go. Danny takes his issues privately, internalizing the idea that this is the way prayer is and that the problem he has connecting to God is his own. Even though he and Tom are friends, and both struggle with prayer even in their partnership synagogue, it seems from their interviews that they may have never spoken about this issue of spirituality with each other. Each one thinks he is alone in his difficulty with the synagogue experience.

Other men find the service boring and uninspiring. Shalom, a new father, called it a "drag" and wondered how he would explain it to his child. Gary said, "It doesn't bother me" as long as he has a book to read. Ehud said he does not like prayer at all, but he always comes, on time, and expects others to do the same. The culture of rote performance that drenches Orthodox masculinity is thus particularly striking in the context of prayer, where the culture stands in opposition to deeper spiritual experience. "I cannot walk into a regular synagogue," Nathan says, referring to all Orthodox synagogues except the partnership model. "I don't connect to it. I felt it was an insult to my intelligence. I don't want to sound like a snob, but it seemed so primitive to me. And then in Shira Hadasha, there is so much content, so much spirituality, so much beauty. It's hard to explain in words." For Nathan, words and spirituality are diametrically opposed.

For some men, participation in a partnership synagogue is an expression of resistance to the lack of spirituality in Orthodoxy. Whether spirituality means connection, God, aesthetics, community, or emotional expression is not entirely clear, but what is clear is that spirituality is something beyond the cerebral, impacting a broader human persona. In these conversations, there is a rhetoric of spirituality that stands in contrast to cold, individualistic, and intellectual experience and is about some form of connection and emotion. Here, the perception of a lack of spirituality is about an overemphasis on intellect, verbiage, and rote, emotionless practice, and an absence of deeper meaning or connection.

Men are seeking different ways to inject their prayer experience with spirituality. The most dominant means is to bring music into the service. "In the *tefillah* [the prayer service]," Zvi said expressively, "the music is one of those means, those meditative means where you feel like it is one of the ways to uplift. There are certain times when the combination of *tefillah* and music is very, very uplifting." This is what Zvi is seeking: a group prayer experience that is uplifting, and when the music is right, he can get there. "There are some very soulful moments when you just feel that everyone is trying to reach some holiness through their davening. I find it very powerful."

For Aaron and his son Lior, the spiritual aspect of Shira Hadasha, especially as it is expressed in collective singing, forms the primary impetus for their participation there. "The davening is so moving," Aaron said, "so much genuine singing and spirituality." For many men, singing *is* spirituality. Aaron, for example, a fifty-one-year-old American academic father of five originally from New York whose job took him to Israel for two years, has become a Shira Hadasha regular because of the singing. When I interviewed him at his home, he and his family were finishing their fourth year in Jerusalem, struggling with high rent and an uncertain future but reluctant to leave the synagogue. His oldest son, about to enter the army, came into the kitchen during the interview, heard his father talking about Shira Hadasha, and decided to join the conversation. "The first time we went to Shira Hadasha," Aaron recalled, "it felt strange because we were used to a modern Orthodox *minyan* where women did not have a role, and it was just odd the first time. But after *shul* happened some more, we came back a second time, and after that we were hooked." Something about Shira Hadasha was unlike anything he had ever experienced. "I really liked the fact that men and women had equal roles. It made for a certain harmony, not only in the voices but also in the whole way that the congregation worked. It truly was more of a community than a men's club." For Aaron, spirituality comes from a "harmony" that is not just in terms of music but also in terms of a sense of social justice—communal partnership. So the gender issue was in fact a significant element of the experience of spirituality, although that was not his initial experience.

Lior's description is even more dramatic. The Shira Hadasha experience, he said, "shook my reality. The *shul* in America, it seemed like it was all about this routine that they had. The men would go to *shul*, women would also go, men would do all the services, some men would go for the Kiddush Club, and everyone would wear their suits and ties and you'd have a big *kiddush* afterward. This is what *shul* was in America. Coming here, it was a lot different. Here, there was a lot of singing. Here, everyone was getting into it." In other words, he was used to *shul* as a social routine, but Shira Hadasha opened up the possibility of *shul* as a spiritual experience. "I'd been to a few *shuls* here that are, in my opinion, bland compared to Shira Hadasha," he said. "It's just what it is—bland—and it's almost boring. And it has no life. But Shira Hadasha has something deeper going on besides just, 'Let's just do it.' Like going through the motions. So that's why I'm going there now. Originally, I went there with the family, but now I wouldn't go anywhere else." Lior's description of synagogue life—"boring," "bland," "no life," "going through motions," "routine," and "wearing suits and ties"—reflects a spiritless prayer experience. Shira Hadasha, by contrast, is the opposite of "no life." It is emotional, passion-filled, moving, and engaging. This is one of the loveliest definitions of spirituality I encountered: *life*.

Other men echoed Lior's sentiment, especially those from Shira Hadasha, where the founders went to great lengths to create a music-based spiritual prayer experience. "*Tefillah* in most places really sucks," Robby said bluntly. "People don't daven with the kind of spirit and the kind of atmosphere. I have been yearning since I was young to be in a community with a *tefillah* where it would really fly for me." Robby was involved with Shira Hadasha from the beginning and said he always expressed his desire to shape the aesthetic of *tefillah* differently. He recalls that at the end of the first meeting, he approached the leaders. "I said, 'I would like to be part of this but I am telling you now that if the *tefillah* isn't worth it, the quality of the *tefillah* isn't worth it, it's not up to it, then it won't stick. . . . I want this to be a very religious experience, I don't want to be some kind of a protest.'" To his surprise, the founders were supportive and "understood it . . . and I discovered that we were on the same page for this." For Robby, creating a *spiritual* protest was a higher priority than changing gender roles. He was against what he called "some kind of protest," that is, a new synagogue all about women's roles. In fact, at Shira Hadasha, spiritual resistance through music and singing takes priority over the "protest" of gender. The synagogue materials reflect that as well. The Shira Hadasha Web site says, "We are attempting to create a religious community that embraces our commitment to *halakha*, *tefillah* and feminism. . . . Within the context of our halakhic duty to daven, we strive to make *tefillah* a spiritual celebration that connects to and nurtures our religious lives as individuals and as a community." In other words, the priorities in the synagogue are first *halakha*, then prayer, and then feminism, and the idea of prayer as a "spiritual celebration" is a central tenet of the synagogue. Robby certainly reflects this approach, which says that the way in which this synagogue is changing the way Orthodoxy is constructed revolves around how spirituality is interpreted in prayer. Making the prayer "fly" was the main motive for Robby in creating Shira Hadasha, and without it, he said, "the community will fall apart anyway."

Actually, Robby is a bit unusual in his vision about the how the music creates spirituality:

> I find *tefillah* more moving and more effective religiously, that it brings me closer to communion with God, when there is a meaningful and serious song. And this is complicated. It's not just a lot of singing. You know lots of *hazzanim* sing, and the

wrong kind of singing and a singing that distracts you from the *tefillah*, rather than carrying the *tefillah*, is not what I'm talking about. Great synagogue choirs are not what I'm talking about. . . . The calm, but very, very musical, very lyrical, perhaps even there is something effeminate about it. There is something effeminate about my voice, that there is a sort of sweetness and a gentleness in the kind of singing that I'm talking about that has a religious meaning for me. It's a vehicle that I can use to travel in *tefillah*, and that was what I very much wanted to give to Shira Hadasha. . . . It means davening slowly, it means taking time over it, but not killing it, not dragging it out, letting it fly, letting it become an experience that you can get enveloped and lost in it, and genuinely feel that you are serving God, in the service, and that's what I mean by a meaningful *tefillah*. . . . I am trying to make it happen.

Robby offers an alluring drama replete with masculinity twists and games. He is not searching but rather "making happen" the "right" kind of singing experience in prayer. Group singing is expressive but calm, dramatic but understated. His description is almost poetic, describing the way a service can "fly" and people can "get lost" and that this is about a "communion with God"—one of only a handful of texts in the interviews that revolve around God. He is in the box but toying and playing and manipulating. He makes a startling gender reference that his own voice is "effeminate." This statement, while reflecting an essentialist notion of gender difference by suggesting that men are pounding while women are lyrical, nonetheless contains within it a subtle but clear element of gender resistance. Robby is creating an entire approach to spirituality in prayer that liberates him from having to sing "like a man" and enables him to express his "effeminate" side. That is, the search for spirituality in prayer is a way for Robby to reject the cerebral, pounding, and authoritarian type of prayer. He rejects typical *hazzanut*, he rejects the man at the center, he rejects the cold and distant, and he creates an emotion-packed, experiential, passionate, melodic group-singing experience.

Nevertheless, this is not a conscious rejection of masculinity. A conscious resistance would be one in which he was seeking out an emotional, lyrical, group experience, *without* claiming to be effeminate. Like Tom calling himself unmasculine for being sensitive, here Robby has internalized his own gentleness as less manly. Robby, like Tom, sustains the box while excluding men who are, in this case, soft voiced. Maybe they are doing their best by comfortably accepting themselves as "less" in a world that values "best," ambivalence and self-denigration in a society that expects all men to reign supreme. He seems to be saying that he likes Shira Hadasha because it allows him to freely be the "effeminate man" that he wants to be. Still, I couldn't help wishing that he would stop calling himself womanly and just let himself say, this is the way I like to sing and I'm still a man.

Although Shira Hadasha is in many ways unique in its sophisticated development of a particular musical experience—the community even produced a digital recording of Friday night services to spread its vision—the emphasis on creating a spiritual experience around music is characteristic of many partnership synagogues. The use of music as a tool of spiritual resistance to Orthodox masculinity predates the partnership synagogue and is a feature of many "breakaway" congregations, as well as a primary feature of the Jewish renewal movement of the 1960s and '70s that has its origins in Orthodox Judaism. In many renegade Orthodox settings, communal singing forms the backbone of resistance to mainstream Orthodoxy, and thus it is perhaps not surprising that many partnership synagogues adopt this practice as part of their mission. Men in many of the synagogues place the goal of spirituality through a group musical experience at the forefront of their attempts to challenge Orthodox masculinity. Jonathan said of Shira Hadasha in Melbourne, "I like being in a *minyan* listening to other people sing, closing my eyes, and just letting the music flow over me." Similarly, Nachshon said of the synagogue in Massachusetts, "The musical aspect of prayer is very important, and always has been" and is intended to make people spiritually "present" via a musical experience that has been "in a coma." Prayer, he said, is about "stretching yourself beyond yourself. It's to open yourself beyond; the ultimate beyond could be God. . . . but the 'other beyond' is first and foremost the other, it is who is transcendent to you. *Tefillah* is about those moments." It is a model of transcendence through music, about rejecting the standard "intolerable" synagogue with its cold individualism and creating an emotional movement through connection to God.

A central component of this spiritual experience for some men is less about the music per se and more about the communal experience of groupness. Aaron and Lior described what they loved about Shira Hadasha as not just the music, but more so the fact that men and women are both included as part of the singing. As Lior said, "People come for the spirituality, and they're coming because it's a total community." In contrast to the mainstream style of *hazzanut* in which one central singer performs as if in the opera, the spiritual music described here is one in which the entire congregation is active. Many men are drawn to group singing as an emotional experience that stands as an antithesis to the cold, individualistic prayer that constitutes the typical Orthodox experience. Moshe, for example, a thirty-seven-year-old musical professional who described himself as "very interested in the musical aspect of prayer," said that "singing together as a group has an effect of really bringing people together [*m'gabesh*]. I would even say that this singing is more communal, welcoming, uniting, than anything else that happens in the synagogue." I think Lior best described the connection between spirituality and social equality, what he calls "harmony," with its double entendre:

> The men and the women are both contributing, and it makes for a harmony and a
> synergy that goes beyond what could be achieved if you have only one side or the
> other running the service. . . . The *shul* that we used to daven in in Teaneck, it's a
> beautiful synagogue structurally, but really, the men are davening and the women
> are sitting behind the partition. The women are actually spectators of the men's
> service, and therefore they comport themselves accordingly, for the most part. It's
> basically a men's service, and it's missing something. Harmony is not something
> that's mellow. Harmony is beautiful. It adds . . . it's a whole different dimension. It's
> a breakthrough in musical tonality. And that's what you're getting—you're getting
> harmony. . . . Men come because they're seeking that spirituality, they're seeking
> that unity, they're seeking that wholeness. . . . [A non-egalitarian congregation
> is] just one-dimensional, and this is two- and three-dimensional. It's a different
> ballgame.

Here, the definition of spirituality is about harmony and balance that comes from full and equal participation from all members of the congregation. Spirituality means not just nice-sounding prayer but also "whole community," of repairing a social injustice in which some people are at the center and others are secondary. It's spirituality as a function of social justice. As Nachshon said, "The Ari"zal wanted to write on his tombstone that before a man walks into synagogue to pray, he has to take on himself, 'Love your neighbor as yourself.'"[7] Without social harmony, there is no spirituality.

I would like to point out that these different forms of resistance are really quite distinct. Many men who seek out spirituality take issue with the cerebral, and by contrast, many of the men for whom cerebral religion is paramount take issue with the spiritual, expressing a distinct disdain for what they consider to be overly music-oriented and self-indulgent religious practice. Netanel, for example, one of the men who most adamantly reject "all that singing," said, "I don't like the Carlebach-style praying,[8] where pauses in the verses go according to the Carlebach melodies rather than the meaning of the text. It drives me crazy. They are the wrong spaces for pauses. Maybe there are other interpretations, or maybe even some kind of kabbalistic meaning that Reb Shlomo wanted to introduce. But I think to co-opt the words for the sake of the tune the way he did it many times, it just doesn't speak to me. I understand that it speaks to other people, and of course the tunes themselves are wonderful. But I have a very hard time with it." In other words, for Netanel, the most important aspect of prayer is the meaning of the words, not the music. If the music creates pauses that contort the "correct" reading of the words, that's wrong prayer.

So many men are seeking a spiritual experience that is distinct from standard Orthodox masculinity, with its overly analytical recitative rote performance of prayer, and seek meaningful connection to God through a group-singing experience. For some, however, this kind of resistance is jarring. It runs completely counter to the cerebral comfort zone that Orthodox men want. So for some men, changing synagogue practice is welcome as long as it does not undermine the intellectual, word-centered ritual.

Paradigm 3: Transforming Social Relationships

Haggai, a forty-five-year-old former kibbutznik turned businessman and father of four, has an easy smile and warm laugh. A big, soft-spoken teddy bear, he loves to joke around, and unlike many Orthodox men, he hugs people, including women, with ease. He spends a lot of time with his children, who surround him in the synagogue, and he was too modest to tell me that he does most of the cooking, cleaning, housework, and child care—that I learned from his wife. In short, he is what Israelis would refer to as a *"hevreman"*—a friend, someone who loves being with people and deeply cares about other people's well-being.

Haggai has had a hard time finding a comfortable place in an Orthodox synagogue. Since moving to Modi'in, he floated between synagogues. "It was *my* issue," he said, not his wife's. *He* was the one searching for someplace "where it would be comfortable for me to pray," he said. He eventually settled on a local synagogue, but "I can't say that we connected to a community there, that we felt part." In fact, now that he's no longer there, he doesn't think that anyone there even noticed. "I don't think I'm missed by anyone there."

Meanwhile, on Simchat Torah, Haggai's wife and ten-year-old daughter attended Darchei Noam, where they "found a place that, in terms of the women and the children, was much better. They were very excited about it," he said. But

Haggai wasn't so easily convinced. It took him months before he agreed to come, but eventually he was hooked—because for the first time in his life, he felt like he was actually "welcomed into a community." Haggai explained that three things happened at the partnership synagogue that were unlike every other synagogue experience he ever had. The first one was a gesture by the prayer leader. "Gvir was *hazzan*, and we didn't know each other that well. But while he was leading, he motioned to me with his eyes like hello, and continued praying." Haggai was touched—after all, nobody had ever noticed him in synagogue before. "Afterward he came over to me and said that he's a *hazzan*—he was very learned and he knows a lot of things—and he said that he did a little trill in the music and he said, 'I did it for you.' That would never happen in [the other synagogue]. Nobody would ever do anything for me, definitely not some music thing. But this gesture really, really touched me. So I came again." Haggai was so used to men being disconnected, detached, individualistic, and serious, and far removed from the class of men who were the "learned" or "*hazzan*" types, that he was shocked to have an experience where he could actually build a connection with men, on the same level—that he actually mattered.

The second story involved his son. "They asked my eight-year-old son to lead *An'im Zemirot*,"[9] he explained. This is a big honor, especially for a newcomer. "I was nervous for him, but a twelve-year-old boy in the synagogue stood next to him, put a *tallit* on his shoulders, and did what a father should do, but he did it a thousand times better. I said to myself, this is how a child should be treated." Haggai was interested not only in feeling like he mattered, but also that his son did—community to the second degree.

The third story has actually nothing to do with the prayer service, which says a lot. "It was before Yom Kippur," Haggai said, "and there was some afternoon program on the book of Jonah. We were still checking out the place, trying to fit in. We sat at the table, our son was nervous, like me, and then another boy gestured to him to come play basketball. My son is not even sporty at all, but he went with him in a second and there they were, happy ever after." What spoke to Haggai was the inclusiveness his son felt not only in the sanctuary but also on the basketball court.

Men like Haggai are using the partnership synagogue as a venue to challenge Orthodox masculinity with its man-on-man gaze by creating a completely new culture of man-on-man *care*. They are also reconstructing fatherhood, since the boy, according to Haggai, was "doing the father's job." Haggai took the standard pose of being "nervous," concentrating on performance; the teenager took the pose of support and care. These events also deconstructed the elite hierarchy that says that only a select group of people can lead by inviting the newcomer boy to lead. The entire experience was one of undoing the standard Orthodox masculinity of distance, coldness, elitism, hierarchy, and gaze. "So these three things made me feel at home," Haggai concluded. "I feel that if one Shabbat I don't come, someone will say, 'Where were you last Shabbat?'" Men are searching out the partnership synagogue for a new definition of *community*, one in which they are actually noticed, where they belong, where someone actually cares about them, and where their presence matters. All of these are a challenge to Orthodox masculinity.

Men are also using the synagogue to create male-bonding relationships. As Isaac quipped, "Synagogue is a *Beit Knesset*, a house of gathering, not a *Beit Tefillah*, a house of prayer. You go to be with other people, not necessarily to pray." Larry, who often spends the entire service setting up *kiddush*, concurred. "I'm all about the *kehilla* [community], not the *tefillah*." Oren agreed. "The elements of community, friendship, connections, these are not just about prayer," he said. "Prayer is one thing, but there are other things as well. Without those other things, the synagogue would not continue." Community here is not necessarily about deep relationships, but it's about relationships. Prayer is almost incidental.

Significantly, this model of community is primarily a man's thing. Efraim also agreed. "Even if you don't necessarily talk to each other much, it's like, you see them every week, you sit near them every week, you wish them Shabbat Shalom," he said. Efraim's relationships are with those sitting next to him—that is, with men. "My wife and I joke that she knows the women and I know the men, and we don't always know who is paired with whom," Amitai said. This gender-segregated relationship building has implications for single men as well. "The women usually do the inviting for Shabbat meals," Adin said, "and since I only really know the men, it's hard to get invitations." In fact, each event Haggai described was between men, and therefore a description of a distinct men's culture. This sense of "community" is a man's thing in that it stands in contrast to the way men have been doing synagogue for so many generations. Men are challenging *their own* gender identities, not those of women. "I could have said that I came to the synagogue for my wife, that she dragged me and I stayed," Haggai said, "but that's not the truth. Today, *I'm* very happy there, *I* feel wanted, *I* feel like I belong, *I* really feel like I'm part of the community. The fact that we also pray is the least important." This is all about men undoing masculinity. It's about men feeling noticed, cared for, and relevant. Even though the men technically count for a *minyan*, this is the first time men actually feel like they truly *count*.

The idea that men are going to *shul* for a reason other than prayer is a bit radical, and I'm not sure how many men would comfortably say this out loud to other men, as opposed to in the privacy of an anonymous interview with a woman. I can imagine men like Robby and Nachshon, who spend quite a bit of energy on the actual prayer experience, hearing this and being pretty offended. ("What do you mean prayer is irrelevant?") Certainly I can imagine the cerebral types like Eitan, Yehiel, and Brian who are watching and measuring the performance and punctuality of other men being horrified that so many men go to synagogue for reasons having nothing to do with prayer. ("You see, that's what I'm talking about," Brian might say smugly, now understanding why it's so hard to get a *minyan* on time.) Men who come late (or hide out with the caterer) are pretty much saying, we are really not here for the ritual. It's possible that all the men who are labeled *hafifnik* are really just men who don't like prayer and come for their friends.

That said, within this paradigm of partnership as an outlet for relationship building, there are several subcategories. The first subcategory, epitomized by Haggai, includes those seeking out the most basic sense of belonging. It is what I think of as the "Norm Peterson" version of community, "where everybody knows your name" and you feel good. It answers a very basic, fundamental human need to feel like others know you exist, and pays no attention to social processes, social inequalities, gender, or culture. Gary described it very simply: "It's nice to be with people you like, you know." That's the very basic model of community: it's comfortable, it feels good, it's possibly therapeutic, and mostly it's a change from the cold, elitist masculinity that dominates Orthodoxy.

Haggai's story creates a really sad portrait of men's lives in standard Orthodox synagogues. Although this may be truer in Israel than in North America, there is something of a universal picture here that the Orthodox synagogue is a tough place. Men are drawn to the partnership synagogue not necessarily out of commitment to equality of women's participation, but in search of relationships. They are seeking out a culture that will allow them and even encourage them to build relationships with other men. The Orthodox masculinity box does not contain relationships, caring or nurturing. These men seem to be yearning for those connections. For many men, it is incidental that it happens in a place where women have more rights. The women's rights do not interest them at all. The partnership *minyan* is just more open and flexible and therefore allows men to play with these constructs. These men are coming to the partnership *minyan* not to satisfy women's needs but to satisfy their own.[10]

The second subcategory of community seekers includes those who value not only belonging but also *equality* as a basic parameter of community. This type of community seeking is not a self-centered act of need fulfillment but a deeper understanding that *everyone* should belong, including others who are systematically marginalized. They come to the partnership synagogue because women and children "count" in a way that redefines community for all. "I really want to be part of a communal *shul*," Hillel said, "and my wife and I want to go to *shul* together. We want it to be an experience for both of us. Our experience before this, for the most part, was that *shul* wasn't an experience for the family. It wasn't really an experience for us as a couple. It's just an experience for men. But here we really feel in all aspects that it's a family environment, and I'm just happy to be part of that and to make it work." Community here is a function of being welcoming to women and children as well as men, something that is new in the partnership synagogue. "I'm looking for a communal religious experience that's inclusive for everybody," Azriel said, "and not just inclusive, but also offers opportunities for everyone to have an active engagement in that experience." Women's inclusion in synagogue life fundamentally reconstructs Orthodox masculinity by making the synagogue experience about community, sharing, partnership, and equality rather than about cold, exclusive elitism or about belonging to a men's club.

This inclusiveness is not only toward women but toward other men as well and is built around acceptance, tolerance, and diversity—all of which are outside the box. "[The partnership synagogue] is nonjudgmental," Jerry says. "The people don't look down if you dress differently. There's just an air of acceptance which is very refreshing to me." Jerry, sixty-one, lives in Manhattan and has been to many different synagogues. At his previous *shul*, "everybody had to wear a black hat and a suit and a tie, in even the hottest of days, and if you deviated, then you were, you know, looked down upon or ostracized. So there's an absence of that where I go to today because everyone's accepted." Here, community is defined by a culture of mutual acceptance, tolerance, pluralism, and nonjudgmentalism.

The third subcategory of partnership as community moves beyond equality and inclusion into collaboration toward a greater goal. "I feel a lot better about [the partnership *minyan*] than . . . the Orthodox *minyan* because I am davening with a group of people who have recognized that there's something immoral about not pushing the line and making it as inclusive as possible," Shalom said, defining community as a purposeful, moral act. "I feel good about it because I'm with a group of people who have made that commitment, and we are acting out that commitment." Community here is about actively collaborating on building a moral society. As Larry said, "That's what every *shul* should be. . . . There are common causes that everyone believes in that you can organize together and you can fight for." This model of community is not only about coming together, but about coming together to fight for something that everyone believes in. Harold believes that community is defined by a shared dedication to social justice. "The *shul* I used to go to in England, the common element I had with people was that we were all Jews and you lived in a dispersed community and you would meet up every Shabbat," he said, offering a description of the very basic Norm Peterson type of community. "But actually I often felt that the people I met there had very different sociopolitical values from me. But from the conversations I had with people [at the partnership synagogue], they had a highly developed sense of social-political awareness . . . in that sense that they are concerned about social justice. . . . They kind of like the idea of change, but they also have a highly developed social justice sense." Here, the sense of connection between people is not about merely liking a person or being with a person who is welcoming. Rather, the sense of community comes from shared dedication to social change and social justice, a connection between people based on the mutual commitment to improving society by first changing themselves.

In other words, the creation of a community that breaks down hierarchies, that builds connections, and that shares an active collaboration on broader issues of social justice challenges multiple aspects of Orthodox masculinity. It shifts some of the most powerful and fundamental aspects of Orthodox masculinity, replacing a socialization that bases a man's acceptance by others on his blind obedience with an acceptance based on mutual acceptance, tolerance, and care. In the typical Orthodox synagogue, men come, perform, and leave, occasionally spreading some jokes and sports scores around in the process. There is no place in this standard *shul* experience where men are forming deep relationships with one another. What these informants are saying is that they are starving for such connections.

Conclusions

The synagogue is the place where Orthodox men have always become men. Through synagogue life, men learn who they are meant to be, what is expected of them, and what is right and wrong. As such, the synagogue is where many men look to form their own identities, pushing and pulling and navigating and negotiating acceptance and rejection through the synagogue experience.

When Darchei Noam, Shira Hadasha, and the other partnership synagogues were formed, the most obvious way in which they challenged Orthodox masculinity was by inviting women to take on roles that traditionally belong to men. As the synagogues evolved into thriving locations on the outer boundaries of Orthodoxy, it became clear that men joined not only for women, but also for themselves. In fact, in some cases, they joined predominantly for themselves. The partnership synagogue is a place where they can challenge and resist the Orthodox masculinity into which they were socialized. They resist the emphasis on cerebral conformity by constructing a flexible *halakha* and allowing themselves to think independently. They resist emotionless rote performance by singing emotively and passionately. And they resist the man-on-man gaze and elitism by building relationships and sometimes even by working toward greater inclusiveness all around.

These processes are not unique to the partnership synagogues. The men who join these synagogues are Orthodox men who have chosen these particular synagogues as an avenue to challenge socialization. But Orthodox men everywhere are going through similar processes, some more than others. Men everywhere find avenues for resistance, whether by bringing books to read during the service, by singing emotively in an unconventional *nusach*, by consistently coming late or not at all, by telling jokes during otherwise serious moments, by stepping outside to look after their children, by having a whiskey with buddies instead of listening to the *haftarah*, or simply by thinking for themselves. Orthodox men everywhere—indeed people everywhere—are in the same process. They internalize some of their acculturation and resist other parts. They accept and conform while they rebel and challenge. That is identity. The partnership synagogue is merely one location for men's resistance toward Orthodox masculinity, but it has echoes everywhere.

Men in partnership synagogues are re-creating their identities, whether consciously or not. Whether through cerebral, spiritual, or social changes, they are changing synagogue life and thus changing meanings of masculinity. There are also interesting underlying tensions. Those who prefer the cerebral find spiritual avenues grating and social avenues lacking seriousness. Those who seek spiritual fulfillment take issue with the overly cerebral aspects of synagogue life. And some men who focus on the social-communal aspect of synagogue have rejected the importance of prayer altogether. All these men are in the same conversation and in the same process. They are all wrestling with the definitions of Orthodox masculinity into which they were socialized.

CHAPTER 5

Jocks, Dads, and Homebodies

Masculinities between the Personal and the Political

∾ ON THE FIRST NIGHT of Rosh Hashana 2006, the first year that Darchei Noam in Modi'in held High Holiday services, Judah led the prayers as his toddler slept on his shoulder. The image was striking, and indicative of shifting trends. In my nearly four decades of participating in synagogue life around the world, I had never seen a cantor hold a child as he sang, and certainly not during the Rosh Hashana liturgy. After all, this was a service that epitomized male decorum and with it male status. The *hazzan* for the High Holidays is expected to be not just any *hazzan*, but the cream of the crop, one who can hold our attention, entertain, rivet, and inspire us with his melodies, inflections, and voice projections. Orthodox men who are considered skilled cantors get paid thousands of dollars for effectively three days, and often travel across the globe, abandoning their families for weeks, during the holiday season. It is prestigious, elegant, and dignified. In short, it is no place for children. More important, it is no place for soft, coddling, unfocused, distracted, and busy-with-their-kids kind of men.

Yet Judah, who had never before led High Holiday services, broke the mold of the Orthodox *hazzan* both by getting up to the podium despite lack of experience and, more important, by holding his sleeping child while doing it. He reconstructed the man as a connected, caring father and brought this example into the center of the sanctuary, where it confronted the model of man as unencumbered, undistracted, and perfect performer. He created this culture shift, and the community was accepting of it. Perhaps more significant, nobody in the congregation batted an eye. There was no complaining by men or women, no attempts to remove the child from his grip, and no tsk-tsking the mother. People simply continued about their business and prayed. Yet there it was, the breaking of social convention and the re-creation of gender for men and women. It is possible for a *hazzan* not to be an expert, not to take on an expert pose, and not to be a sterile individual free of all constraint. It was the reconfiguration of the cantor as a regular Joe, perhaps a radical notion, especially on Rosh Hashana.

It was clear at that moment that something was happening to men in this synagogue, something beyond synagogue life. Men were not simply moving over to allow women to take some of their formerly men-only jobs, but were redefining their own identities and value systems, challenging many of their former notions of masculinity. They were trying to escape from the competition between men and the man-on-man gaze not only in religion but also in their relationships. They were rejecting the model of man as singular, detached, cold, separate, emotionless expert performer and trying to replace it with a more comfortable model, different from that of their fathers—a model of man in connection, caring for his child as he cares for the community, singing not as expert but as father to father and father to son, enabling the congregation to connect with him as a whole person, just like them, rather than as some kind of superhuman representative of God.

This chapter explores the broader context of men's socialization into Orthodox masculinities. It examines the ways in which Orthodox men grapple with masculinities in the wider context of marriage, relationships, career, and the overall male "persona," and examines the ways in which Orthodox men are changing beyond the walls of the synagogue.

Change in the Kitchen

Zvi was very nervous about being interviewed. Before we started, he asked for a pen and paper to write down his ideas before he answered—a request I had never encountered before or since in an interview. The thirty-eight-year-old former librarian turned fund-raiser mulled over his responses and paused frequently to think about what he wanted to say next. I tried my best to let the silences settle without feeding into the awkwardness.

But his pose soon broke. When Zvi said he "firmly believes" that "men and women should be treated with equal dignity," I responded, in good ethnographic form, "How does that find expression in your life?" Zvi then took a deep breath and laughed. "I was dreading that question," he said. "I've been thinking about it all today, and all yesterday." Zvi then proceeded to elaborate. "I put the kids to sleep usually, which is a long task and takes up a good part of the evening. [My wife] does more of the cleaning. I have never been a particularly good cleaner, but I do laundry, and I fold. She folds more, and she does more of the housework." Then he said, "Sorry, [Karen]," and started laughing.

For many men, the kitchen sink is where the first conversations about gender identity often take place. When men hear the words "feminism" or "gender," some reply with an almost knee-jerk reaction, "But I help with the dishes."[1] When I told men that I'm studying men and gender identity, many were certain that I was asking about division of home labor. What this says is that for many men, home "work" is the first place where they think about gender.

Sharing home duties is a primary expression of changing gender roles—for both women and men—and a different way for men to view the women in their lives. "We try as much as possible to be equal in the way we share household chores," Avi said. Isaac, who also shares fifty-fifty, said, "I'm just doing my work because it has to be done. I don't believe that I should sit down, relax, and watch television while my wife does all the cleaning up." For many men, shared home duties predate joining a partnership synagogue and emerge from a similar rationale. "I am a feminist," Ehud said, which he explained as, "In terms of house duties, it's fifty-fifty, and I belong to an egalitarian synagogue." Similarly, for Netanel, "The synagogue is a natural outgrowth of what we do as a couple at home. We both work, we both educate, we are equal in everything. Each of us takes on all the tasks. Why shouldn't it be the same way in the synagogue?" For other men, though, there is no connection between gender at home and gender at synagogue. Robby, for example, after talking about the division of home duties, stopped and said to me, "None of that was relevant at all. The sharing of house duties bears no relevance to what is happening in the synagogue." Unlike Netanel, for whom the private and public arenas are intricately linked, Robby sought to separate the two.

Robby's discomfort, expressed in an attempt at compartmentalization, reflects an underlying tension and multiple pulls on his masculinity. He wants to be a good man, but changing definitions of masculinity have left him with a lot of insecurity, uncertainty, confusion, and self-doubt:

> If you ask my wife she'll say I am a hypocrite. Because I am crap. I don't cook. I clean a lot. . . . I am terrible. No, in the middle of the week I will fry up sausages and that sort of thing, but when it comes to cooking for Shabbat, I am not good. I come home at the end of the day exhausted. She also comes home at the end of the day exhausted. She just has much more energy than I do, or much more willpower than I do. In theory I'm a feminist at home; in practice, I'm OK. I'm not brilliant, I clean the house a lot. . . . I wash the floors. I really do that. That's my thing. I do washing as well. I also serve on Shabbat. There I am the guy who does that. I would argue

that I carry about 40 percent of the household responsibility, my wife will agree. . . . I am not as good as I should be.

This is a tormented but incredibly illuminating text about the different pulls on men, the deliberations, the ambivalence, the self-doubt, and the attempt to measure up in all directions. The man-on-man gaze that tells men to measure up has now morphed with a perceived woman-on-man gaze, a demand that he be not just a guy but also the kind of guy who helps at home. Of course, the female-on-male gaze does not necessarily come from a position of power wielding, but is likely to be an expression of seeking help, partnership, justice, and compassion. But Robby is caught in what feels as multiple responsibilities and as such has no recourse but to say that he's "crap." He is saying he wants to be a good man, a good husband, and a good father, but finds himself lacking in all those areas, and this adds to his sense of not measuring up. Here is a man under pressure from all sides, confused and a bit tired, not sure what the world wants from him as a man, or perhaps what kind of man he wants to be.

This "new age man" is confusing for men who are still stuck in old paradigms. They are trying to be both the alpha male breadwinner and the sensitive supporter, and in both cases they are just trying to maintain their own sense of masculinity. Interestingly, when I rang Robby on a Friday morning about an interview, he was in the middle of cooking for Shabbat, which he later claimed that he doesn't do! So Robby is self-punishing for not being egalitarian enough at home—and possibly not man enough—though this is a somewhat dubious self-report. In practice, Robby's house duties are similar to those of Netanel, but Netanel admits that his wife does all the cooking for Shabbat and he does all the dish washing. But despite their almost identical roles in practice (if anything, Robby does more), Netanel calls his role a proud full partnership and Robby calls his a reprehensible 40 percent. Although it is hard to know what really happens at home, what is certain is that Robby is still trying to measure up, while Netanel is perfectly happy with himself. Robby is trying to be a good man, but definitions are murky, and he is caught between old paradigms and new ones, between a desire to change and a desire to have the security of knowing that he is a correct and approved-of man. Netanel, on the other hand, calls his arrangement "partnership" and feels good. Robby has maintained the "not measuring up" anxiety of masculinity, perhaps adding to it a certain ambivalence and self-doubt that is not part of the male culture, whereas Netanel takes on a classic male confidence that he and his wife are "partners" and therefore he measures up. Complex times for men, indeed. Actually, though, I think that Robby is breaking down masculinity more that Netanel just by this admission. Netanel's proud and non-self-critical stance (labeling it equality despite an admission that he does not cook, for example) is much more classically "masculine" than Robby's ambivalence and self-denigration.

It seems that while men are talking about sharing of household chores, they are not necessarily unpacking the underlying issues of masculinity. Men are also not necessarily unpacking the gender power-relations involved in housework. It is a real challenge for men to give up the privilege of being served, cooked for, and looked after in order to become the cook and cleaner. Some men feel pressured into the change and are clearly resentful. So while masculinities are changing and men are challenging gender at the kitchen sink, this is not necessarily indicative of a deeper shift in gender relationships. Binyamin, for example, who describes his wife as "the queen of the house," admits that his wife does all the cooking every Shabbat, as well as all the serving. "I sit," he says, referring to Shabbat meals, "and she runs things," because they typically have ten to fifteen people at a meal. In other words, she works and he gets served. But interestingly, Binyamin describes himself as a feminist and says "we are a very open house." So some men not only maintain old-style gender, but they do so while claiming to be new and open. And significantly, most of the old-style gender is connected to Orthodox life—the Shabbat ritual. His wife may be seen as a "queen" as she cooks and serves, but there is no doubt that Binyamin is king.

It seems, then, that although for some men household work is a place where masculinity is changing resistance, for others it is not changing at all. What is changing, however, is that men feel the need to answer to feminism. "My wife is a much better cook than I am," Eitan said, for example, justifying their classic division of labor. "I'm a better cleaner-upper, so that becomes more my role, and I do the books and the financial things. She is definitely the one who sets up our social calendar. She's gifted in that way. She truly is." Perceptions of women's "gifts" sustain a masculinity that includes economic management and excludes cooking (though, to be fair, it includes cleaning). Even men who advocate for breaking down gender roles in the public spheres (synagogue) may retain traditional masculinities at home—and vice versa. Home life, therefore, is the chosen site of resistance for some, but not necessarily for all, and may or may not be related to changing gender roles in public. For almost all men, however, there is a growing awareness that housework is a place for reconfiguring masculinity—and not always to men's liking. Home duties, especially around Shabbat, are for some Orthodox men a location of gender renegotiation and for others a mere perception of that renegotiation.

Soft Fathers

It's easy to understand why men are resistant to taking on home chores. Frankly, it's a big pain with little apparent reward—unless one counts a happier spouse and possibly a cleaner home. This is undoubtedly one of the hardest privileges for men to abdicate. There is, however, one household "chore" that holds enormous rewards for men: child care. While washing dishes offers little emotional reward, child care is about building strong, lasting relationships. In classic masculinity, the persona of detached "provider" frees men not only of child care chores but also of involved fatherhood. As Isaac reported, he was offered a job in which the interviewer said, "Bring a photo of your children, because you will never see them," and he did not take the job. Just like the "sterile individual," a classic father in the "be a man" box is distanced, alone, unencumbered, aloof, and home only in the early morning and late evening, Orthodox man is a religious version of the bourgeois, successful, professional, distant workingman.

Many men challenged the "box" first and foremost by building different models of fatherhood. As Azriel said, fatherhood "changes your perspective on everything. You see things with different lenses. It's not just seeing things about how everything affects your own journey, but now you're seeing things for how they affect another person's journey." For him and others, fatherhood formed a major point of socialization and change within the development of the Orthodox man.

For Yossi, a sixty-nine-year-old father of two sons, the topic of fatherhood was a formative component of his identity. He describes his father as an "authoritarian dictator type" who would "denigrate everything that I would do." He recalled his father being very "tough," saying things like, "You don't touch it. You'll break it." For Yossi, this harshness was particularly difficult because he was a boy. "A girl can find other roles," he said. But for Yossi, this was all he had to teach him what kind of person he wanted to be. "A father is supposed to be an image for you, a role model. The fact that he attacks you all the time, and I was a male" made childhood a very painful experience. Yossi's entire adult life has been a rejection of this model of fatherhood. "I try never to get angry," he said. "Anger is one of the worst things." He also uses a lot of humor and joking around with his sons, and now with his grandchildren. Unlike his own father, he gives his children a lot of love. "I'm a very loving person," he said, "and I love the kids. I worry about them, take care of them. I think I respect them. I think I'm a very good father." Yossi became a different kind of man because he became a different kind of father.

Significantly, however, although Yossi has been Orthodox for over fifty years, his father was not. So for him, becoming a more caring father was connected to becoming Orthodox, as opposed to rebelling against Orthodox manhood. His father tried to force him to become nonreligious, so for Yossi, the forceful imposition of masculinity worked in the reverse direction from most other men in this research. He worked on building his own model of masculinity, and care and religiousness went hand in hand.

Half a century later, however, Yossi started to question his whole story. The glue holding his model of masculinity together began to disintegrate as he questioned whether becoming religious was really an expression of resistance toward his father:

> When my mother was in the hospital dying and it was Yom Kippur, and my father wanted to go to the hospital, I knew he couldn't go because he wouldn't be able to walk it. So I had to go with my father, to take him by bus because he was already not all there. So it was Yom Kippur, and here I was on Yom Kippur getting on a bus, handling money and everything. It was a really big break for me. . . . I didn't want to do it, but I felt I had to, because I felt he should go to the hospital, but I had to go this way because otherwise he wasn't going to go. You're doing it, but it was a strange feeling, and it is still a strange feeling. But that was a point where I think I kind of saw futility of the religion a little bit.

In this description of the strained father-son relationship that spanned more than a half century, Yossi describes being pulled by the different parts of his identity as a religious man and a son. There was pressure to be a good son to his mother and bring his father to see her. There was the tension between taking care of his aging but abusive father who was "not all there" versus his lifelong practice of not riding the bus on Shabbat. All this took place in the context of a situation in which a man in his sixties was forced to undo his religious practice in order to care for his difficult father, who wanted him to have a different religious practice. As a teen, Yossi fiercely resisted his father and ended up living four decades as an Orthodox man. But now, years later, he gets on the bus on Yom Kippur and is not even sure that he believes in being religious anymore.

What Yossi's story agonizingly illustrates is the central role of fatherhood in the formation of masculinity, and the complex and often painful interplay here between religion, compassion, and fatherhood in the socialization of the Orthodox man.

Harold's story is a bit gentler and perhaps more typical of the men interviewed, in that he was brought up Orthodox and stayed Orthodox, and changed his fatherhood socialization along the way. A sixty-five-year-old retiree from England and father of four living in Israel, Harold reports that he has a "very close relationship" with his children, unlike his own relationship with his father. This is due in part to the fact that his father was "away from home much more," but perhaps more due to cultural shifts. "I think that just life was very different then," he reflected. "Our kids have a very different relationship with us than we could ever have possibly had with our parents. My parents were more formal in that sense. There was more of a distance between me and my parents. There was a much greater sense of respect and tradition and authority." Times have changed, Harold said, especially when it comes to "the kind of relationships that children have with their parents today." Harold's father was perhaps not as tough as Yossi's father, but they both reflect a larger sense that men today are doing fatherhood differently than in the past. Actually, from these accounts, the larger cultural shift in fatherhood from hard to soft has been going on for over thirty years, arguably an entire generation.

Comparing Yossi and Harold sheds some light on how agency emerges, how we garner the ability to resist our socialization. One of the interesting differences between the ways Yossi and Harold tell their stories is in attribution. Yossi says that he made a conscious, overt, and often difficult decision to be unlike his father, whereas for Harold it sort of just "happened." A second striking difference is about trauma. While Yossi talks about boyhood interactions with his father in a way that the pain is almost still raw, for Harold there is no expression of real trauma. These two differences suggest that perhaps agency is a function of pain and trauma. I think it's possible to argue that sometimes the people who truly fight against the entire set of dynamics from childhood that worked to mold them into a correct member of society are the ones who were most hurt. Perhaps agency or resistance is a function of systematic trauma, something that jars the foundations of a person's existence. One might even argue that, for some men, resistance is a process of *healing*.

There is another significant difference between Harold and Yossi that raises a vital question about the role of fatherhood in Orthodoxy. For Yossi, resistance meant becoming religious, whereas for Harold, resistance was merely about shifting fatherhood and remaining religious. This leaves us with an unanswered question about how Orthodox men are socialized into fatherhood, and whether changing fatherhood is a function of Orthodox masculinity, or of masculinity in general. Many interviewees grew up with difficult fathers, whether the men were brought up Orthodox or otherwise. Of the fifty-four interviewees, approximately three-fourths grew up Orthodox, and they have father stories that run the gamut from Yossi's abusive, autocratic father to those whose fathers were the nurturers, cooks, and carers in the family. What is more interesting here is why some men, like Yossi, resisted the fatherhood models of their childhood, while others did not.

Binyamin, who is nearly twenty years younger than Yossi and was brought up Orthodox in Israel, in some way embodies the tough obedience model of Yossi's father more than the model of gentle care that Yossi constructed for himself. "I think that as a father I am warm and embracing and close to my sons," he muses, and then adds, "but everyone knows that I am very demanding and tough." He says that his children sit with him in synagogue, and "they would never think to be outside during prayers." Unlike Yossi, Binyamin says he has "one principle: when I am angered, I get angry. That's it." Whereas for Yossi anger is the great evil, for Binyamin it's his "one principle." Binyamin is not abusive like Yossi's father, but he embodies a tough, unbending, angry masculinity that Yossi has specifically resisted and rejected. Binyamin is proud of his toughness, of raising his sons the way he was raised, with strict boundaries of right and wrong, but with what he calls "warmth." For Binyamin, fatherhood is not about doing masculinity much differently than the model he received.

Men's resistance is, perhaps counterintuitively, not a function of age or generation. Younger men are more likely to talk about "fun" relationships with their children, like thirty-two-year-old Judah, who said, "I think I'm a good dad. I love my kids, I think they love me, and we have a lot of fun together." Nevertheless, the patterns of fatherhood that men expressed did not fit a generational pattern. Harold and Yossi are of the same generation and adopted a much "softer" fatherhood model than Binyamin, who is much years younger than them and still takes on some elements of authoritarian style. It is also not really a function of Orthodoxy per se. While much of Binyamin's strictness revolves around Orthodoxy—like insisting that his sons sit in synagogue, next to him, quietly, from beginning to end—Yossi's father was equally strict about being *not* religious. The differences between men ultimately boil down to the fact that some make the choice to be a certain kind of father and others merely follow what they were taught. Binyamin's brand of fatherhood, I would argue, has little if any reflection or resistance at all. By contrast, Yossi's and Harold's forms of fatherhood are all about looking at how they were brought up and doing it differently. There are men who reflect and resist and men who don't, and this is not a function of age or generation but of something else. For some reason, Harold and Yossi are different from their fathers—more caring and nurturing—while Binyamin merely replicates the old models. Why does Binyamin conform rather than resist like Yossi and Harold? It's not yet clear.

One of the ways in which men are doing fatherhood differently is when it comes to the actual hours and chores of child care. Approximately twelve men described a routine in which they share child care duties equally. Netanel, a forty-year-old academic and father of four, says that he and his wife regularly negotiate their daily timetables and arrange child care depending on what their workdays look like. Danny, a thirty-eight-year-old academic and father of two whose wife works in high-tech, describes quite a busy life as a father. "I do a lot of stuff," he says. "I get them up in the morning, I get them breakfast, give them a bath, take them to the doctor, take them to the dentist, make them dinner, play games—I'm the board games person—those kind of things." At the same time, he says his wife does more "logistics." "She is better at doing the homework with them and like when they need speech therapy and things like that. She's going be more organized and talking to the speech therapist about exactly what's wrong. But I will take them to the speech therapist." His wife may be organizing the children's lives, but he is carrying it all out. Other men have different forms of negotiation, such as Stuart, who takes the morning shift as well as bedtime while his wife takes afternoons because she works at night. Tom, a teacher, also frequently picks up his daughter and can often be seen walking with her in the park and supermarkets in the afternoon. In short, many men are willingly and happily taking over the day-to-day parenting, from going to the park to speech therapy to making dinner—and as a result are benefiting from close and caring relationships with their children.

The overwhelming majority of men, however, are still living lives with uneven child care duties rooted in ideas about "natural" gender differences. Even Judah, who says he is a good dad and has a "special relationship" with his daughter, admits that he works very late and often sees his children only for breakfast. He is a fast-tracked lawyer, and his wife is a stay-at-home mother. Many fathers of young children, in fact, continue to maintain an unequal burden of child care, even as they try to be warmer, more-loving fathers. Approximately fifteen interviewees described an uneven division of child care, with women still making the difficult personal choices about working part time or from home or not at all, or maintaining the primary responsibility for school pickup even if both partners work full time. Despite the fact that Gad's wife is an engineer with greater earning potential, his comment that she is "naturally better" at parenthood becomes a justification for patriarchal child care divisions. Efraim, an engineer whose wife has a doctorate, said that she is "definitely the more active one in terms of housework and raising the kids." Like Gad, he says that if they were in a situation in which she was earning more money than he, he could not see himself as "the husband [who] quit his job . . . and raised the kids, the home husband. . . . I think it would be difficult for me." Moshe, a self-described feminist whose wife works until 4 PM every day while he works sometimes thirteen-hour days, said, "In that respect, we have not really implemented equality in our relationship." Similarly, Gary said that his wife "takes more of a role than I do. . . . Maybe she likes it more." In other words, men—even feminist men who are actively promoting women's advancement in public life and trying to be good fathers in some ways—continue to use the language of natural differences to maintain a second-class fatherhood.

That said, a very small number of men do *more* child care than their wives. Levi, a senior academic whose wife works long days in the financial district, takes the brunt of the afternoon duties. Similarly, Amitai, also an academic whose work schedule is only part time, takes the brunt of the child care duties.[2]

One thing that is significant about the men who are active fathers is that they are almost all either academics or teachers; they are in professions that have a bit more flexibility of hours than high-tech. The correlation between men who are active fathers, academics, and go to partnership synagogues is very interesting. Perhaps it's not a coincidence that academics are more-active fathers. Perhaps the choice of academia, the choice to parent, and the choice to be in this synagogue all reflect men who are making active choices, who have a bit more agency than the average man. Academics, almost by definition, are free-thinking people with creative and highly intelligent minds who thrive on the rejection of old ideas and the creation of new ones. Perhaps the men of this study are more accustomed to breaking from the herd, and the correlation between academics and active fatherhood suggests that one of the first sites for active resistance is in the reconstruction of fatherhood.

Another interesting point is that for the active fathers, share in child care is not necessarily correlated with their share in house chores. For some, like Netanel, who said, "We share in everything equally," there is clearly a guiding thread of equality. But that is not the case with all the men. Hillel, for example, said, "the cleaning, no, but the child care, yes [we shared equally]." For Hillel, fatherhood is more of a site for renegotiation of masculinity than housecleaning; for some men it's the opposite. Oren, for example, whom I met while he was washing the floors and listening to a Torah class on his earphones, said, "I haven't been available for child rearing the way my wife has been. My wife has more of a tendency to care for the kids than I have. Even when I am home, I'm not really with them." Oren, who is a freelance business consultant who sets his own hours, is more likely to be home to wash the floor than to look after his children. He describes his wife's "tendency," a vague allusion again to natural differences that is used as a tactic for keeping gender roles fixed. The language of "tendency" masked a desire to avoid too much change.

Zachary, though, completely rejects the language of natural differences and has formed his own type of fatherhood:

> Personally, I completely don't go for the bullshit of men are like this and women are—you know, men are the "take the kids out to play ball" and women are the emotional center, and men do the bills and women do [other things]. . . . I just personally don't relate to it at all. I'm the emotional center more like for a lot of things and all that—more understanding. They come to me to hug me and to cry with me and like things like that. She's more practical, she does things and gets up early and makes them food and does a lot of practical things. And she takes out the garbage—just because I don't.

Zachary's complete rejection of natural differences has given him the ability to be a father who is the "emotional center" for his children.

The Low-Power Career

Men may be turning into active fathers, but few do so at the price of their own career advancement. The fact that so many of the active fathers are academics highlights the extent to which those who are willing to take on more duties are the ones who have enough time flexibility to do so without damaging their careers. I asked Stuart, for example, a forty-eight-year-old father of two and one of the most active fathers I interviewed, whether he chose to work an overnight shift for a daily newspaper so that he could be home for his children during the day, and he replied immediately, "Not at all." In fact, when I asked him if he had ever felt he made a career sacrifice to enable him to be an active father, he said, "No, definitely not." In other words, even active, engaged fathers are not necessarily constructing work life around parenthood, at least not the way women are.

There are, however, a few exceptions. Efraim is living out career choices based on a different model of masculinity. Early in his sixteen-year marriage, he moved to a different city, leaving behind a high-powered government engineering job to enable his wife to pursue her dream of getting a doctorate. "My mother was unhappy in her traditional role," he recalled, "and that's why she ended up leaving my father. I did not want to be the kind of man who makes his wife unhappy." After their children were born, he worked in an 80 percent position, and then 50 percent, which he does from home. "Your kids only grow up once. I want to be there for them, to make sure that they get the support they need," he said later in a focus group. Listening to Efraim's description, Isaac added, "What he means is that he loves his children. It's not about watching them grow. It's about just wanting to be with them."

Amitai takes fatherhood even further. A thirty-four-year-old father of two, he is the only interviewee who actually stopped working at a certain point, the way so many women do, in order to raise his children while his spouse worked. "I was very involved with the family. I took care of the girls, more than normal men—much, much more. I was home for a while, and I would walk my daughter to school, etcetera." Amitai, who compares himself to "normal" men, is an academic who works eight months a year as an adjunct professor and collects unemployment the other four months. He has worked in half-time jobs, or not at all, or sometimes as a flex-time freelancer. Although he says proudly that "we have equality at home," he feels that it's "a little problematic" in that his dedication as a parent has infringed on his professional advancement. "It hurt me. I'm a little stuck because of it. I feel like professionally I haven't advanced enough, because I wasted time on the family." Even though he's happy with his decisions, he feels that as a man he does not have the social approval for his choices. "Women do it all the time, but nobody makes any claims about it. With men, people say things." Like the unemployed man who feels he cannot walk into *shul*, Amitai feels the male eyes of society watching and judging him. "There's this thing about how a man has to be assertive and demanding, socially and in terms of earning. There's a real problem here. Because society is defined a certain way, even a man who wants to be a feminist, they'll come to him afterward with issues." By looking after his children and taking a less high-powered career track, he has placed his masculinity in question in the eyes of other men. So although he is trying hard to resist "marketplace man," he painfully demonstrates that such resistance is not without personal cost.

Despite the pain, Amitai does not really regret his choice. "I think most men do not understand what it means to raise children. It is an experience that is very, very powerful, that a person should experience as much as possible. Many men do not know how to make time for their children, do not know how to handle them. They don't see the other side of it, the interpersonal aspect. I think that because I was with my girls more than most men, I gained a lot." So while he paid a certain social price for being an active father, what he got in return was a deep and active relationship with his daughters.

For a man to be anything less than fully ambitious and high-powered, he has to be willing to endure this male gaze that tells him to be *man* and not *woman*. Judah had an experience when his wife went away for a week and he worked until 3:30 every day. "It was hard," he admits, adding that, "at my office a lot of women do it." Despite the discomfort of working the "women's hours," Judah says he would "be absolutely fine" if his wife had a high-paying job and he worked until 3:30. This is in stark contrast to the men who would not consider it, even if their wives do in fact have more earning potential than they do. Gad, a forty-two-year-old salesman and father of two, insisted that he would not even consider switching places with his wife. Although she is more educated than he and earns more money, at the time of the interview he was working late almost every night, while she was working in two subcontracted part-time jobs, leaving the house at 6:15 AM in order to be back in time for the 4 PM pickup. His reason was about natural differences. "By nature the woman's role tends to be more focused on the home, and it's even with working women," he said.[3]

Other men choose to switch from self-centered career ambition to family-centered career ambition. Noam, for example, a forty-two-year-old computer engineer and father of four who holds a senior position in a large, NASDAQ-traded computer company, said that he switched his attitude after his divorce. "I understood at a certain point that I don't want to be CEO," he said, "because it's confining. I don't want it. I make compromises. I seek out balance." He is a self-described "former workaholic," he said, working until after nine every night. But now not only does he go home, but he urges others at his office to do the same. "I see people who work for me who don't leave at five, six o'clock, so I tell them, 'Go home!' Sometimes it's taken like, 'Are you nuts? You're sending me home?' I say, 'Yes. Come back tomorrow.'" Noam is actively and forcefully trying to help men find a better balance. "I once said to a guy, 'Show me your diary. Show me all your meetings.' It was full of meetings," Noam laughed. "I used to be that way, too. Every hour, my entire Outlook was blue, full of meetings. I said to him, 'Show me all the meetings you have that if you don't show up, the meeting would be just as effective. Delete all those meetings, and then you'll see how much free time you suddenly have.' I think people create meetings for themselves to avoid going home." Noam makes the startling but probably accurate suggestion that men create back-to-back meetings for themselves not just to be a good "provider" but also to avoid going home, as excuses to avoid becoming an emotionally engaged father, or perhaps to avoid extra chores. Noam worked on changing this in himself, and now he's changing the men around him. He says, half joking, that his ex-wife says it's a shame that he discovered this only after their divorce. As if to say, being a different kind of man may have been beneficial to their marital health.

Although Noam has enormous confidence in his own process of change, other men are not quite as secure. Amitai, for example, feels like men look at him as a lesser man. Tom, a forty-one-year-old high school English teacher, is very self-critical about his "lack of professional ambition," a derogatory quality in a man. "The flip side of sensitivity in men," Tom says, "is maybe a certain lack of initiative, lack of aggression, a lack of competitiveness in life, a lack of professional ambition." Even though he calls himself a "sensitive man," and even says that he is "more effeminate than other men," he wavers about himself and says that the kind of "masculinity" he lacks is "good for society." "I think that that drive, that certain ambitious quest, can be good, if it is funneled in certain directions. I think maybe the Western world is pushed by that spirit." Tom, who by his own admission has rejected the "professionally ambitious" type of masculinity, has sadly internalized the man-on-man gaze and sees himself as stuck in the role of not-such-a-man kind of man. Rather than being proud of his "sensitivity" and his ability to reject behaviors that do not suit him, he says that society is right and ambition is good. Like Amitai, Tom has made great strides in breaking down masculinity but also has trouble settling into being comfortable with his decision. The rejection of masculinity demands explanation and justification and seems to riddle some of its proponents with a sense of inferiority.

One of the most moving stories I heard about challenging the career ambition aspects of masculinity came from Oded, a single forty-year-old who overcame some powerful social messages about being a married provider in order to switch from a career in management to a career as a fourth-grade teacher. Oded didn't even want me to interview him. "I'm not married, so I'm not a normal part of the population you're looking at," he told me, emphasizing the extent to which men who reject the "provider" aspect of masculinity feel "not normal." Oded's story is both touching and heartbreaking, and emphasizes the power of socialization to damage a person's spirit:

> As I was getting out of the army, I didn't know what I wanted to study at university. My father said, "I have a friend who's an organizational graphologist. Send her a writing sample, and she'll tell you what profession to go into." So I sent her all these different writing samples, and after a week or two she gave me an analysis and recommendation. One of the areas that she recommended for me was organizational psychology. I said, "Why not clinical psychology?" She said, "You're the type of person who takes everything to heart. As a clinical psychologist, you would have to treat people and hear their difficult stories. You won't be able to tell a patient to stop, and you'll take it all home, and that's not healthy." She then recommended other areas: advertising, tour guiding, international relations, and political science.
>
> So I asked her, "What about education?" I had been in education my whole life, as a summer counselor and youth group leader, and I loved working with children. She said, "You can, and you may even be successful. But it's my job to tell you what will be most useful to you in life, what will make your life better, what will help you provide [*l'hitparnes*]. So if you can study and learn organizational psychology and succeed, why would you go into education and work hard? Especially as a man, you can't provide for a family that way." So in the end, I majored in organizational psychology and studied informal education as a minor, at least that. But a few weeks before starting class, I switched from education to economics. People said, "You have nothing better to do than study informal education? Learn something useful that can help you in life." So I studied economics. I didn't really do well in economics, and I never connected to the subject.

The pressure on Oded *not* to be a teacher, despite his love for the work and his skill, came from multiple sources. The father-backed "expert," coupled with "people" at university and elsewhere giving an impressionable twenty-two-year-old advice, created a formidable wall of attack. It is no wonder that Oded caved in and ended up studying a subject that he did not connect to and working for ten years in a field that he did not like. Most significant, however, was the graphologist's comment that "you can't provide for a family that way." This is masculinity par excellence: the man's feelings, desires, interests, and passions are put aside so that he can fit in, be like all other men, get married, and work to support his family. Interestingly, the scenario that Oded has lived out—that at the age of forty he has been in the workplace for nearly twenty years and has never been married—was never even considered.

Oded's crisis came in his late twenties with a rebellion that he said is "not finished yet":

> After five years of working in a human resources company, measuring and evaluating projects, I quit. It all started at a Hanukah party. There were twelve people there, all around my age, all with first and second degrees, working people. Toward the end of the party, the host asked, "Who wakes up every morning with a smile on his face when he goes to work?" Everyone said no, except for one who dealt with high-tech. Two weeks later, the guy who asked the question quit because he did not wake up every morning with a smile. I said to myself, "He was very brave. What's happening with me? I'm also not happy. I also don't wake up every morning smiling to go to work." So on Passover eve I let my boss know that I'm going from slavery to freedom and quitting. He didn't even try to convince me to stay, didn't do anything, didn't talk to me about how important I was to him. Just told me what projects I had to complete before leaving.

Oded craved a "smile on his face" and had the courage to seek that out despite societal objections. Sadly, most of the other men in the office did not even know how to say that they wanted to experience the emotion of joy. The masculinity that he encountered at his workplace was one that acts not out of passion and interest, but out of obligation. Emotional expression is absent, just like in the performance of religious ritual. It is hard to know whether Israeli Orthodoxy borrowed masculinity from the office or whether an emotionlessness originating in religious masculinity was imported into the Israeli workplace. In any case, there is a fascinating overlap between religion and work, as the pivotal moments in Oded's transformation correlated with Jewish holidays. Even the metaphor of finding agency—slavery to freedom—is taken from Jewish culture. In short, Oded offers a poignant glimpse into the cold, heartless Orthodox masculinity expressed in the guise of "professionalism."

Despite Oded's courage and personal awakening, he still had to face harsh social expectations, especially that of his parents:

> My parents were in shock. To leave a steady job with a good income and throw it away? To leave something that has a future and be left with nothing? With no other

job? You don't quit a job unless you have something else! You can't be left without a job! . . . But it didn't do it for me. I asked myself, what are the things that are fun for you in life? And I thought about summer camp at Ramah in Canada, when I worked for the Jewish Agency teaching Hebrew and Judaism, and I really enjoyed it. It was good for me. . . . I was offered a job teaching the following year in the Midwest. After a week there, I knew it was the place for me. I spent five years teaching there.

In order for Oded to turn his life around, he not only had to fight social convention, but also had to have a difficult emotional conversation with himself about his unhappiness. The first key to his transformation was acknowledging his own right to joy. Significantly, Oded has the same "Does it do it for me?" question that Zachary had about religion. But while Zachary was self-critical for even asking the question, Oded found it was a pivotal life moment.

Today, Oded continues to grapple with these decisions. "Is it wrong to keep moving around instead of concentrating on trying to get married?" he asked me. "Is it wrong to continue making my parents so unhappy?" Although he was offered an administrative position, Oded stuck to teaching fourth grade. He thus rejects the model of climbing the career ladder at all costs in order to do what he loves. Nonetheless, he still has issues to confront. "Men in education," he muses, "it's not the greatest profession. It's not easy for children to say, 'My father is a teacher.' It's easier to say, 'My mother is a teacher.' But it's easier to say, 'My father is a lawyer, a doctor, a bus driver.' Maybe in fifty, sixty years it will be different." In other words, the gendering of professions has an impact on both men and women. Just as women are pressured into low-status jobs, men are pressured into high-status jobs that they may hate. These gender boxes are difficult for men as well as for women.

A compelling portrait of resistance is beginning to form. It seems that developing independent agency in the face of societal expectations can be a very painful and even traumatic process and demands the ability to be courageous and withstand severe pressure. It also requires the willingness to be uncertain, even ambivalent, and make difficult choices even in the face of doubt.

Sensitivity and Nirvana

When people ask Oded about his decision, he does not know what to say. "I don't know whether to be sorry or not," he says. This ambivalence is itself not part of the box. Deborah Tannen,[4] writing about gender and cultures of discourse, says that men are socialized into being decisive and solution focused, while women are socialized into being ambivalent, process oriented, and indecisive. Oded's decision to go to Ohio came after a lot of ambivalence and indecision, which, in Tannen's terms, is culturally very female. Similarly, Tom, in being self-critical, unsure, and indecisive, is rejecting society's masculinity just by virtue of the language he adopted. One of the interesting things, therefore, about the way men challenge masculinity is that at times the language itself is nonconforming in its softness and ambivalence.

For some men, rejecting masculinity is less about the particulars of life decisions, careers, child rearing, and relationships, and more about a stance, a personality, or a way of walking through the world without aggression, assertiveness, and competitiveness. Tom has described this in terms of being nonaggressive and nonambitious. "I think I am a sensitive man," Tom said with characteristic uncertainty. "I am a good listener. I think I am compassionate. . . . I always tried to avoid conflicts, I never felt comfortable with conflict." Yet he wavered about whether to admire himself for his nonviolence. "When I look back at my childhood, I maybe wish that I was maybe a little bit more aggressive, a little bit more assertive. That was just me. I mean, I stood up for myself, I defended myself . . . and I was shy." Tom's focus on "sensitivity" means that he is not pushy, confrontational, or aggressive, all classically masculine traits; but he is also reluctant to say that this makes him a good man, a strong man, or even a better man.

Other men shared Tom's experience of being the sensitive one among aggressive men. Moshe, for example, described his own nonconfrontational approach to life. "I am the type of person who doesn't like confrontation," he told me many times, and indeed he speaks very gently and carefully. Even when he leads services, he has a soft, gentle voice and the skilled demeanor of a man who has studied music. Mostly, however, his gentleness is a way of escaping from the aggressive, assertive expectations imposed upon him as a man. "I used to come to synagogue late—I would plan to get there forty-five minutes late just so that nobody would ask me to lead," he laughed, "because of this pressure. It was scary. There was something about that big forum, the men's section, that was not good for me, on the personal level. I just didn't like it. I didn't want to deal with it." Significantly, he feels that in the partnership synagogue there is more room for him to be the kind of man he wants to be. "Now, when we came to this new synagogue, there is much less pressure to perform to a certain standard, and that has liberated me. I can lead services the way that feels good to me, softly, in my own voice. I hadn't done it in twenty years, but now I'm doing it again, and it feels good." Like Tom, Moshe has liberated himself from the assertive, "macho" aggression and competitiveness of masculinity. The partnership synagogue has been a place for Moshe to liberate the soft-spoken man inside.

There is an ongoing tension in Orthodox masculinity between aggressive and disciplining conventions and men's desires for more softness and flexibility, and many men struggle with this. "I think that the *tefillah*, when you are doing it correctly, is both a discipline and an art form," Zvi said, "and it takes an incredible amount of discipline and also openness, and I haven't been in that place for several years." Before Zvi had children, he had an intense, concentrated experience at synagogue. "I feel that I used to have a relationship with God. Now I am not sure that I do. That's hard. . . . It's difficult for me to have *kavana* when I'm going in and out,[5] or it just takes me time to get there. I mean I wish I had time to invest in it, and the time to do it right. I don't always like rushing through it. . . . I would like to have more time to daven, to have more *kavana*, I would like to be in a place where I was a long time ago." The Orthodox man is meant to be someone who prays with "intent," or, in the language of the "be a man" box, is "serious." Child rearing, however, has gotten in the way— "going in and out" refers to Zvi's experience with looking after his three little children during prayer services. Thus, Zvi finds himself negotiating expectations on the Orthodox man to be "serious" and "striving," versus his real life of phenomenological experience of having three children who need care. The partnership synagogue, then, relaxes some of the pressures on men, but some men do not see that as necessarily a good thing.

The issue of letting go of "standards" or "striving" and relaxing with one's own self became an extended topic of conversation at one of the focus groups, where men debated the Orthodox emphasis on men's "striving" versus a resistance that allows a man to just be okay with himself and live comfortably in his own skin. We looked at Zvi's comments and then engaged in an extended conversation about pressures, expectations, parenting, and the missing sense of being okay with oneself. The conversation began with Zachary, who talked about his guilt about not living up to expectations:

> I think there's a certain sense of guilt, at least for me, because there's a certain standard that you're expected to be, and the standard is very difficult to be up to, you know? You know you're supposed to pray three times a day, and with *kavana*,

you know, and on Shabbat all these rules and laws and this and that, and you need to know how to read *Gemara*,[6] and you need to know how to layn. . . . You need to know everything, and if you don't know everything then you're a failure, basically. I don't know what other people know, I don't know what other people do, but there is this sense of, like, well, you're not living up. You're not there, and therefore you're inadequate in some way. That's how I feel.

Zachary expressed a sense of being overwhelmed by all that is in the box—learning, practicing, knowing, leading—and always feeling "inadequate." Like Kimmel's marketplace man who is always trying to live up to standards, here Orthodox men are under pressure to live up to expectations. Stuart, on the other hand, who experienced and understood what Zachary was describing, offered a striking portrait of resistance to this male "persona":

When I was growing up, and I grew up in a traditional home, and I went to a day school, I kind of felt that the idea of striving to be better was kind of engrained in my mind. Not at home, but within the community, within the world that I lived in. I think that as I got older I got to the point where that doesn't necessarily have to be the case. That I can be happy with where I'm at, and that there are other factors in my life that are also, you know, relevant and important. I feel like maybe sometimes I do strive and sometimes I don't, but if I do strive, it's coming at the expense of something else which is also valuable and which is also important to my life. . . . Your priorities are different. The whole idea of the children, for example. I think that for me, if I don't daven three times a day, and I'm not saying I do or I don't, or if I don't get to *minyan* three times a day, so it's not because, you know, I'm goofing off and doing other things and not striving in other things. I'm striving in other things.

Stuart, combining a reconstruction of fatherhood and career as "shifting priorities," thus constructs a male persona who gives up the need to constantly "strive," because he wants to be "happy with where I'm at." He adds a vital element to the portrait of men's resistance: *letting go*. Whether it's letting go of expectations, of constructs, or the need to always be "striving," Stuart has made a choice to resist by abandoning the process of constant striving for more.

For other men, however, this idea of letting go was difficult because it went against their whole concept of being an Orthodox man. This is what Efraim added:

For me there's a dialectic. On the one hand, I feel like I'm inadequate because I don't match up to the standard. On the other hand, there's supposed to be a striving, isn't there? I mean isn't . . . the whole point of being religious is that there's supposed to be a striving to be better, to be better people and to serve God? We can never be perfect. We can never do it all the way, but there's always got to be some striving. So in some ways that's a positive thing.

For Efraim, then, who values Stuart's description of making time for children, the idea of "striving" is effectively the "whole point of being religious." Stuart's description of resistance clearly hits a nerve. There's no nirvana for Orthodox men. This issue sparked a lot of discussion:

> Stuart: That's kind of a depressing thought in some ways because it's always, you know, Efraim's feeling of being inadequate, maybe that's something. If someone is really truly Orthodox, maybe that's how everyone feels? You know, that they always have to strive and then they're always going to feel inadequate.
>
> Zachary: This describes my whole struggle these days. It's exactly this. It summarizes my whole thing. When I pray I try to—I always think I should have *kavana*. It doesn't happen a lot, but I really want it to happen.
>
> Efraim: You used to have a relationship with God, but you don't anymore?
>
> Zachary: I certainly don't feel that—or it would be a long time ago.
>
> Efraim: . . . I don't think I ever had it in the full sense, I never felt it completely, and I definitely strive to be in that place. I'm not one of these, how do you say, "national religious" Israelis who just grew up with the sense that's the way it is and there's hardly any striving. Maybe that's not true; maybe I stereotyped it. But it just seems like that, that they're set, that's the way it is, and with me it's a constant struggle.

Orthodox men are striving and struggling. They are trying to live up to expectations and trying to be good men, good husbands, good fathers, and good Jews. Everything they do requires effort, and the standards are impossible to achieve. The Orthodox man is in constant dialogue with an unattainable ideal. Only Stuart seemed to have rejected the notion of striving, because he understands that every time a man is so focused on one goal, something else falls by the wayside. Stuart quite remarkably rejects the whole persona and says he just wants to be "okay." How very telling, and perhaps a bit sad, that being "okay" with oneself requires men to reject an entire stance of Orthodox masculinity.

Bisexuality and Euripides

One of the most difficult situations in which an Orthodox man cannot conform to the box is when he is homosexual. Adin, a twenty-seven-year-old graduate student from a well-known Orthodox family, went through an entire process of struggling against Orthodox masculinity that revolved primarily around sexuality but was really about the whole box. While the focus of his resistance is sexuality, his struggle reflects a deconstruction of the entire Orthodox male persona. "I sort of went through a general sexual identity—not crisis, but questioning, in college, about whether I was bisexual or not," he said. "At some point I realized that I was not, and I realized that the question has its roots in different misdirected psychological or just existential questions about whether or not I felt like a man. For a short time, my gender identity felt very sort of transgender. I sort of felt that I didn't fit the mold of either gender properly." Adin questioned whether he was a man altogether, so that his sexual orientation became the focus of his struggle. He discovered, however, that his difficulty had nothing to do with sexuality, but with the male persona he was socialized into. "Basically, because of my connection with my emotions and my need to express them and have them be a part of my life, I drew the conclusion that I was bisexual." Because he did not fit the mold of the men in his life—particularly older brothers, since his father had died young—he felt like he must not be a proper man. Because he also had behaviors that he saw as masculine—for example, getting angry in "a male way"—he did not feel like a woman either. His "connection with emotion" led him to the conclusion that he must be gay or bisexual.

Perhaps what is most striking about Adin's story is that he says he had no example in his entire upbringing of a straight Orthodox man who was emotionally expressive:

When I was talking with my girlfriend, I would often get mad at her, and she would cry when I would get mad at her, and it was very confusing to me because it's usually, in my family, either the person wouldn't respond or would shout back and be angry, and that was the way my brothers and I interacted when we were upset with each other. You know, we didn't cry to each other, and that was the way my sisters and my mother interacted with us, even though amongst themselves they would cry. Also just in terms of rational thinking, being very mathematical and scientific, all my brothers are strictly rational thinkers and would make fun of me when I wouldn't know something. In college, I was studying Greek drama, and I would make a mistake in division or something at the table, and they would make fun of me and I would say, "But you don't know about Euripides!" I'd be thinking that, but I found it ridiculous in terms of the model that they were for me, as men, to sort of participate in that, and so it felt that I was more like my sisters or my

mother. [I thought it] must make me, you know, not gay, but bisexual. The first
question was . . . you know, what am I inside? I don't feel the need to have a super
outward gender identity. I don't need to dress a certain way, but, you know, there are
people—I can't remember his name, but this famous British comic who says that he's
not a straight man, he's a lesbian. He thinks he's a woman in a man's body who likes
women. So that was sort of where I thought I might be, somewhere in that category.

Adin offers a striking montage of masculine identity in Orthodoxy. His oldest brother, a practicing Orthodox rabbi and author, is described as analytical,
emotionally stunted, mocking of boys, and directing a powerful man-on-man
gaze. Adin describes a remarkable process in which he challenges or discon-
nects from this model—and as a result comes to the conclusion that he is either
transgender, a lesbian, or bisexual. He eventually concluded that this was a
"classic psychoanalytical homophobia" and he has been living a straight man's
life with a monogamous girlfriend for the past five years. But getting to that
place required a process of reconfiguring the entire box. To quote John Stoltenberg, Adin was "refusing to be a man."[7]

In some ways Adin's story is unusual, but it also somewhat reflects a phenomenon of men struggling with homosexual exclusion from Orthodoxy. Azriel, a twenty-nine-year-old married father of one who spent much of his college
time as an activist in the lesbian, gay, bisexual, and transgender (LGBT) community, offers a touching portrait of a straight men reaching out to enable homo-
sexuals to be Orthodox men. Azriel was brought up in the Chabad community
but left it in his late teens and traversed many different Jewish communities and
outlooks before settling into the partnership *minyan*. The Orthodox approach to
homosexuality is a major point of Azriel's disillusionment with Orthodoxy:

When [the movie] *Trembling before God* [about Rabbi Steven Greenberg's struggle
with homosexuality] came out, we were recruited to help to try to reach out to the
Orthodox community and try to promote it locally. My discussions with various
local rabbis and my own rabbi were frustrating. They weren't willing to go as far as
I thought they needed. Only one *shul* was willing to screen the movie, but they
had to do it behind closed doors. They weren't willing to sign onto any way a
formal agreement about how they would be inclusive to gay and lesbian Jews.
What disturbed me most was that they weren't willing to admit that this was an
issue, or that this was something that needed to be attended to. They kind of felt
like, "Oh, right now people are bringing it up, so we'll talk about [it], but then we'll
brush it under the rug. It's not crucial to our community or to our Judaism." For me

that was like, wow. For me, issues of sexuality and gender are the key issues to the postmodern Orthodox Jew. There's nothing right now in the twenty-first century that is more relevant to the conversation.

For Azriel, sexuality and gender are the most important issues that modern Orthodoxy needs to challenge, and he is actively and courageously working to bring about that change. As a result, he has experienced the resolve with which Orthodox rabbis refuse to unpack the Orthodox man box. The exclusion of gay from the box, then, is emblematic of the overall power and resolve of Orthodox masculinity.

Conclusions

Orthodox men are changing, not only in strictly Orthodox settings, but in other aspects of their lives as well. The manifestations of these changes reflect processes of challenging masculinity in general, and especially challenging marketplace man. They also reflect particularly Orthodox dynamics of marketplace man.

The tension between family responsibilities and synagogue responsibilities is a central location for navigating identity. The demand to be a meticulous synagogue performer comes into conflict with the demand to be an active father, a conflict that finds expression in a myriad of ways. Similarly, the demand to be a family man sometimes conflicts with the demand to be ambitious. Men are under enormous pressure to be reliable, dependable, strong, and responsible in both the religious and personal realms, and some are actively seeking ways to reduce that pressure.

Although the synagogue is one outlet for challenging gender expectations, some men have found other outlets for change. One location for change is in marriage relationships and home life, where men are making choices about what kinds of fathers they want to be, and what kinds of husbands they want to be. Many men are rejecting older models, while other men reject selectively. Few if any men are completely deconstructing expectations of being the provider, but some privately wish that they could. Another location for change is work. Some men are choosing professional paths that fly in the face of expectations by being less ambitious than is socially acceptable for men. Some men resist simply by being less aggressive, less competitive, and less unequivocal, while others resist by taking on the strictures of heterosexuality.

Many of these acts of resistance overlap, whether between child care and home chores or sexuality and persona, or between roles in synagogue and roles in the kitchen. But at other times, there is no obvious connection. Some men reconfigure career or persona without any connection to women, relationships, fatherhood, or child care, but rather out of a general sense of wanting to be a different kind of man. What is certain, however, is that this is one area where men have begun to create a language for re-creating masculinity not only around singular ambition and control, but also around relationships, negotiation, and care.

While many of these processes reflect broader social trends, there is a particular face of Orthodoxy here. For one thing, Orthodox men are told to be constantly "striving," creating an added pressure to perform. Similarly, if marketplace man is meant to be also "family man," here the pressure to have a large family and provide for them is even more intense. Finally, the issue of religious ritual, especially Shabbat, gives the struggle of Orthodox men its own color and form. Shabbat is certainly one of the most gender-focused rituals in Judaism— women prepare for Shabbat, women light candles, men make the blessings, women sit passively in synagogue (if at all), while men perform at synagogue and do what the community expects of them. As such, Shabbat is one of the unique locations of the negotiation over gender. Men's descriptions of who prepares for Shabbat cut deeply into Orthodox tradition and create one of the most interesting battlefields over gender, a parallel to the entire discussion of what women do in synagogue.

Sometimes, men's changes are subtle and easy to read as something else. Singing more softly in synagogue is not just about musical taste but also about reconstructing power, control, and hierarchies, as well as an entire persona of masculinity. Moreover, expressions of ambivalence, self-doubt, or a willingness to just "be okay" are ways for men to let go of the overwhelming aggressiveness that so often characterizes masculinity. Certainly the letting go of an all-encompassing ambitiousness is difficult for some men, but the changing of the masculinity persona is probably at the core of all these shifts.

Perhaps the most striking illustration of how difficult change can be was from Adin, for whom the epitome of the Orthodox man is an overpoweringly heterosexual, angry, demanding, insensitive father figure. The socialization into this type of masculinity was so strong, and yet so uncomfortable for him, that his form of resistance was to shift at the core and explore homosexuality, as if to say the entire posture of aggression around Orthodox man comes from a relationship to women, a stance opposing and controlling women, and that in order to abandon that stance, one has to abandon manhood altogether.

CHAPTER 6

Men Encountering Feminism

Women, Feminism, and Orthodox Men

〜 MEN WRESTLING WITH their identities may mistakenly think that they are alone. A man challenging his socialization may make changes in his personal or professional life, in his relationships, or in his persona. These informants are all in a process of one kind or another, challenging bits and pieces while internalizing others, changing and moving while staying within expected boundaries and norms. Each man has his own story and his own journey, and each is unique.

In the partnership synagogues, however, there has also been a different kind of process taking place, a collective process, based on the fact that men have actually come together in a particular place to search for something different. The partnership synagogue is by definition a location of social change, and men have arrived there—or in some cases, created that location themselves—out of desire for that collective experience. The result is a new kind of space that is shifting the landscape of Jewish life and Jewish practice.

A Note about Men and Feminism

Over the course of this research, I have often been asked if men can be feminists. The question stems from the notion that men cannot write from the perspective of the female experience and therefore can only be "experts on" feminism rather than through-and-through feminists.[1] For men, the question may also be about whether feminism is or ought to be a "woman's thing." Some argue that if men call themselves feminists, they should be welcomed.[2] Although there is not necessarily a true correlation between feminist self-identification and feminist practice among men,[3] I believe that feminism is a worldview, and as such anyone with a mind can ascribe to it. Would anyone ask if, say, Haitians can be capitalists, or if teenagers can be adherents of macrobiotics? It seems obvious to me that men and women can believe in anything they want to. Furthermore, as much as personal experience sheds light on particular issues, I believe that empathy exists. Just as not all oncologists have had cancer, so, too, not all feminists have had the experience of living femaleness. It is this very belief that informs this research. Not only am I exploring the feminisms of men, but I am also assuming that I can be a woman and still come to an understanding of men. The process of understanding "otherness" should expand horizons and not just confine us to our own lived experiences. Certainly men have that capacity for empathetic wisdom as well, and I would rather call them feminists and honor their work of mutual understanding.

Not only *can* men be feminists, but it seems that some men *have* been feminists since before the advent of the word "feminism." Peter F. Murphy, in *Feminism and Masculinities*,[4] traces "pro-woman" or feminist men back twenty-five hundred years and includes a whole slew of British, French, and American writers and thinkers from the past 350 years, such as Defoe, Montesquieu, and Thomas Paine. Similarly, Kimmel and Mosmiller document the writings of feminist men from the past two hundred years,[5] some of whom, such as Frederick Douglass, were even plenary speakers at the nineteenth-century Seneca Falls Convention. Kimmel noted that Tom Paine favored equal rights for women before the United States was founded and that Ralph Waldo Emerson promoted women's suffrage.[6] Lest one think that feminist men of yesteryear had lighter issues to discuss than today's men, it is worth noting that while twenty-first-century Americans continue to debate abortion and the day-after pill, during the French Enlightenment, men were arguing not only for suffrage and economic equality, but also for birth-control rights for women. It is not only logical but also historically illustrated that men can and most certainly have been proponents of feminism throughout history.

Nonetheless, there is discomfort around men who are led by women, both in Orthodoxy and in Western culture in general. As Doris W. Ewing and Steven P. Schacht write,

> Too often feminism has been seen as a "woman-only" arena or defined in competitive terms of male versus female privilege, rather than a cooperative effort to improve the quality of life for everyone. The few men who have attempted to embrace a feminist worldview often have been marginalized by women who view them with suspicion and by men who see them as gender traitors (or as a friend says, "The worm in the sperm").[7]

In other words, it is indeed possible for men to be feminists, but feminist men, like feminist women, have to survive some formidable societal hurdles to be comfortable with that attribution. Geraldine Fabrikant wrote an article in the business section of the *New York Times* titled "Would You Hire Your Husband?" about men who work for their wives. The fact that she has to even ask the question indicates that society is uncomfortable with men being led by women. "The woman may make a conscious effort to ensure that her mate is getting appropriate recognition," she wrote, adding that "the men interviewed for this article seemed comfortable working at family companies controlled by their wives. . . . It was the wives who tended to be more sensitive about the potential pitfalls of having their husbands on the payroll. A wife's fear of making her husband feel emasculated in the workplace is a real consideration."[8] In a counterintuitive reversal, the men Fabrikant interviewed were more comfortable with their feminist stance than some of the women. Feminist men in a tenaciously patriarchal world, both three thousand years ago and today, still have an uphill battle.

Men and the Partnership Synagogue

When I embarked on this research project, I assumed the partnership synagogue to be the most feminist place in which Orthodox Jewish men could belong. My *own* misguided assumption was that men are knowingly entering this feminist place as an expression of their negotiation with feminism. I sought to understand the identity processes that this entry entailed, by simultaneously exposing both the world from which those men emerged and the world that they were entering. I thought I would get almost two for the price of one—both understanding Orthodoxy and understanding male-feminist resistance to Orthodoxy.

Late in the research, however, one of my informants, who has been involved in several partnership *minyanim*, told me, "If you're looking for feminist men at the partnership synagogues, you're going to be disappointed." Indeed, it was not very long after I began that I realized this population of men is hardly what one could call a predominantly feminist or even profeminist group. As the previous chapters indicate, men come to the partnership synagogue for a whole host of reasons, the overwhelming majority of which have nothing to do with feminism. In fact, even when gender issues factor into their reasons for coming, they are often a minor subtext, or even an afterthought. Several men told me that I would not want to interview them because, as one man said, "I'm not here for the reasons you think I'm here." They come because they are grappling with their own inductions into Orthodoxy and are challenging issues of self, relationship, and community and seeking avenues to further their own liberation, much of which often has little to do with women. I would say that the dominant reason men come to these synagogues is social. They are looking for connections.

For some, feminism is not even on their radar screens. When men explain that the synagogue experience is nicer now that the entire family comes together, they sidestep the fact that the "entire family coming" is a function of the fact that women now have a *reason* to come. When men talk about liberation from perfect performance, they ignore the fact that women's voices have created space for alternative sounds. When men talk about feeling welcome, they ignore ways in which including women creates a larger culture of inclusion, or "niceness." Women are often irrelevant to men's experiences and descriptions, leaving feminism and social change outside their motivations. So much of what is going on in the partnership synagogue is incidental and subconscious, not only ignoring women's liberation, but also at times impeding it.

Nevertheless, there is a cadre of men who come to the synagogue out of a strong and dedicated feminist ideology, for the reconstruction of gender in Orthodox culture, and they make some intriguing points about their own identities. Men's feminisms contain gradations and ideological distinctions that parallel some of the disputes in feminism in general, as well as some particularly Orthodox quirks. The feminist resistance among these Orthodox men fits roughly into three categories: a moral-liberal feminism seeking equality and fairness; a broader, cultural feminism seeking to change Orthodox cultural institutions; and a radical feminism seeking the transformation of men. There is no balance between these different outlooks; the first, which relies on a liberal-feminist ideology of equality, is undoubtedly the most common, and the third is extremely rare. Nonetheless, there are indications that some voices are calling for broad change and male transformations within Orthodoxy.

Abdicating Male Privilege

Men who participate in a partnership synagogue are, knowingly or unknowingly, engaged in the process of shifting gender identities. "It's not manly to be open-minded," Hillel said. "A manly thing to do is to keep women in their place." Joining the partnership synagogue is a rejection of that manliness. As Mendel Shapiro said, "You're giving something up; this is something that was yours and now you have to share it."[9]

The issue of men's roles in places where men have abdicated privilege has been a heated topic of discussion in the American Reform movement, with headlines about the "men's crisis" spurring debates everywhere. Even among the "moderately affiliated," women are taking the lead, sometimes to the exclusion of men altogether.[10] Michael G. Holzman writes of the multiple grapplings and journeys of Reform men in response to the decline of men's participation in Reform temple life. "Jewish men have scaled every mountain . . . in the secular world, and they have (almost) every opportunity imaginable in the religious world," he writes. "Yet many remain anxious, squeamish, and awkward when the time comes to actually consider their selves. And if we ask them to consider their souls, that might send them into conniptions."[11] Holzman argues that the Jewish men's crisis has a lot to do with feminism. "The term 'feminism' inspires a great deal of anxiety among some men," which leads to a "great deal of resentment" because "very few men think of themselves as proudly misogynistic, and most will resent feeling branded with that term for no other reason than our membership in the male sex." He adds that the anxiety also comes from a "fear that feminism means a loss of power."[12] Holzman works to deconstruct these "misunderstanding[s] about feminism" by advocating a feminism for men that is "more than a movement for equal access, opportunity, rights and remuneration as men."[13] He advocates, in fact, for a radical Jewish men's feminism:

> Feminists decided to look at gender, to embrace it, and to redefine how it applied to them. They decided that not only did they want equal access to the vote, schools, sports, jobs and salaries, but they also wanted to bring their perspectives, their methods, their preferences, and their style. Mere access was not enough. They wanted to change the environment once they entered. They taught us all that gender matters. It matters for all of us. Women and men.[14]

Holzman's important essay reflects a certain ambivalence, even among enlightened and feminist men, about their relationships with feminism. He is both completely supportive of gender equality and feminism and sympathetic to men's anxiety about feminism.

The tension between men and feminism, even feminist men, finds expression in many ways. Rabbi Rona Shapiro discounts the crisis as male discomfort with the abdication of privilege: "If Jewish men, young or old, are turned off by women's leadership, then our commitment to justice requires that we call this what it is—sexism—and work to change the attitude instead of accommodating it."[15] Holzman countered that there is no zero-sum game of victimhood, and that both men and women are hurt by patriarchy. "This either/or binary think-ing is counterproductive for a healthy response to the needs of both sexes. . . . The absence of men and boys implies a deeper problem that affects us all."[16] At issue here is the debate among male feminists about whether feminist men should be focused on relieving women of their oppressions or on relieving men of theirs. Holzman argues that it does not have to be either/or, though the argu-ment begs substantiation. The women's crisis from patriarchy is more systemic and more oppressive than that of men, but the men's crisis from patriarchy, which is also at the root of their discomfort with female power, has barely been acknowledged or understood.

This tension between feminist women and feminist men, which today can be seen most readily in the changing dynamics of the Reform temple, has fasci-nating implications for the partnership synagogues. Both arenas are locations of feminist intervention in a patriarchal structure. If the Reform movement, which has had a few decades to grapple with this, is now in the midst of a major struggle, one can only imagine where Orthodoxy is vis-à-vis these issues. The discussion of Orthodox masculinity may be starting, frankly, right here.

In order to try to elicit some thoughts about power, privilege, and masculin-ity, I confronted informants with the remark of my friend at the beginning of this book: "If women are doing everything, what is left for men to do?" I used it as a "text" during interviews, asking men how they would respond to this state-ment. Their responses shed light on the complexity of reconstructing masculinity.

Some men were perplexed. "That's ridiculous," Avi said. "That makes no sense," Judah agreed. "I don't come to *shul* because I'm a man." Even when I practically spelled out the issue of masculinity and power, some men were dumbfounded. "I have no idea what this research is about at all," Haggai said several times—even after a three-hour focus group. "You say masculinity, but I have no idea what you're getting at." Others said they did not understand the question. "I have no problem with that. This *minyan* is about religion. We come to pray," one of the men said simply. Michael said, "I guess it could be argued that maybe the synagogue is the last refuge of a purely male domain, but I just don't relate to it in that way." For many men, the topic of male power and the abdication of privilege was a foreign formulation.

Others acknowledged that bringing women into the synagogue required a certain shift in these elements of masculinity, but that men would find other ways to fill the void. "There's still a lot left for a man to do," Zeev said, referring not only to all the leadership jobs that women are barred from but also the ways in which the tasks are carried out. "If the synagogue is in a bind, if they don't have someone to read on a particular Shabbat, and they need someone, it's almost always a man who can pick it up." Men retain their superior knowledge or position in other ways.

Some men are comforted knowing that female takeover is not absolute. "I can see that loss of power being disorienting for someone, which is classic," Harold acknowledged. "People are used to having a position of authority and power, and you take authority and power away from people, they are lost to know what their role is. And it's a common experience to feel resentment, anger toward that, so that doesn't surprise me." Yet although Harold understands the sentiment, he says that it doesn't bother him at all because "it seems to be pretty fixed what women do, the bits of the service they're allowed to and they do. . . . I don't experience any sense of resentment or being pushed out." He is able to live with what he called the initial "strangeness" of women's roles by virtue of the fact that they are limited and "regimented." Women are not taking over the service but just "bits," a point that actually distinguishes the partnership setting from the Reform setting.

There are some men who offered reflective, feminist responses to the issue. Isaac, for example, when confronted with the story of the man who said "What's left for men to do?" responded, "It's a load of rubbish," and countered that the "only reason why he feels that way is because deep down he believes that these should only be men's roles, not women's. I mean, he's very happy to see women doing nothing while they watch him do stuff, that's fine with him. But when the roles are reversed, he doesn't see it as fine at all. So, you know, its just contradicting logic." Moreover, the sentiment is based on perceptions of a female takeover, not an actual takeover. "None of these *shuls* are saying that women do everything," Isaac said. "They're saying that men and women do things equally. The fact that he can't do everything anymore but he can only do half and saying that he doesn't know how it's affecting his manhood, I think that's just rubbish." Zvi added, "What do you mean, there are no jobs left for you? Like, you're there, like you're davening with 100 percent kind of *kavana* all the time, you're progressing with your relationship with God that's really, really hard work."

Ehud, who like Isaac is fully cognizant of the power issue, voluntarily and purposefully abdicates an entire white male privilege and then some:

The whole issue of status—I was asked once why I go to the egalitarian synagogue. After all, I am giving up something, and I have a lot of power as a man to lead the service, to see about what goes in the service, and I was asked how I am willing to give up on that. I have power, so why would I want to share it with other groups, or the other gender? And it struck me as a very strange question, because what does that mean? It shouldn't be. I really do not believe that one group should have more power than another group, and I have no problem sharing that power or giving up my uniqueness as a man. . . . If I wanted to retain my power, I would have stayed in the army, continued to stand at the checkpoints. There I have a lot of power. I didn't like doing that either. I still don't and I try not to. The army experience, the check-points, the territories, it all really influenced me that way. I don't want power. Power is bad. And certainly power that I have just by virtue of the fact that I am a man, or a Jew, or an Israeli or an Ashkenazi or white or educated or rich or—not rich but bourgeois. . . . I have no problem losing power. I don't want power.

More than any other informant, Ehud has made a purposeful, conscious decision to abdicate privilege. This applies not only to gender, but also to eth-nicity, nationality, and class. He has made this decision following experiences of having extreme and absolute power, and purposefully decided that this was not a stance that he wanted. Whether he made this decision out of morality or for some other reason is a bit unclear. Nonetheless, he is one of the informants most conscious of the issue of abdicating masculine and other privileges.

Like Ehud, Azriel also understands the privilege issue and voluntarily abdi-cates privilege. He too takes a staunchly feminist, pro-women stance:

There's the "supposed to" that I don't agree with. You know, that this is ["supposed to be"] men's domain and we've emasculated men by taking it away from them. I don't think it was always man's. I think it was given to men and it should be given to everybody. And so, the "supposed to" is a fallacy to me. That's not *halakha* or Judaism talking. That's classic male fear that they're going to take away from us the power and we're not going to have anything to do and we would be what they were. I mean the part of that whole statement that really gets to me is God forbid we should have to sit in a *shul* the way we've made women sit in the *shul* for thousands of years.

Azriel effectively suggests that men's fear of abdicating privilege is about the fear of being like women—perhaps the epitome of being "outside" the box.

A Feminism of Empathy

The prevailing expression of feminist motivation among informants is what Jonathan termed a "moral logic." As Shalom said, "I think there should be gender equality for the same reason I think women ought to vote. I don't have to defend that argument. Why shouldn't they [vote]?" It is a line of liberal thinking informed by changes in society at large, especially the comparison between women's *professional* status and their *synagogue* status. "It was always just totally logical to me," Jonathan said. "I just never ever saw why a girl could not layn. Being an academic, I never saw a difference between men and women in the academic sphere. It seems so overwhelmingly logical to me." Jonathan, a physics professor, who works with female professors on a daily basis, fully believes that this equality should carry over into the synagogue as well. Zeev, a pediatric neurosurgeon and the father of three daughters, also compares women at work with women at the synagogue. "Like the doctors here in the hospital, I'm always pressing the women to make sure they do good fellowships, that they don't sell out on their career," he said proudly. "I think they should learn, I think they should have independence financially, they should challenge themselves as human beings." The synagogue is another arm of societal culture that demands equality. "Even in religious society, women are allowed to be teachers and professors, career women and decision makers active in the spheres of education, public life, economics, and professional life," Netanel said. "Meanwhile, in synagogue, they are there behind the partition, not active at all, not seen. This dissonance is ultimately what drives the process of equality in the Orthodox world." Zeev added that the partnership synagogue is a "really important change within Orthodoxy and an important way to give opportunities to people." The exclusion of women is damaging for society, he said. "You've got to figure out and work it out so that you can use all this intelligence. . . . This is one of the ways to manifest that by being able to participate in *shul* and show that skill set." The alternative, he said, "seems ludicrous." "In today's world, women have equal knowledge as most men in Jewish subject and thought," Yossi concurred, "and this is a place where they can at least have a physical expression of it. It is important. Otherwise I'm afraid we will lose a lot of really intelligent people." All these men value women's intelligence and skills and want society to benefit from women's active participation. This is the abdication of privilege not only for the benefit of women, but for the benefit of society as a whole.

Despite the obviousness of this "moral logic," there is an incredible amount of resistance among Orthodox men to many of these ideas. Brian, who grew up Conservative and is now an ordained Orthodox rabbi, says that some Orthodox men suffer from a "disconnect" or "cognitive dissonance" regarding women. "If you live in the world where women are Supreme Court justices, women can run for president, women are your professors in school, women are business executives, so you spend 144 hours of the week in that environment, and then come Shabbat and you walk into *shul* and all of a sudden we have the gender dichotomy that we do. . . . If you're socialized in an Orthodox environment, either you have some sort of barrier that cushions that blow and you say, all right, this is the way it is for the time that I'm in *shul,* or you just don't see it. It's like a veil that enables people to experience this sort of cognitive dissonance, that there's this disconnect." Brian thinks that he does not have this disconnect because he did not have the Orthodox socialization, and finds himself torn between the "authenticity" of Orthodoxy and the social norms of Conservative Judaism. "Walking into an Orthodox *shul,* I feel like I'm not being genuine about who I am because I don't believe in treating women as second-class citizens," he says. "At the same time, how can I do that in an environment that doesn't feel like I'm also getting rid of what feels authentic about *halakha*?" The dissonance is not just between Orthodoxy and secular life, but between Orthodoxy and other aspects of his Jewish identity.

One of the interesting aspects of this "moral logic" is that it cuts across cultures and countries. Brian, a twenty-nine-year-old who was brought up as an American midwestern Conservative Jew, Jonathan, a fifty-one-year-old Australian professor brought up in modern Orthodoxy, Zeev, a fifty-two-year-old doctor from a liberal Jewish New York family that marched in the civil rights movement, and Netanel, a forty-year-old religious Zionist Israeli who grew up in the ranks of Jerusalem Bnei Akiva, have all reached very similar conclusions. The similarity, in fact, between these narratives effectively dismisses the claim that Conservative Jews are dominating these *minyanim,* or that there is something inherently different going on in Israel and North America. Fundamentally, the processes that men are experiencing are parallel. Around the world, in different places, men are coming together to challenge Orthodox masculinity.

Another recurring element of men's feminist resistance goes beyond moral *logic,* and that is moral *empathy,* the sense of internalizing another's offense or pain. "It's interesting," Zvi reflects. "For so long, *kavod hatsibur* [congregational dignity] prevented women from taking part in the communal life of the *tzibur* [congregation]. And for me, it's very much the opposite. *Kavod hatsibur* necessitates it. In our *tzibur* where women are educated and halakhic . . . and when woman can read, to *not* let them read is equally insulting. *Kavod hatsibur* would require any community that saw its women as educated [to enable them] to fulfill this duty, and not allowing them to do so would be a problem for the *tzibur.*" In this clever rereading of the halakhic argument, which makes the radical suggestion that women are part of the "congregation," Zvi is able to access a woman's emotional and visceral experience and make it part of the male Orthodox discourse. He interweaves the language of law with the language of empathy. "I think that's why a lot of us are here," he concluded.

A more direct feeling of empathy for women's experiences emerges from men's personal relationships with women in their lives. "I didn't want my daughter going to a *shul* where implicitly she would understand at a certain point, there are two types of people, people who are on one side of the partition, and people who are on the other side of the partition," Tom said. "I think girls understand it at a very young age, and I didn't want her . . . to internalize the reality that somehow she is on the wrong side of the *mehitza*, she's not as good as the people on the other side . . . that there are two groups of people and they belong to the group of people that are somehow and someway less good. I didn't want her to have that." Tom, whose daughter is two years old, asserts that even young girls can feel the insult of being relegated to second-class-citizen status. Tom's care for his daughter's emotional well-being forms the impetus for his support of the partnership *minyan.* In fact, I think that men's concern for their daughters is one of the most powerful forces driving men's feminism. Jonathan, for example, initially came to feminism out of the desire to give his daughters opportunities to layn:

> Given that many women were genuinely disenfranchised for no good halakhic
> reason, the beginning [of my involvement] was the women's *tefillah* group, and I
> was fully supportive of that, and I taught my children and my daughters to layn. I
> was very happy to be in the kitchen when my daughter layned for her bat mitzvah.
> I never thought about Shira Hadasha coming to fruition, but when it did, I found it
> completely comfortable and just completely logical. My daughters all tell me that
> in fact now they can't go to a regular *shul* because they just find it offensive. My
> daughter layns better than many, many men. She's a delight to listen to.
>
> People said, but why do women need it? And I said you know, a boy, regardless
> of how much he knows or how much he doesn't know, when he has his bar mitz-
> vah, [he] comes along and holds the *eitz hayim* [tree of life] of the Torah scroll. That
> act of grabbing the *eitz hayim* is basically saying this is mine. It's everybody else's as
> well, but I'm now taking hold of it, grasping it—this is mine. And that symbol
> cannot be replicated by having a bat mitzvah party or a white dress or whatever.
> That's a symbolism that means that girls take the possession of the Torah just like

boys take possession of the Torah, and it's a logical outgrowth of everything that's happened in the last fifty years. I mean, you can't have a situation in which girls don't know how to layn, but girls know Talmud and they are full-fledged learners and even in some cases judges.

Jonathan's love and empathy for his daughters drives his entire belief system. Unlike Zvi, his argument is less rooted in *halakha,* and more in his feelings about girls' experiences. Significantly, men often come to feminism through relationships with women and girls whom they love and empathize with, regardless of their own age or stage in life, and irrespective of the actual age of their daughters. The empathy is an emotional stance that leads to thinking about exclusivity, insult, and social hierarchies, and perhaps men's expressions of the personal are political. Empathy seems to be a key element in the emergence of liberal-socialist feminism among men, and it creates a formidable weapon in men's struggle against conformity. A man's love of his daughters can be stronger than his desire to fit in.

Empathy, however, is not a function of a man's marital or parental status any more than it is a function of being brought up Conservative or Reform. In fact, Michael, a thirty-nine-year-old single man who describes himself as a feminist, says that his feminism "stems from just a greater feeling of egalitarianism, of just leveling the field of not having gender barriers overall." But beyond that abstract description lies empathy. "It's the way that I saw my mother approach religion and my sisters approach religion and the education they got and the opportunities that they were denied, and the way then they approach Judaism and spirituality, it's sort of a limited world. I'm just unhappy with that limited world." Michael feels the pain of women in his life who were denied opportunities and access to spiritual expression. Oded describes a similar empathy he feels for his mother. "My mother, who grew up in a 'regular' religious family and did not go to a religious school, and she never learned [Torah], she would only come to synagogue if there was a special occasion, a holiday or an event or bar mitzvah, but normally not. And when she would come, she would also not be able to follow, so she has no connection with prayer." Like Michael's sisters, Oded's mother was denied connection to her heritage and denied access to religious practice.

Empathy can also be toward strangers. Efraim described feeling physically and emotionally "uncomfortable," such as when a building committee refused to have a woman member. "I think that a lot of the rules regarding women are completely ridiculous and arbitrary because they are based on cultures that existed two thousand years ago, which are completely anachronistic and totally unfair," he said. "It's pathetic." Oded, who teaches bar mitzvah boys in an elite northern Tel Aviv neighborhood, built empathy around relationships with women he did not even know. "When I would get to the part where I start to explain to the parents what happens in synagogue, it was always very hard for me to say to the mother, 'You'll be over there, behind the partition, with the grandmothers and sisters, and you'll see your son through the little window there, and we'll let you throw the candies.'" A feminist resistance to the Orthodox synagogue can be based on empathy for women who are wives, daughters, sisters, or even strangers.

Men's feminism, the kind that is rooted in empathy or "basic fairness" or "moral logic," is not a function of a man's upbringing, location, age, religious commitment, education, family structure, or generation. It is about seeing others and rejecting conventions that are shaming to others. Steve, for example, recalled his first experience as an Orthodox teenager in the 1970s working in a Conservative camp, where he was confronted with women as "other" for the first time. "A woman was given an *aliyah* right after me, and I was standing up there at the Torah, and I actually thought to myself, 'What do I do now? Do I—how do I feel about this? Do I shake her hand, do I stay there, etcetera?'" These thoughts were running through Steve's mind as he had to choose between Orthodox norms and an internal sense of empathy. "Whatever I was going to ultimately do, I cannot publicly shame a person by refusing to deal with them as an equal there, so I shook her hand and realized that I was fine with it." Now, thirty years later, Steve, although he has continued to dwell mostly in Orthodoxy, takes this empathy further, as he wonders whether there is room for compassion in Orthodoxy, and whether there is room for him. After thirty years of activism, he is currently debating whether to publicly resign from a public position in Orthodoxy because of an announcement that neither a convert nor a woman can serve as an officer. "I find that absolutely disgusting." He is neither a woman nor a convert, but he feels another's shame.

Orthodox men are not socialized into empathy for the other. The very notion that men will form an ideology and even a new ritual practice based on that sort of sympathizing with people who are of a different status is, in itself, almost revolutionary. It is about thinking through gender not only via cerebral, halakhic argumentation and cold distance, but also using one's entire range of emotional and visceral human experience to feel the pain of another and to work to alleviate that pain.

For empathetic men, the partnership synagogue rectifies social injustice and collective insult. "I think to myself, if my mother would go to a synagogue like Shira Hadasha . . . maybe even get an *aliyah*, she would be more interested in the Torah portion, maybe even come every week," Oded said. The synagogue would transform her connection to Jewish life, which would affect his entire family, "because when a whole family comes together to synagogue, there is a common experience." Efraim concurred. "When I see something like [the partnership synagogue] where they are willing to push the limits of what is considered acceptable, I love that. I think you should push it. You always have to push the bleeding edge in that situation, because it needs to be pushed." For some men, feminism stems from a deep care for women, and seeks social change.

Challenging Surrounding Structures

The liberal feminist outlook of equal rights for women in the synagogue is one facet of a feminist approach to social change. Another facet, which integrates critical theory to deconstruct surrounding structures, also finds expression among men in the partnership synagogue, albeit to a lesser degree. Some men have used their empathy as a springboard for broader thinking not merely about women's rights but also about the exclusivity of synagogue life in general. Others, like Danny, take a very strong emotional position to women's inequality based on his reading of other minority groups in society. "I can't bear it," he said. Isaac compares women's experiences of inequality with those of other social groups. "It hurts me because when you go into *shul*, and they don't have rights for women, it goes against justice and what's right in the world," he said. "The same thing, if you were to go to a *shul*, and they say, 'All the blacks in the back,' or you go to a church and all the blacks are in the back, people shouldn't pray in those places. It's not a *shul*." Isaac offered the radical idea that a synagogue that is unequal is "not a *shul*." In other words, he is not just trying to throw women a bone but is offering the radical interpretation that the presence of inequalities in the synagogue detracts from the very definition of a synagogue as a spiritual place. "I cannot even go to a 'normal' Orthodox synagogue anymore," Isaac said. "It's just offensive." In other words, he is here to change the way the synagogue—even the Orthodox synagogue—is defined. He is reversing the structural hierarchy that makes the partnership synagogue marginal within Orthodox culture and says that the partnership synagogue is not marginal— rather, the "mainstream" is "not a *shul*."

Admittedly, Isaac is in a small minority among the respondents who have difficulty entering a "standard" Orthodox synagogue, one of only a handful of men who expressed similar views. Noam, for example, also said that he would not walk into a "regular" Orthodox synagogue "because of the inequality," as did Elitzur Bar-Asher Siegal, who has made a hobby of helping establish partnership synagogues; and Jonathan does not understand why anyone would go to a "regular" Orthodox *shul* and not a partnership one. Beyond these few men, the sentiment that Orthodoxy globally should restructure its entire set of gender norms was not widespread.

For some men the partnership synagogue is part of a broader world vision of alleviating human injustice and inequality, perhaps a more universal mission of social change. Getting back to Steve, whose empathy for women generally went beyond any particular woman, the partnership synagogue is but one expression of a worldview that focuses on alleviating oppression. "Nothing started with the *minyan*," he said. "I think that it is one of the touchstones of society and human interpersonal relationships. I think that there is a tendency both halakhically and socially in Judaism to objectify women in certain ways. . . . Fairness, equality of human rights, were issues that going back as long as I can remember, I cared about." Steve is trying to work Orthodoxy into his sense of "fairness" rather than the other way around.

These men offer a glimpse into the idea of promoting a broad, systemic feminist revolution in Orthodoxy. It is not a widespread idea, nor is it taken to its logical conclusion by most of the informants here. Still, this type of feminism has faint appearances, startling in places, even here amid this very patriarchal community of Orthodox men.

Transforming Men

Although there are no loud calls for a systemic feminist revolution in Orthodoxy, there are some men who have thought through a transformation of masculinity. Adin, for example, explored his own victimhood from the men in his life who tried to socialize him as an aggressive, competitive, unemotional heterosexual. Adin's story is distinct because it points out that men are both *perpetrators* of the patriarchal gaze, as well as its *victims*. Adin is not only exploring women's experiences in Orthodoxy, but also exploring men's experiences, and the ways in which the male gaze damages men as well as women.

Overall, only a few select men even engaged in this direct discussion of masculinity suffering from patriarchal gaze, and it is possible that in nonpartnership synagogues, the number of men discussing masculinity would be close to zero. Among informants, feminism, when present, was relegated to the realm of liberating women, with only a handful of men taking feminism further as a tool for deconstructing masculinity. Even men who understand this were reluctant to take ownership of the idea. As Shalom said, "I think the impetus [for change in Orthodoxy] has to come from them, from women. . . . It would require a significant change in the consciousness among men also, but I think the impetus has to come from women." In other words, even men in favor of gender change still take a passive approach to changing men.

One of the most radical feminist men is Azriel, a married father of one who grew up in the Chabad community and today spends a lot of his time advocating for gay and lesbian rights. His goal is the transformation of Orthodoxy via the feminist transformation of men:

> I think it's our responsibility to teach our sons to be feminists, and I think it's a responsibility to teach straight people to be advocates for everybody who is another. But it goes beyond that, and it's our lives that are enriched with everybody who is fully engaged, and so it's not just on those that have the power to engage to carry that. I mean, we'll be a stronger community if everybody feels that they have a place in it, and I don't mean just a minor place in it. I mean, that's the problem with some of the feminist Orthodox movement . . . that okay, so we got a little chunk of the apple, this is—okay, at least it tastes good. We're at least happy with that. You know, I want people to be able to bite into as much as they want to.

In this poignant account, Azriel argues that men and boys should also be feminists, that feminism makes for a better society, and that even Orthodox feminists should be more feminist and not complacent and satisfied with minor changes. Azriel offers a rationale for his unusual approach that is a stunning cross between feminist drive for social change and a religious compassion and love for all God's creatures, an ideology that actually has some provocative Chabad echoes:

> You need to be a man who is willing to recognize that what connects the *neshama* [soul] to God is not the fact that you are a man. You have to be open to the reality that your manhood is not the answer and not the only avenue. So if you recognize those voices being a true soul, that soul is reaching to God at that moment, then you know, you are okay. . . . To look at the child and to see potential to be able to go there and hear those voices—something completely holy, and not just holy, em-

powered. I felt empowered by those voices. I felt those voices were lifting me much more than when I go into 99 percent of the other *shuls* I go into where most of the voices I hear are a *hazzan* davening either too fast, too slow, or with tunes that don't make me really feel uplifted, and with men talking about their stocks and their sports score.

In this soulful account, Azriel strips men of their masculinity and unveils an inner, "true" soul, as a search for God. Seeking out the "true" connection to God through spiritual soul-searching and holiness, he offers a radical feminist ideology of rejecting masculinity in the process of reaching God. He also has a strongly developed sense of empathy tied to fatherhood, and thus blends feminist and religious forms of compassion. Significantly, he is also critical of the bourgeois "talking about their stocks" form of marketplace man Orthodoxy and injects a certain element of Marxism into his account. Azriel therefore offers a strikingly religious form of radical Marxist feminism for men, placing him as one of the most religious as well as one of the most feminist informants. He is not only deconstructing Orthodoxy and gender identity, but also reversing an entire religious hierarchical system that would see him as "less religious" for having left Chabad and standard Orthodoxy. He is in fact radically feminist because of his religious beliefs, and he is promoting a transformation of men. Personally, I found his description breathtaking.

His vision of radical male transformation is not only for men, just as feminism is not only for women:

> I don't want a profeminist women's movement at all. I don't want a men's movement, I want a feminist movement that has human beings fighting for feminist ideals. . . . Do you really feel (a) you're going to have an impact this large in the community if you're not utilizing the entire community? (b), what kind of message are you sending to the communities? It's like we're doing this without you and not for you. So it's like I don't want a profeminist men's movement. I want a movement of feminists that are men and women, and it shouldn't be that men have to prove themselves to be feminists in the same way that I wouldn't want women to have to prove themselves to be a feminist.

Azriel lays out a feminist ideology that includes men as equal partners in the struggle for systemic social change in Orthodoxy. For him, not only is it possible for Orthodox men to hold radical feminist ideologies, but it is also expected and desired. He is without question a minority among the informants, but his is a beautifully stirring voice.

"I'm here for my wife"

It is not easy for men to be feminists. Whether because of people's reluctance to abdicate power and privilege or the discomfort of bucking social expectations, feminist men have to endure perceptions of emasculation and even mockery as they work at building a different society.

One of the ways that men put down feminist men is by ridiculing those men who say or are perceived as saying, "I'm here for my wife." I first heard this line from Binyamin, who said, "The problem with the synagogue is like that joke, 'I'm here for my wife.'" He began laughing, but I was not familiar with the joke, so he explained that there was a famous stand-up comedian who did "a whole skit about men who come to different places and don't fit in. 'I'm not really here, but what can you do, my wife made me come, so I came.' It was a whole evening about 'I'm here for my wife.'" Binyamin said that this is what the men in the partnership synagogue reminded him of because "they were not as strong as the women." It was a joke, but not really. Similarly, Shlomo ran for a seat on the executive committee with a flyer that announced, "Why am I here? Most men will simply answer, 'I'm here for my wife.' But I'm here for myself as well." His brother, Moshe, said that most of the men come because "their wives dragged them. . . . They seem bored, they don't want to be here." Avi also said that there are a lot of men "who are dragged by their wives."

"I'm here for my wife" may actually denote the opposite—a man who wants to be there but cannot admit it. Noam says a man who says "I'm here for my wife" is shirking responsibility for that decision, almost apologizing for being someplace men are not meant to be. Jerry says that it's a camouflage. "People say they do things for their wives, but they really enjoy it themselves. The wife is a convenient scapegoat." Aaron Frank explains this shirking of responsibility, "Like saying, 'My mother made me do it.' Like, it's not really you, but it is you. Or like when you're in the pharmacy buying diapers and you meet another guy, and you're like, 'My wife sent me to buy diapers'—it's the same kind of thing. It's you but you don't want to admit it in front of other guys."

Whether the man there for his wife is the caricature of the man dragged somewhere he doesn't want to be, or the man who is there willingly but cannot admit it, the image is of a man who is spineless and weak—the quintessential non-man. He is a man who follows his wife outside the box, designated as less manly. It's the modern, enlightened, new-age version of the caricature of the henpecked husband. Only he's not really henpecked; he just loves his wife and wants her to be happy. Perhaps this caricature is a reflection of how emphatically outside the box empathy lies.

"I'm here for my wife" also highlights one of the most important and obvious aspects of the box: the persona most emphatically outside the "be a man" box is *woman*. The very worst thing a man who wants to be a man can do is become a woman. By being in a space that is dominated by women, where women are leading and demanding and taking over—especially the space that is meant for men to be men—men put their entire identities at risk. A man who comes for his wife is essentially trying to reconcile the perception that he is entering a place that was once a men's space and is now a woman's space. In order to avoid feeling like he has become a woman, he basically says, I am still man, but one who is attached, or in this case, married, to a woman.

Although men who come for their wives are perceived as effeminate or weak, the men do not perceive themselves that way. Harold, who says proudly that he comes to the synagogue because it makes his wife happy, adds, "This is a good thing." Isaac similarly says that he was initially motivated by his wife's happiness and that he is proud of that. "It's good for people to care about one another's happiness and well-being." Gary, too, says that he likes seeing his wife "have a place where she wants to come. . . . It's good to see." And Ilan, who is single, says, "It's great that they support their wives and their wives' endeavors, and I think it's good. I think a husband should support his wife." So there is in some sense a profound joy that comes from helping one's spouse find fulfillment. In fact, coming for one's wife may be an indication of a powerful resistance to masculinity. "When a man says he comes because of his wife," Levi said, "it must really be out of ideology."

There is another compelling aspect of the "here for my wife" narrative: it reinforces the idea that feminism is for women, inhibiting men from a direct, personal encounter with feminism. Still, several men overcame all that, and reflected on how masculinity, patriarchy, and privilege are damaging to both men and women, and how feminism potentially liberates men from being powerful oppressors. I believe many more men experience this than have a language to express it. Nevertheless, by highlighting what feminism does for women, and by emphasizing that men are "here for their wives," men are deprived of a language for their own liberation.

The statement "I'm here for my wife" is loaded with meanings. Its use as self-description by some men is shirking of responsibility, by others a reflection of care and compassion for women. Used as an other-description it is a form of mockery, a tool of gaze that removes some men from the box by turning them into women. Some men who say "I'm here for my wife" are both internalizing the gaze and looking for an excuse to do masculinity differently. Maybe this is their way of saying that they do not want to be in that man box.

Conclusions

Men of the partnership synagogue are not only navigating personal identity, but are also agents of social change in a feminist setting. Yet, to be a man who simultaneously dwells in the patriarchal structures of Orthodoxy and the feminist structures of partnership is tricky. Feminist men face enormous obstacles from both men and women, even from feminist women, and some people even doubt that they can exist. The voluntary abdication of privilege makes them seem both noble and effeminate, and those are difficult gazes to grapple with. In some places, it might have the same effect. To be a feminist man in a patriarchal religious culture and society requires layers of armor and resistance to an anti-feminist backlash.

It is hardly surprising, therefore, that many men do not even go there. They join partnership synagogues because it is a comfortable way to make certain changes, but perhaps not too many. The partnership synagogue is still within the "camp," and the men are still "men." They are changing, but without going too deep into social change. Perhaps more surprising, and encouraging, is that there are in fact men who are working toward social change by grappling with masculinity. There are several variations on this theme, and men take feminism in different directions. But signs are evident that men are rethinking the social structures that create patriarchy and masculinity in the broad, cultural sense.

Still, all this comes slowly and reluctantly. Most of the Orthodox men interviewed have no idea what male gender identity means, nor do they have the language or tools to formulate ideologies around its deconstruction. Even in this potentially feminist space of the partnership service, the language of deconstruction of gender identity has not caught on in any kind of sweeping way; it is scattered, secluded, and perhaps a bit bashful.

Feminist social change is happening in certain corners of Orthodoxy, although it is struggling to find its own contours and its own stable presence. It rears its head and shows distinct signs of life as a poignant expression of the ways in which Orthodox men are changing their surroundings.

Part III ～ Orthodox Men Creating New Boundaries

The greatest deception men suffer from is their own opinions.
—LEONARDO DA VINCI

A woman simply is, but a man must become. Masculinity is risky and elusive. It is achieved by a revolt from woman, and it is confirmed only by other men.
—CAMILLE PAGLIA

CHAPTER 7

"Just Not Reform"

The Outer Boundaries of Orthodoxy

⁓ IN THE SUMMER of 2007, the Darchei Noam community began a process of writing a vision and mission statement. Over the course of several months, the community conducted a series of brainstorming and writing meetings, at the end of which approximately forty-five people created a "vision document" outlining the general philosophy of the community.[1] Five value pillars were outlined: community, *halakha*, equality, education/family/youth, and *tikkun olam* (literally, "repairing the world"), or social justice. Each of these values was given an elaborate definition, which was further fleshed out by five different subgroups. People freely signed up for the subgroups, and the larger group created a two-sentence overarching vision:

> Kehillat Darchei Noam is a halakhic-egalitarian community built on the values of community, family and *tikkun olam*. The central aspiration of the community is to enable maximum communal and religious participation of all community members both in and out of the prayer service, and to actively ensure that all who want to be part of the community will be welcomed and will find a house of prayer that is also a home.

The most controversial aspect of this statement, indeed the entire process, was actually not the word "equality" but the word "halakhic." During the first meeting, the group working on the "halakhic/religious/Orthodox" topic was bursting at the seams, whereas the groups working on *tikkun olam* and equality were nearly empty. The "halakhic" subcommittee was not only the hot spot, but was also the most contentious group. At issue was the word "Orthodox." Some argued vehemently that the community must unequivocally call itself Orthodox. "If we do not call ourselves Orthodox," Limor opined, "many people will simply leave." Others disagreed. "We don't have to give ourselves any particular designation," Monica countered. "Why do we need to call ourselves anything?" Limor told me that she was eventually convinced that "Orthodox" does not

hold as much significance as she originally thought. Despite the extensive process, and the attempts to be somewhat inclusive, it quickly became apparent
that the question of "Orthodox" versus "halakhic" was not entirely resolved.

At the annual general meeting at the end of December 2007, which again
some forty to fifty people attended, the vision statement was formally presented,
after having been distributed to the entire community by e-mail, with several
points highlighted for discussion. There was a very brief discussion, many rounds
of congratulations on a job well done, and a vote to approve the document. Approval was *almost* unanimous; the three dissenters were Gvir, his wife, Sigalit,
and Limor, who sent an e-mail saying she was angry that there wasn't a more
in-depth discussion of the issues and that there appeared to be an attempt to
sweep issues under the rug. Her point was not so much about the content but
about the last leg of the process. She thought the *va'ad* was so worried about
causing discord that they quickly pushed this document through without a
proper debate. She was so upset about the process that she did not come to
synagogue for weeks and wrote a few more angry e-mails before sliding back
into regular attendance.

Gvir had a more aggressive protest. Unlike Limor, he had not attended any
meetings other than the first and did not take part in the work process, but was
nonetheless very angry about the document. Over the next two weeks, he went
from one male member of the community to the other on a campaign to build
up a movement to protest the document, specifically to protest the absence of
the word "Orthodox." He did not approach me, nor did he approach any of the
women I asked about it. ("He approached my husband," several women reported, which is how I eventually learned that he was mainly asking men.) Gvir
ultimately found his greatest ally in the unassuming Reuven, whom he convinced of the urgency of this issue. Reuven, who told me he hates meetings and
synagogue politics, bonded with Gvir over Talmud classes and a shared love of
meticulousness, and decided to act on the absence of the word "Orthodox." In
January 2008, Reuven and Gvir sent a petition directly to the entire congregation via e-mail:

> Many members were greatly irritated by the fact that the opening paragraph does
> not include the word "Orthodox.". . . . In a conversation conducted with Rabbi
> Daniel Sperber, he [Sperber] sided with the position that the phrases should be
> examined from the social perspective. That is, how we see ourselves and with which
> religious stream we want to associate. In light of that, and according to the views of

the members signed on this document, we demand a change in the introduction
from "Kehillat Darchei Noam is a halakhic-egalitarian community" to "Orthodox-
egalitarian" for the following reasons:

- In Israeli society, three main religious streams are recognized: Orthodox, Conservative and Reform. The term "halakhic community" indicates a social
  framework that is not clear and needs definition and arouses social suspicion.
- "Halakhic community" is an undefined and unclear term that creates stigmas
  and distinctions that are unacceptable, such as "The Reform *minyan*"—because
  the point of discussion is in terms that are not generally acceptable.
- The uniqueness of the community is that it is Orthodox and rests on the Orthodox discourse. Halakhic changes that we took upon ourselves are within the
  framework of Orthodox discourse, that is, we come to the discussions about
  changes with the Talmud and its interpreters over the generations.
- A community that defines itself as Orthodox makes an outward-facing statement
  that we see ourselves as belonging to Orthodox communities, despite differences we have with the Orthodox community on certain points.
- A significant number of members who comprise the community define their
  lifestyles as Orthodox. The way of life and way of education that they and their
  children come into contact with obligates the use of the word "Orthodox."
- Part of our attempt to recruit new members seeks out the Orthodox public, such
  that turning to them with the term "halakhic" creates reservations and suspicion
  that is not in its place.

In this e-mail, Reuven asked people to sign the petition in advance of the
next meeting. By the end of January, Gvir's wife, Sigalit, presented the petition
to the *va'ad* with the claim that they had twenty-eight signatures. One woman I
spoke to said she signed simply to appease Gvir, who she said was "clearly very
upset." Another man I spoke to said that Gvir was mostly concerned about the
reputation of his oldest son, who goes to the local religious boys' high school.
Amitai similarly reported that Gvir approached him saying, "I need this because
my sons learn in the yeshiva. We do not want to be outside of the camp. That's
why this Orthodox thing is so important. The Orthodox camp is something
you grow up with, that forms you. You learned in the state religious schools, in
yeshiva high school, religious army, and then Bar Ilan [University]. It's part
of your identity, the *kippa*, something about who you are, and it's something
you want to be part of." This petition was based on a fear of losing membership
or belonging in one's "camp," perhaps a smoke screen for that fear of being os-

tracized. An Orthodox man's entire identity here is a function of how others will accept him.

Others denied that this was about fitting in. "It's about *halakha*," David said, "and letting people know that this is a halakhic *minyan*." He did not catch the irony of that statement: the entire purpose of the petition was to *replace* the word "halakhic" with the word "Orthodox." In this bizarre, counterintuitive argument, the petitioners claimed that only the word "Orthodox" means "halakhic," and the word "halakhic" means "not necessarily Orthodox," so in order to be perceived as "halakhic" they have to write "Orthodox." No, this is not a Laurel and Hardy show, but synagogue politics. Ultimately, the proposed changes to the document were about maintaining membership in the club, about the fear of being labeled with social and religious identities deemed "unclear" and consequently "out of the camp."

The fear of being placed outside the "camp" not only causes men to construct bizarre rhetorical twists but also brings them to take strong and angry actions such as writing petitions. Even the release of Gilad Shalit did not merit as much social activist energy as the issue of the word "Orthodox." This was a huge eye-opener for me, both personally and as a researcher. The contrast between the energy expended on the Orthodoxy petition and the energy expended on actual social activism was astounding to me. Moreover, the fact that so many people signed was a striking indication that the congregation did not entirely disagree with this set of priorities. Though this may have been a partnership synagogue, part of a worldwide trend toward inclusivity and equal rights in Orthodoxy, its members' greatest fight was to maintain a perceived status in the club.

To be fair, the petition was not received by the *va'ad* with enthusiasm, though the committee members were upset less about the petition's content and more about the subversive way it was spread. The *va'ad* tried to calm the waters and regain some firm standing by urging the entire congregation to refrain from sending out incendiary letters without going through the correct channels. "We felt that it was not an appropriate way of addressing an issue," *va'ad* member Stuart told me. "People should not be sending petitions around and calling for changes for any particular thing that just bothers them. I think it needs to be addressed in an organized fashion and in a way that shows respect for not only the *va'ad*, but as well as the conversation as a whole." *Va'ad* members were distressed at having been pushed against a wall before they even had an opportunity to discuss the issue.

These events were part of a change in the culture of the synagogue from one of open dialogue and communal activism to one of top-down control of discussions and a fear of confrontation. The *va'ad* announced that only e-mails that have been approved by the *va'ad* could be sent to the entire congregation, thereby activating a centralized, authoritarian model of control, one that fits in well with Orthodox culture generally. The partnership synagogue, which was once a place of fluidity, change, and dialogue, was transformed overnight into a place of fear and control, first by two men who chose an aggressive form of attack over participation in a communal process of dialogue, and then by a *va'ad* that, instead of dealing with the communal rift, forged a culture of tight authoritarianism. "There is something terribly wrong with this whole process," Noam often said. He claimed that the *va'ad* lacked transparency and openness and that *va'ad* members were more interested in control and power than in community process.

This story is about the ways in which "Orthodox" evokes fears and anxieties, and about the culture of authoritarian control over communal discourse in Orthodoxy, beyond *halakha*. In Shira Hadasha, decisions are even tighter than in Darchei Noam. As Yehiel, who is on the Shira Hadasha *va'ad*, said, "It is a very closed, tight circle. At Shira Hadasha, they are careful, they are afraid, there is backup, there is a *halakha* committee, there is consideration. The *halakha* committee is busy all the time holding back all kinds of radical issues." This fearfulness is often unstated. Gvir and Reuven's petition rested on the unspoken fear of being labeled not "Orthodox" but perhaps "Conservative" or "Reform." This story is about the wielding of power in order to keep the synagogue "in" and not "out," and about the extensive measures some men are willing to take in the service of that aim. It reveals the enormity of the shadow of "Reform" or "Conservative" hanging over Orthodox culture, and it exposes some of the political dynamics underlying men's attempts to retain their membership in their desired camp.

This and the following chapter look at the other side of changing men: resistance to change. If Orthodox men are changing and challenging their socialization by redefining and recreating masculinity, they are also fearful of taking that change too far, of exiting their comfort zone, of being outcast and perceived as completely out of the box. These chapters revisit the boundaries of those changes, first the boundaries of "Orthodox" and then the boundaries of "men." They focus on the points of tension, the places in men's identities where they get stuck and perhaps fearful, where they backtrack and hold on tight to their reserved place in the known and therefore comfortable world of Orthodox masculinity.

Conservative and Reform in the Eyes of Israeli Men

The "Conservative" and "Reform" labels, the most direct and perhaps obvious definitions of "Not Orthodox," undoubtedly threaten Orthodox men. In Israel, where both these movements struggle to maintain a presence, this sense of threat is particularly odd, an irrational panic based on that which is mysterious, unknown, foreign, and strange.

The overwhelming majority of informants used "Conservative" and "Reform" interchangeably,[2] and the petition mentioned the "three main denominations" in Israel, when in fact most sociologists would say this is a much more accurate description of North America.[3] The Conservative/Reform identifications fall on the same national-cultural axis as the partnership synagogues: foreign, American, and threatening to Orthodoxy. "If only the Israeli public knew what Conservative was, but they haven't the slightest clue, even among Modern Orthodox," said Professor Asher Cohen, who has done considerable research on the Reform movement in Israel. "What does an average Israeli know? There are tremendous differences, and they are not aware. If you ask, they'll say, 'They're nuances of Americans.' . . . It's an American thing.'"[4] Conservative and Reform Judaism are thus constituted as one big block of "not Orthodox" and "American," epitomizing "outside" or "other."

This chapter explores the ways in which informants construe Conservative and Reform in relation to their own identities. It sheds light on the outer boundaries of identity, the limits of change, and the dynamics within which Orthodox men struggle to find definition. Although part of the focus here is on Israeli informants, there are strong implications for American Orthodox men as well. At the very least, this chapter demonstrates unequivocally that Orthodox men are in conversation with one another across oceans, and they are in conversation with non-Orthodox Jewish men as well. More significant, the function of "Conservative" and "Reform" as boundary markers of Orthodox masculinity is apparently shared across cultures.

Halakha

Just as one of the first ways men describe Orthodoxy is "halakhic," the initial description of Conservative and Reform is along the axis of *halakha* as well. Gil said, "What actually characterizes an Orthodox person is the degree to which they will consider the *halakha* as being an important part of the process by which they live their lives and by which they draw guidance. . . . For most Jews, if you ask them any sort of question about a moral issue, they will not naturally reach for the Jewish sources in order to express an opinion about abortion or stem-cell research or cloning or even animal slaughter. But the Orthodox Jew will at least ask a question about what precedents are there in the *halakha*." Jonathan concurred, saying that Orthodoxy, as opposed to Conservative and Reform, "takes seriously the halakhic process."

Related to *halakha* is the notion of Conservative as not observant, and not serious. Gary called Conservative "nonobservant," as well as "big, bland, and boring," and Efraim said of the Conservative synagogue he attended for a few years, "terrible. I hated it. It was a big *shul*, the people were talking all the time, the women were dressed with the fancy hats and the makeup, and it was like a fashion show. . . . It had no spirit, the people just sat there, and the cantor did everything, just like a Conservative *shul*." By contrast, he says Orthodoxy is difficult because women have no roles, but "at least [in] the Orthodox *shul* you could see people were into the davening, if nothing else." In other words, Orthodox is sincere but unjust, while Conservative is egalitarian but shallow.

The comparison is also knowledge-based, and Orthodoxy is seen as superior in knowledge and authority. For Efraim, who always wavered between both worlds, Orthodoxy ultimately won out because, as he explains, "I needed to be with people who are more knowledgeable and observant than I was, because it wasn't serving me to be with [the Conservative synagogue]. It's better to be a tail to lions than a head to foxes, and I always interpreted that to mean it's better to be with people who are better than you, so you can learn from them, than it is to be with people who are inferior to you. When I say inferior I don't mean socially, I mean people with less knowledge or less observant." This perception of Conservative as thin in knowledge and observance led him to Orthodoxy. The partnership synagogue is very satisfying because it incorporates the seriousness of Orthodoxy with the egalitarianism of Conservative. It's "religious but not with the blinders on. I also like the fact that it is observant and there are knowledgeable people, and even Eitan when he does his crazy, correcting, trivial Torah mistakes, or making sure that we do *Bracha Achrona* after the *kiddush*.[5] I myself might not do *Bracha Achrona*, but . . . it's good that there are people here who take this seriously."

Efraim offers a synopsis of the Orthodox man versus the Conservative man: seriousness versus slacking off, knowledge versus ignorance, commitment versus "cheating," precision in Torah reading versus cutting corners, hierarchy versus equality, all of which are connected to *halakha* or "observance." The undercurrent of hierarchy around *halakha* and knowledge echoes the "scale" of "commitment" and "seriousness" or "authenticity" that many men mentioned, as Efraim sees ideal Orthodoxy as striving to be like the men who are "higher" or "more" on the scale, always moving upward. Indeed, Efraim's metaphor about tails and lions is very telling and fits into the idea of Orthodox as superior to Conservative. This is particularly true in light of his further comments about Eitan, someone who is seen as "superior" in terms of *halakha* and observance. What is clear is that Orthodox men find themselves embedded in a set of hierarchies, a "scale" of those who are more versus those who are less.

The idea of "Conservative" being lower than Orthodox on the scale of seriousness, commitment, and *halakha* came up elsewhere as well. Zachary, who also deliberated between Conservative and Orthodox, says he never felt "comfortable" in the Conservative world because it wasn't considerate enough of *halakha*. "Conservative egalitarian practice just cut it all down the middle to be egalitarian 100 percent without considering. They just said it's not fair and that's it." Orthodox is deliberative, studious, serious, and committed to tradition, and "checks out everything and makes adjustments according to *halakha* and not based on everyone's personal need." Conservative is considered a bit like the *hafifnik*: selfish, hedonistic, and shallow—the antithesis of the Orthodox man.

Conservative/Reform as "Outside"

Although the simplest distinction between Orthodox and everyone else rests on *halakha*, or knowledge and observance, beyond the language of *halakha* lies a description of hierarchical social groupings. Note, for example, that the purpose of Gvir's petition was to explicitly undermine notions that Orthodoxy is the equivalent of halakhic and instead proclaim that Orthodoxy is a social grouping. Indeed, many informants used language of "inside the camp" (like the petition) to distinguish between Orthodox and Conservative. "It is very important to me to be part of the Orthodox public," Koby said frankly, "because, what can you do, that's the only spectrum in which I can identify. There are many things that I personally would be able to live with that are much more radical. But in terms of community, I think that overall the more moderate approach is right." The desire to stay "inside" restricts changes, even changes that ought to be welcome from a strictly halakhic view. "Whoever wants a Conservative community, you can find one, and I even know some people there and they are very nice. I am definitely in a different spectrum. I am part of the religious public in Israel, which is a public that knows that it's an Orthodox public with all that it is. That's where I want to be, somewhere else in that spectrum. I will not break the boundaries." Orthodoxy is a "public," a club with specific people, more than an ideology. As soon as a person attends a synagogue that is called Conservative, that person is not in the same public as the speaker, not on the same "side" of the metaphoric fence. There is also a difference between private practice and public practice in that even if a private practice or ideology may seem acceptable in Orthodoxy, the "public" has to refrain from it in order to retain its Orthodox identity.

Avi also used the language of public groupings to describe Conservative versus Orthodox. "What can you do? A person needs a social group," he said. "Today, in the social reality in Israel, there is either the religious grouping with its entire spectrum, or the secular grouping with its spectrum. It's hard to be Conservative and be part of society. What can you do? I want my children to function in the spectrum of religious society, so I pay a certain price with my ideology in order for them to have it better." Avi, like Gvir, places what he calls his children's "education" in the rationale for these definitions, a euphemism for being accepted in certain social circles as "religious." Effectively, it means that all his social associations are with people in his "religious spectrum," defining himself not so much by ideology as by the social need for group acceptance. "I was debating about whether to search for a Conservative community, but that space is not a space that I live in," Oren said. "It's about being in a space with people where I'm at." In other words, the Orthodox identification as "where you're at" has to do with being around people who are like you.

Although some men think that this inside/outside approach to Orthodoxy versus Conservative/Reform is an Israeli phenomenon, it actually seems to be remarkably international. Harold's description of British Orthodoxy paints the same portrait. "In England you are either Orthodox or you're not, and that's it," he said. "If you're not Orthodox you're considered Conservative or Reform, which has an element of being renegade, rebellious, or however else you define it." Harold's descriptions of the Conservative and Reform "outsiders" as "renegade" or "rebellious" go directly to the issue of who is acceptable and mainstream and who is counterculture and marginalized. Harold, who moved to Israel fairly recently, also wonders how these concepts translate into Hebrew, demonstrating that Gvir's insistence on the word "Orthodox" is actually an adoption of an Anglo construct. There is a strange irony here, in that Israelis have co-opted

English-language constructs to signify that which is absolutely rejected (Conservative and Reform) and that which is absolutely correct (Orthodox).

The boundaries of the Orthodox versus Conservative social groupings are kept in place through a culture of fear, especially a fear of the "slippery slope." "These are tags that we've put upon ourselves that make people feel safer with their status quo," Azriel reflected. "The status quo is really important to the Orthodox community, just keeping things secure, keeping things safe. It's like the survivalist mentality is that we've got to protect our borders. If we try to change things too quickly, we'll run into problems. I mean I can't stand how many times I've heard the term 'the slippery slope' used relating to women's rights and Orthodoxy. I don't know what this slippery slope is related to, but the people are afraid of it, and I don't know what to do about that. You know, it's the thing that keeps people the most from actually making changes in their life for a positive." The "slippery slope" is an argument that reflects fear. It's about veering toward the unknown, the forbidden, the abyss. As people create their own identities out of difference, they create space in contrast to that which they are not. Conservative and Reform provide the social contours of Orthodoxy by reminding men who or what they are absolutely not. Even when the practices resemble one another, the definition as "Orthodox" and not "Conservative" has the effect of stamping the person as "normal" and not "outsider."

Conservative/Reform as Social Class

The language of Conservative versus Orthodox social hierarchies and groupings has echoes of a socioeconomic class system. "We" are not like "them," "we" are "better," and we just don't associate with "them." It is as if Orthodox Jews have co-opted this snobby, cliquish language of exclusion. Just as there are certain places I would never play golf, there are certain synagogues I would never attend. It is in some ways a classic superiority complex.

This notion that Orthodox men view Conservative as a lower social or ethnic class was faintly present in many interviews. Efraim, for example, could not belong to a synagogue where the entire group was "less" observant than he. Reuven describes himself as having the status of the "true Jew," and Reform Jews are not really Jewish because they do not own the same knowledge. Harold also described Reform as "deviant" and questioned adherents' entire status as Jews. The underlying theme, then, is not only a hierarchy of observance or a hierarchy of knowledge, but on some deeper level perhaps a hierarchy of authentic Jewishness.

There are many symbols and behaviors that classify people as being of lesser ilk. Haggai, for example, said that those who are not Orthodox are "esoteric," a euphemism for deviation from group norms. Another man said, "The second you define it as Conservative, it repels certain people." It's as if "Orthodox" gives men the status of superior quality. "When you define something, you create a boundary and then you put other people on the outside of it," Danny reflected. Orthodox Jews "want a super *hechsher* [kosher seal of approval], so that the *shul* is kosher. There's that psychological need to say this is Orthodox, this is kosher. . . . You want that status." There is a clear need for hierarchy within the definition of Orthodoxy, where people are judged and labeled according to "okay" and "even better." Danny calls this a "malady" that has roots in psychological processes and fears of that which is new or different. The "*hechsher*" is the creation of a form of social classes labeling those who are acceptable and those who are not. "There are things that threaten the identity of the framework," Yehiel adds. "That's why some Orthodox people will say, 'Those people cannot be part of my story.'" "Those people" who cannot be in "my story" are Conservative and Reform Jews.

Strangeness as Gender

Orthodox men have many ways, then, to describe Conservative and Reform Jews. They are other, not serious, not halakhic, esoteric, following personal whims, in a different spectrum, outside the spectrum, inauthentic, or not in my space. This collection of signifiers raises more questions than it answers. *Why* is Conservative/Reform considered so "strange" as to be outside an Orthodox man's entire social sphere? What is it about the Conservative or Reform congregations that places them so definitively outside "normal" for an Orthodox man, like an inferior social class? What exactly are Orthodox men so afraid of?

In many cases, when men say "strange" they really mean "strange in terms of gender." "When I first heard a woman cantor, it was strange for me," Oren says. "When you hear it for the first time, the question is, wait a second, I'm in the Reform? What's happening here?" The strangeness is a woman's voice, which immediately triggers "Reform." Judah describes as "strange" the first time he saw a woman take out the Torah scroll from the ark. He reports being "in shock" because he had "never seen it before" and it seemed "very foreign . . . even wrong. I just didn't seem right to me. . . . I guess in my mind, thinking of women's role in the ceremony is, I guess, a Reform *shul* or Conservative." For Judah, hearing a woman lead put him in "shock," feeling "foreign" and "wrong"—all because he says he never came into contact with Conservative and Reform. Eitan said explicitly that he was against women wearing a *tallit* because "we are not Reform, and we have to protect this, our Orthodox image, with all our might. A woman who wears a *tallit* . . . is some kind of red flag toward society. Because it has a symbol of Reform." Amazingly, the very sight of just one woman in the sanctuary wearing what is considered an icon of masculinity threatens an entire community with being labeled as "out"—something the community must "protect" itself from.

Just as the language of Reform and Conservative as "strange" masks gender, so too the language of *halakha* is often a smoke screen for gender. Binyamin, for example, who also cannot tolerate a woman in a *tallit*, said, "A woman in *tallit* burns my eyes [because it] looks Reform to me," couching his very visceral discomfort in the language of *halakha*. "I am halakhic. . . . I do not go near the Conservative horizon, and most certainly not the Reform horizon," he said. He claims that what distinguishes his "framework" from Conservative and Reform is *halakha*. Yet the one example he gave in practice has little if anything to do with *halakha* and everything to do with gender visuals. The language of "burns his eyes" is a strong visceral description that goes beyond the merely "strange" into a deeper, all-consuming revulsion. The sight of *tallit* on women somehow threatens his physical being as an Orthodox man.

Almost every example of a practice or an icon that men evoked as symbolizing their discomfort with Conservative or Reform congregations revolved around gender. The partition, for example, is a huge issue for men in retaining their definition as Orthodox. "We are not Reform," Reuven insists. "Every second sentence when people ask you, 'Where do you go? Are you in the Reform synagogue?' 'No, it's not Reform.' Everyone says it. *We have a partition.*" For Reuven, the partition is the penultimate dividing line between Orthodox and everyone else, "proof" of being Orthodox and not Reform. "When people say, 'You're Reform,'" Haggai said, "I usually correct them. . . . Usually, the sentence goes, 'You're Reform, the boys sit next to the girls.' So I say to them, 'There is a partition, boys and girls are separate.'" This idea came up time and again. "I don't see [the partnership synagogue] as such a monumental departure because we still daven with a partition," Zeev said. It is the partition, then, separating men from women—or, from a man's-eye view, keeps women invisible in the main sanctuary—that keeps the synagogue Orthodox. If the presence of female voices in the sanctuary renders the community "trailblazers," nagging at gender

and threatening to send the community off into the dangerous territory of Reform, then at least the partition keeps Orthodox identity in place.

The partition is the first of a series of gender icons that define Orthodox
versus Reform. Amitai says, "When people come and think about the synagogue, they want to know, is there a partition or not? Or, are women reading
from the Torah or not? Or, what can women do? It grabs headlines." This is why,
he believes, calling the synagogue Orthodox is "very important. Because it's an
outward statement." It's a question of identity; gender defines Orthodoxy. "A
community needs to have boundaries," Moshe says, "what it is and what it isn't.
The partition is one of those boundaries. Even the most open communities
have their borders: dress, head covering, and modesty [of women's dress]. For
some people, that's the border. If not, we will not only be egalitarian but we will
also be *hafifnikim*." There it is, all wrapped up together: women's bodies, the
partition, and *hafifnikim* as the defining icons of Reform versus Orthodox.

In some nonpartnership Orthodox communities, Reform and Conservative
icons share the space of "outsider" with the partnership synagogue—hence the
petitioners' obsession with being seen as Orthodox—because they share a function vis-à-vis gender identity. As long as a synagogue maintains correct gender
definitions, it is "inside" the camp; otherwise it is over the edge. "I do not want
to be Reform," Avi says. "The change in the status of women has to come as part
of a change in approach. For this to happen, the community has to speak in one
voice, even if this voice is moderate, but it means that more people can feel at
home. There are enough people who will be shocked if a woman will say a *dvar
Torah*, even before a woman reads from the Torah." Shifting gender in synagogue is so threatening that it needs to be taken in moderation. "If someone
comes from outside, the very fact of hearing women is what's different," Oren
concurs. "The difference is threatening and repelling. It doesn't matter what is
happening there, does not matter if it's halakhic or not, doesn't matter. I'm saying, psychologically, [what matters is] the fact that it's different." Oren thus confirms that what threatens men with being labeled outside of Orthodoxy is not
halakhic but the psychology of gender. "So we have to do it gradually. It's easier
to digest." Communal changes in how gender is performed can be frightening
for men.

The synagogue structure, with its partition separating men and women, the
tallit preserving male and female iconography, and the assurance that only
men's voices will be heard, comprises the most powerful symbols for defining
Orthodox masculinity. The threat of being labeled "out" comes from the shift-

ing of some of these symbols, and the protection from being ousted comes from maintaining others. If the synagogue is going to be so bold as to toy with one of these symbols, it had better do it carefully, slowly and moderately, otherwise men will lose their entire identities as Orthodox men. "My sense is that these men [in the partnership synagogue] would prefer a Conservative or a Reform synagogue," Binyamin lamented. "There is no strength on the men's side." In other words, Reform and Conservative are places where men can be weak, if they so choose. In this sense, to be Conservative or Reform is ultimately *to be less of a man*.

Conservative/Reform as American

Following the idea that Orthodox men are threatened by being labeled "Reform" because it threatens their masculinity, I would like to revisit Asher Cohen's analysis that Conservative and Reform have not taken off in Israel because they are seen as American imports. Until this point in the analysis, there has been a strong overlap between the narratives of Israeli and non-Israeli informants. That is, the idea that Conservative and Reform are seen as not legitimate because they shift gender boundaries cuts across nationalities, even if Americans have a keener awareness of the differences between Conservative and Reform. The analysis thus far also cuts across religious upbringings; men from all backgrounds, whether they were born into Orthodox families or not, whether they were born in Israeli, America, or Australia, all have a connection to this narrative of Orthodoxy as a social "camp" that is based in large part on gender symbols. But there is a point where the analysis diverges between Israelis and Americans: in Israel, Conservative and Reform are taboo because they are construed as "American." Given the understanding that much of the fear of Conservative and Reform is about gender and the loss of masculinity, I will now turn to this narrative about the American import and look at it in more depth.

Israeli men had a lot to say about the "American" character of Conservative and Reform—although just as they do not distinguish between Conservative and Reform, they do not distinguish between British, Australian, South African, Canadian, or American men. Haggai, for example, recalled being called up to the Torah when a woman was reading Torah, and he was told that he had to use his mother's name as well as his father's name, which he found "disturbing." "It bothered me on the psychological level, because I didn't have that custom," he said. "I have never in my whole life been to a Conservative synagogue, or Reform, because I grew up here in Israel." The strangeness is linked to Conservative, which is linked to gender, which is linked to non-Israeli. (It does not even occur to him that there may be a Reform or Conservative synagogue in Israel, though there is one a few blocks from his house.) Similarly, when Amitai first heard a woman being called up to the Torah, he said, "It seemed to me a little like something American and not Israeli. It's something that does not really fit here. . . . It's like, playing football is American. Israelis play soccer or basketball. That's what it seemed like to me. Something American. Not authentic. American." Gender is connected to the "inauthentic," to a foreign, imported culture. When women upset the gender order, it has the effect of switching teams, or being inauthentic. It's a violation of one's masculinity, like misplaced identity.

The connection between nationality, Conservative, and gender, was clearly a subtext of Reuven and Gvir's Orthodoxy petition as well. According to Stuart, the entire petition to make sure the synagogue was called "Orthodox" and not "halakhic" reflected Israeli sensibilities and a fear of American culture. "It's important in terms of our identity vis-à-vis the Israeli public that Orthodoxy's important because otherwise people won't understand it, or they'll understand it in a way that isn't respectful of the *halakha*," he said. "They might understand it as something that's, you know, Conservative, Reform, or something else." So in Israeli culture, "Orthodox" means "halakhic," while "halakhic" means "Conservative." "For the Israeli mind-set," he added, "you need to use that Orthodox terminology, because otherwise it won't be perceived as something respectful of *halakha*." Stuart had trouble wrapping his head around this because "Orthodox" does not actually mean "halakhic" but rather membership in a club with understood unbending gender identities. "Halakhic" is also riskier for men than "Orthodox" because shifts in gender roles that are halakhically acceptable might not be socially acceptable. "Halakhic" actually includes Conservative Judaism, which begs the question. If Conservative is also halakhic, why is it so bad? The answer is becoming painfully clear: Conservative is bad because although it acts within a halakhic discourse, it breaks down gender roles, which puts the entire identity of Orthodox man at risk. It's not *halakha* that the men are afraid of, but the social roles, specifically gender. They are afraid of being seen as incorrect men.

American culture, thus conflated with Conservative/Reform, is seen by Israelis as being weak and excessively flexible, especially around gender. Put differently, Conservative/Reform American men are construed as lesser men because they allow women to take over their masculinity. They are the quintessential *hafifnikim*: weak, wimpy, effeminate men.

Between Secularism and Egalitarianism

A really interesting side story emerged in this research. At the same time that the partnership synagogue in Modi'in was developing, another synagogue was also being formed—the Yachad (literally, "together") Minyan, a product of the Yachad school, which prides itself on being a place where religious and secular students learn together. Many of the men in the partnership synagogue also dabbled in the Yachad synagogue, and the interplay between the two activities sheds light on the connections between masculinity, Orthodoxy, secularism, and women's roles in the synagogue.

When the Yachad synagogue was being formed, the question of women's roles came up and was eventually voted down. According to Asher Cohen, who has not only written extensively on religious politics in Israel but is also heavily involved in Yachad and marginally in Darchei Noam, Israeli men who do not want to be Orthodox will sooner become *hiloni*, or secular, than Conservative or Reform.[6] This phenomenon finds expression in a variety of ways. Shlomo, who was involved in both in Darchei Noam and Yachad, had his own perspective on this topic:

> In the synagogue of Yachad, people are willing to include men who do not keep Shabbat. Here in my neighborhood, we wanted to create a Yachad *minyan* as well as a branch of Darchei Noam, so we thought it would be nice to combine the two things, to create a Yachad *minyan* that was also egalitarian [partnership]. So I brought it up and I saw the incredible objection to what we call egalitarian. Despite the fact that there were, in the group, some who really wanted it like that. . . . There was a long and stormy discussion about it. In the end, he [the discussion leader] got up and summarized the issue. "Here, at Yachad, we decided that we are going according to *halakha* and we are not cutting corners." Period, end of story. So egalitarian was perceived as "cutting corners," as in, you must be Conservative, there is no way that you're Orthodox. People were like, "You are definitely Conservative. You can't be Orthodox." Or [you are] Reform. In Israel, people don't really know the difference. Reform, Conservative, doesn't matter. "It can't be that you're going according to *halakha*."

This narrative is fascinating because of the strict adherence to the status quo regarding gender in a group that had not shown great adherence to other religious issues, and the forceful opposition to the possibility of being labeled "Conservative." This is an intriguing window into secular Israeli thinking about the Conservative movement. Here, secular men share the perspective of Orthodox men in their fear of the threat of the Conservative label—a threat that only comes as a result of discussions about gender in synagogue. The school demonstrates flexibility on a whole host of religious issues, from dress codes to Bible instruction, without fearing the Conservative label. Moreover, it is baffling that such a secular population would even care about being labeled Conservative. If the argument is that the secular families do not care about the Conservative label but the Orthodox families do, then the question becomes this: why are the Orthodox families who are flexible on every other issue and fully at ease mixing with secular families so frightened about being labeled Conservative? And why does this conversation revolve around women's roles in synagogue?

This narrative powerfully demonstrates the centrality of gender in men's identities and its connection to the rejection of Conservative in ways that extend beyond Orthodoxy. As Shlomo continues, the men's opposition was not really about *halakha* at all but about gender and masculinity:

> I saw that even though people were open to a mixed religious-secular prayer service, they had actually been very brave, but they didn't know it. After all, to include in the service people who break the Shabbat in public is against *halakha*, period. That is not cutting corners; it's not a question or a doubt. Of course, today, if you ask a rabbi, he will find all kinds of twists and ways. . . . Take those seventeen arguments, and put them in front of the people at Yachad who don't keep Shabbat, and tell them that these are the reasons why we agree that they can come, and they will turn around and leave. What is unique to Yachad is that it is made up of people who keep Shabbat in some form or another, and there is complete equality between people. Nobody says, "You came by car, so sit in the back." We respect everyone. We accept everyone.

The Yachad group, which Shlomo points out is composed in large part of formerly religious men, views secular as an acceptable identity, while Conservative is frightening. Shlomo was expecting support for egalitarianism here, which has basis in *halakha*. Yet even among people who are secular or who have chosen to leave Orthodoxy and who publicly do not keep Shabbat, he encountered the fear of breaking gender structures.

Israeli men who completely resist Orthodoxy are doing it by becoming secular, and not by becoming Conservative. This is because leaving Orthodoxy is not necessarily about resisting gender constructs. Being secular poses no threat to one's gender identity, whereas being Conservative does. They may be interested in breaking down religious hierarchies, but they are clearly not interested in breaking down gender hierarchies. They are more than happy to let go of the dictates of *halakha*, but not of the dictates of masculinity.

It is clear that what rests at the core of Orthodox versus Conservative identities is not *halakha* but gender. If it were *halakha*, then there would not be an issue with women's participation being cast as "cutting corners" and therefore "Conservative." As Shlomo pointed out, there are many other halakhic issues in Yachad that cut corners far more than women's Torah reading. Rabbis and other Orthodox men will make tortured, disingenuous twists in *halakha* to create equality between men. This is precisely the point: men are more than happy to break down hierarchies among themselves, as long as women stay behind the curtain. The equality of Yachad is an all-male equality, not a cross-gender equality. At the end of the day, the deconstruction of gender hierarchies—which is reduced to a fear of being labeled "Conservative"—is threatening to men's identities. To be Conservative is to be less of a man.

These identities cannot be separated from the power issues they involve. The role of women in this entire conversation was quite significant. "There were some people in the group—mostly women—who wanted the egalitarianism," Shlomo said, "but they themselves said, 'We want it, but there is no chance.' They didn't even really try." Even here, where "equality" between religious groups is promoted as a primary value, men retain powers in multiple realms. Asher, who took part in some of the Yachad discussions as well, said that at a certain point it was decided to allow women to give sermons. "A mother in the school, a secular woman, heard the description of equality [as allowing women to give a speech] and burst out laughing," he told me. "'Tell me, you're doing me a favor that you're giving me a little corner in your synagogue? What world are you living in?'" The woman was nonplussed. "She said, 'Tell me you're Conservative, and either I'll come or I won't come, whatever I feel like. But don't tell me a story. What you're describing to me is very, very chauvinistic, that you're trying to give me some kind of cute little corner.'" It is impossible to separate the process of defining Orthodoxy from the process of male exercise of power. Even as men stretch boundaries of religiousness—even becoming nonreligious—they are much less willing to stretch gender. Becoming nonreligious is fine, but being less masculine is a whole other story.

Conclusions

Men in partnership synagogues are border dwellers. Standing as if on the edge of a cliff, afraid of falling into an abyss, the men stand firm in their locations while trying to change. They are on an edge between what they perceive as mainstream Orthodoxy and everything else. Some men do not care. Some informants did not sign the Orthodoxy petition, others did it without a passing thought, and still others have no interest in whether the rest of the world identifies them as Orthodox. Some men are comfortable with nondefinitions and even revel in the ambiguity. Nevertheless, the energies poured into processes of being called "Orthodox," coupled with men's reflections on the meaning of Conservative and Reform, shed light on some of the most significant tensions within the identities of Orthodox men.

For Orthodox men, definitions of "Orthodox" are critical for maintaining a perceived stable place in their immediate social surroundings. The Orthodox label, like a stamp of approval, is a pragmatic tool for attaining "credentials"— schools, camps, and safe passage into the world of Orthodoxy. To be labeled not Orthodox, or "Conservative" or "Reform," risks ostracism, or what men described as crossing a boundary. For the overwhelming majority of informants, crossing that boundary is not an option. They want to be perceived as Orthodox, because that is how they perceive themselves.

In my attempt to understand what constitutes "over" the line, the answer pointed definitively to one component: gender. Certainly men talked about *halakha* and knowledge and observance. But when these texts were unpacked, it was clear that they were virtually all about gender. To be Conservative or Reform is to be a weak man, one who lets go of his power. To be an American Conservative or Reform man is to be a little less of a man. Significantly, even among nonreligious or formerly religious men, this fear of abdicating power and losing masculinity is paramount. This fear blocks forces of change, forces of equality, and women, even in some non-Orthodox settings. Men are content to bend halakhic rules for a whole host of reasons, but to bend gender norms is unacceptable. So while Orthodox masculinity may be in transition, especially in partnership settings, the forces resisting that change—that is, the dynamics of fear about losing Orthodoxy by losing masculinity—are formidable indeed.

CHAPTER 8

The New Patriarchy

Orthodox Men Reclaiming Their Power

〜 ONE SATURDAY NIGHT in December 2006, Kehillat Darchei Noam held its first-ever annual general meeting. On the agenda were burning issues such as should the *kiddush* after services be monthly or weekly, and should herring be on the menu. The atmosphere was jovial and warm, as members were happily getting to know one another and the year-old congregation was forming its character. Before the meeting broke up, Yuval, a member of the founding *va'ad*, asked to raise an issue that he called "sensitive." His son was about to become bar mitzvah, and his uncle, who is ultra-Orthodox, "cannot walk into this synagogue." This placed him in a difficult bind, since he wanted to make the bar mitzvah in his new community but also wanted to include his uncle in the festivity. He asked the community whether they would be willing, for this one weekend of his son's bar mitzvah, to hold a "standard" or "normal" service— that is, for one week only, women would step back from their roles in the service and stay silent, passive, invisible, and uninvolved behind the partition.

The question caught me off guard. I had not yet learned that Darchei Noam adopted the Shira Hadasha model by merely one vote (Yuval was one of the strongest opponents), and I did not realize how fragile this model was. I had mistakenly assumed that all were in agreement that this was the correct course of action for the community. "We can make a section outside for relatives," I responded, unsure how real this situation was. The truth was, however, that many members of the community struggled with family members for whom standing in a synagogue in which women's voices are heard is a sin worse than eating pork. In my interviews, the question "How do you explain this synagogue to your relatives?" had become standard. The idea that an entire community would reinvent itself for an ultra-Orthodox uncle seemed absurd to me. The phrase "He cannot come in" was also difficult to digest, as if the *shul* had failed to make itself accessible to certain segments of the population, like failing to build a wheelchair access ramp. The accurate description is that he *refuses* to come in because he is offended by women's voices and presence. I was surprised that Yuval would ask this of the women in the community, including his wife.

Responses were vast, varied, and intense. In opposition were arguments that this was a slippery slope, and that if we allow this then we will have to allow other changes, even changes in the opposite direction to accommodate uncomfortable guests; that in five years' time, given the current demographics, we may have a bar or bat mitzvah every week, and making such accommodations would cause our synagogue to lose its character; or, as one woman said, "It's time for you to come out of the closet." Yet there were a surprising number of voices in support of his proposal, more than I expected. One woman argued that it would be terrible for such a "vital" family in the synagogue to feel that they had to go elsewhere for the bar mitzvah, and others added, "Well, we'll do it for you but not necessarily for everyone"—comments that created (or merely highlighted) a new social hierarchy between those who deserve special treatment and those who do not. One woman said, "You know, we all fix things up in our homes before the mother-in-law visits. Why is this any different?"—as if women's voices were dirt that needed to be cleaned. Another woman said, "Of course we'll help you. My children won't step foot in the synagogue either." A whole conglomerate of femininities was recruited for this discussion: be accommodating, be considerate, avoid causing discomfort, and don't be so loud or so difficult. There was arguably more agreement to preserve this particular version of femininity than agreement about breaking down formal gender barriers.

This discussion formed a striking encounter between men's resistance and women's resistance in Orthodoxy. Orthodox men may be resisting certain aspects of their identities, and in many cases this resistance takes on a feminist character of shifting patriarchal dynamics between men and women. But in many cases, the resistance to patriarchy is severely limited by the men's desire to maintain certain aspects of their own power and control.

This chapter explores these points where resistance ends and patriarchy digs in its heels. It examines the incidences of male muscling and the accompanying rhetorics of power, and highlights the ways in which men still insist on power over women, even in the partnership synagogue.

Moments of Power

Melissa, a thirty-eight-year-old woman and regular layner in Darchei Noam, was slated to read the first three sections of the Torah on the holiday of *Simchat*

Torah. This is a particularly busy holiday for Torah reading, because it is customary for every member of the synagogue to be called up for an *aliyah.* The logistics of this holiday, which include setting up several concurrent "stations" of Torah reading around the sanctuary, were arranged way in advance, with extra e-mail reminders and precise schedules for all the readers. That morning, Melissa was told where to go, and she approached her station and prepared to read.

As she was about to start laduring, Gvir approached the stand and put his hand up, silently signaling to Melissa to stay away, and then proceeded to layn. Melissa stood there confused and asked me if I knew anything about it (I was slated to layn at that station after her). I shrugged, and we both set out to search for our station. We asked the main *gabbait*, who confirmed that this was our station. We asked around, we received shoulder-shrug replies, and Gvir kept laning. Eventually Melissa approached Gvir and asked what was happening. "There is a man here who is not comfortable with women laying, so I just read for him," he said. Finally, after the final *aliyah*, Gvir stepped aside and Melissa took over the next round.

Gvir had not discussed this with anyone, asked anyone for approval, or received permission from Melissa. He also did not confirm the synagogue's policy about accommodating men who are uncomfortable with female layners. Gvir simply took over the entire process, and in some ways the entire congregation, and layned. It never occurred to him—or to anyone else in the synagogue besides Melissa—that he could not push aside a woman layner just to accommodate a sexist man in a partnership synagogue. Melissa later discussed this with members of the *va'ad* and asked them to take steps to ensure it would not happen again. Not only did they not deal with it, but the following year on *Simchat Torah*, the *gabbaim* gave Gvir the center and main Torah stand, making him the only member of the synagogue to have a station all to himself. Thus, rather than ask Gvir to apologize to Melissa for the affront, the synagogue leadership sent the message that he had superior status in the synagogue. His tenacity, irreverent control, and sexism were rewarded with power.

The synagogue's troubling relationship with Gvir became even more pronounced later that year, when his public humiliation of a young woman in synagogue went completely unchallenged. Miri, thirty-three years old and one of the founders of the synagogue, was the designated *hazzanit* one Friday night in July. This particular night, Miri added another new dimension to synagogue life as she altered a key word in the *Lecha Dodi* liturgy that welcomes the Sabbath:

she replaced the word *ba'al* with the word *ish*. The original four-hundred-year-old text reads, "*Bo'i beshalom ateret ba'ala,*" which literally means, "Come in peace the glory of her owner," since the word *ba'al*, meaning "owner," is the biblical word for "husband."[1] Miri, following her feminist consciousness and without asking approval, simply sang this liturgy as "*Bo'i beshalom ateret isha,*" and continued praying.

Sitting on the other side of the partition, Gvir seethed. He began talking frantically to the men around him, riling them up. At the end of the service, Gvir preempted the announcements and took center stage to make his own announcement: "On behalf of the community, I apologize to all our guests for what happened. This is not who we are. We are Orthodox. This woman does not represent the community."

Miri was, understandably, mortified; she was publicly shamed and written out of the mainstream. "She" became the one who is out, who does not represent "us," while "we" became Gvir.

Moshe, one of the men Gvir had frantically approached during the service, was very upset by the incident. "They were both wrong," he told me a few days later. "I felt like they both raped the congregation."

"Raped?" I asked.

"Yes," he insisted, "violated. They both set their own agendas on the congregation without asking permission."

"How can you compare what she did with what he did?" I countered. "She changed one word that has no halakhic significance whatsoever in a part of the service that has so little status that even women are allowed to do it, which by your own admission you wouldn't have even noticed had Gvir not told you about it. He, in turn, publicly humiliated her and ostracized her from the congregation. How do these compare?"

Moshe thought for a moment and said, "See what you're doing? You're putting me in a position of having to defend Gvir."

To this day, I am not sure how this became my fault, or why Moshe felt like he had to defend Gvir. This remains one of the most difficult exchanges I had during this entire work.

Shortly after these events, Miri stopped coming to the synagogue. Gvir, on the other hand, has not only continued to come, but remains strong and empowered, since, once again, nobody in the community confronted him about his actions toward women. "It doesn't pay to say anything to him," Yossi's wife, Cindy, who is close to both Gvir and his wife, Sigalit, told me. "He won't hear anything you say anyway." So for now, the dynamics of enabling abusive practice remain in place, and the muscling of women remains part of the culture.

Liberating Men, Liberating Women

There is a certain tension among feminists about liberating men from patriarchal structures versus liberating women. While some men claim that social change should focus on men's painful experiences—for example, the damaging effects of the man-on-man gaze—others argue that men's liberation should be secondary to women's, or the man-on-woman gaze. Kimmel explores his own hesitation about asserting male disenfranchisement by asking, "How can I claim that men have no history? Isn't virtually every history book a history of men?"[2] Jeff Hearn concurs. "Studying men is in itself neither new nor necessarily radical. Men have been studying men for a long time, and calling it 'History,' 'Sociology,' or whatever." Moreover, Hearn writes, "Men's Studies, as conceived in some versions, is not in women's interests. To speak of 'Men's Studies' is at the best ambiguous: is it studies on men or studies by men? It implies a false parallel with Women's Studies. At worst, it is anti-feminist."[3]

Some feminists, men and women alike, are ambivalent about men's liberation as a feminist objective. Their main objection is that while both men and women need to reconstruct gender identities that are *not* built around privilege, competition, and the domination of women, ultimately women's suffering far outweighs that of men. Explaining what he calls the "disempowering-privilege" paradox, Harry Brod argues that "society confers very real rewards on men who will conform to these self-destructive, self-alienating behaviors [of patriarchal privilege]. The appearance of being less emotionally vulnerable makes you appear more rational, makes you appear more capable of wielding authority and power. All this is really the price of privilege."[4] Although patriarchy harms men, it also offers men some serious benefits, which is not the case for women. For a society or community to break patriarchal structures, men have to first be willing to let go of their privileges of power and only then focus on their victimhood. Moreover, John Stoltenberg believes that men's role in deconstructing patriarchy is about "confronting their own role" as perpetrators of violence against women, not as victims,[5] and his goal is simply "to end men's war against women."[6] He says that while men may one day "share in the struggle against injustice as honest allies of feminist women . . . at this point in time . . . none of us can presume that we have yet done enough in our own lives to eradicate our allegiance to masculinity. Unless we change, we cannot claim to be comrades with women. Until we change, the oppressor is us."[7] Hearn adds that, "What is at issue here is the persistent presence of accumulations of power and powerful resources by certain men, the doing of power and dominance in many men's practices, and the pervasive association of the social category of men with power."[8]

Kimmel promotes a blending of approaches. He writes that "feminism is about transformation, both for women and for men."[9] While he is primarily looking to liberate men from man-on-man power relations, he also takes an actively feminist approach of seeking to undo the damaging effects of patriarchy on women as well. He brings a fascinating vignette written in 1914 by pro-feminist Max Eastman that illustrates the complexity of this point:

> "Are you a feminist?" we asked the stenographer.
>
> She said she was.
>
> "What do you mean by feminism?"
>
> "Being like men," she answered.
>
> "Now you are joking!"
>
> "No, I'm not. I mean real independence. And emotional independence too—living in relation to the universe rather than in relation to some other person."
>
> "All men are not like that," we said sadly.
>
> "Then they should join the feminist movement."[10]

As this fin de siècle stenographer so eloquently observes, the liberation of women is not just about equalizing hegemonic power relations and "becoming like men," but also about liberating men from the constructs that deprive them of "emotional independence." In this vignette, neither men nor women are in an ideal cultural-political situation. Significantly, however, the woman sees feminism as benefiting both men and women simultaneously—creating a situation in which feminist *women* can actually liberate *men*.

The partnership synagogue, which is ideologically premised on liberating women from exclusive patriarchal practices, has become a place that liberates *men* from patriarchal practices as well. The premise of this analysis, based on Paul Kivel's "'be a man' box," is that both processes are intertwined. In order for men to liberate themselves from the effects of patriarchy, they have to be willing to confront the ways in which patriarchy socialized them into their particular roles. These roles are damaging to women, but the process of socialization is damaging to men. The process of opening up the box, a process that in some ways is at the heart of the partnership synagogue enterprise, should achieve both objectives. The tension between women's liberation and men's liberation, however, has come to a breaking point in some very difficult moments.

Patriarchy is deeply entrenched in many locations in Orthodox society. Even in this partnership setting, where resistance to gender is presumably part of the mission, there is a whole range of formal and informal dynamics, some subtle and nuanced and others overt and aggressive, all of which construct an Orthodox masculinity that is about power and control over women. Even in this partnership setting, which seeks to make change, strong forces are at work that resist liberation for both men and women.

Women's Bodies

One of the central obstacles to change is reflected in the discourse about the woman's body. One Shabbat, I stood at the back in Shira Hadasha in Jerusalem, as two female board members came over to me anxiously. "Do you know that woman?" one asked me, pointing to my colleague. "Yes," I replied. "She's a Reform rabbi visiting from the Midwest. She's lovely—"

"A rabbi!" came the horrified response. "You would think she would know better."

"Know better about *what*?" I asked.

"Wearing sleeveless," she replied as the two of them stepped aside, frantically whispering. A few weeks later, I learned that Shira Hadasha began keeping shawls on hand to make sure that women's shoulders would not show.

Menachem explained that the reason for the shawls was to maintain a certain "standard." "Shira Hadasha is not just to give women *aliyot*," he said. "This is really a well-run *shul*. It's a *good shul* by any standard. . . . They have shawls. They're prepared for that sort of thing." A proper synagogue is tightly run, in control, and managing women's bodies. The sight of women's shoulders undermines the synagogue order and decorum. The most astounding part is how *women* internalized this male gaze on the female body, as if women are now so comfortable in men's roles that they have to watch women's bodies.

Discourse on the female body forms a significant component of Orthodox masculine identity. Certainly the insistence on the partition as the symbol of Orthodoxy indicates that women's bodies need to be hidden from men. As Efraim said, "When the partition is drawn open, I find that a little distracting. . . . I find myself actively looking away from that area, so I don't have to look. . . . There are some gorgeous women at Darchei Noam, and I don't want to have to be thinking about them during *shul.*" The partition protects men from their own gaze on women, serving both as a reminder of women's bodies and as a form of containment. The objectifying discourse of women's body is not necessarily challenged in the partnership synagogue and may, in fact, be at times bolstered.

Dr. Gili Zivan, director of the Yaakov Herzog Center for Jewish Studies and a renowned Orthodox feminist scholar, was invited as a scholar-in-residence at Darchei Noam—the first and only woman ever to be invited. As part of that weekend, she was offered the honor of being called up to the Torah. As she approached the Torah, the *gabbait* asked her to cover her head. She stepped down and declined the honor.

The issue of women's head covering was raised at one of the synagogue meetings—by a woman. "We are trying to be recognized by people in a certain camp," the woman had argued, "so we should be conscious of how we appear to others." A woman without a head covering sends the "not-Orthodox" message. "There has to be some kind of minimal threshold of observance if it is going to consider itself halakhic. That means head covering," Binyamin told me in his interview. "We are not Reform." The language of "Orthodox and not Reform" hinges here on the woman's body, and the woman's appearance becomes the masthead of the synagogue. Exposure of hair acts like a measuring stick for the entire synagogue, determining levels of correctness as viewed by others, or by oneself. Both men and women internalized this idea of women's body as a definer of identity of an entire community. Thus, although there are at least six or seven married women in Darchei Noam who do not cover their hair in synagogue, they all cover when they are called to lead.

Still, the treatment of Zivan was jarring. Darchei Noam decided at that meeting *not* to make women cover their hair. Interestingly, men from different synagogues expressed discomfort with women's bare heads. "It's often very frustrating to see that there are lots and lots of nonmembers and that sometimes people are immodest in their behavior . . . women who are inappropriately dressed, and it creates discomfort," Robby said, but added that despite the discomfort, the official position was not to comment to women. "There are different opinions, and I am one of the people who believe in biting their tongue," he said. "I don't see the point in *tefillah,* when it makes other people feel ashamed. All you can do is wish it was otherwise." Even among men for whom women's incorrect body presentation causes discomfort, there is often an understanding that shaming a woman is worse. When Zivan was the guest of honor at Darchei Noam, such understandings were set aside in favor of women's body cover.

When Asher found out about what happened, he was "shocked that they could insult someone like that. . . . The story of Gili Zivan is so angering, because it screams out that what interests us is not our value system that guides us, but what interests us is this new set of rules that we have created."

The issue of women's body cover as an identity marker for the synagogue came up in other contexts as well. "Should women be allowed to just breast-feed in the middle of services?" a woman said at a Darchei Noam meeting, justifying the practice of asking a breast-feeding mother to leave the sanctuary, as if women's hair, shoulders, and nursing breasts are the archetype of the profane. The male gaze on the female body finds expression in the issue of women wearing a *tallit* as well. Amitai called a woman wearing *tallit* "provocative . . . like she's trying to be a man . . . like putting on a fake beard," and Koby said "It's like if I would wear a skirt." The *tallit* is almost seen as an extension of the man's body, like a beard, foreign for women. Binyamin, who said that a woman in *tallit* "burns my eyes," sees it as the "classic feminism that women are supposed to be like men," adding, "I am in favor of absolute difference. Why should a woman look like a man?" Put differently, a woman wearing a *tallit* is an incorrect female body. Avi said it is "out of place," signifying lack of gender order; David called it "weird"; Harold called it "jarring"; Zachary said it "causes confusion" and makes him "uneasy"; and Eitan called it a "red flag" marking the community as "Reform." This incorrect female body has the power to unravel the entire Orthodox male identity, threatens masculinity, challenges the "order" of society, forms a harbinger of chaos, and breaks with *halakha*.

In short, the changing of women's outward appearances, including the adoption of male "garments," elicits fearful stances revolving around the need to maintain a gender order.

Women's Voices

Related to men's anxiety about incorrect women's body cover is alarm about women's singing. Just as women's uncovered hair or shoulders are out of bounds, so, too, for many men, women's voices are out of bounds. Men describe their first time hearing a woman singing in synagogue, like a woman wearing *tallit*, as "weird" or "jarring" or "Reform." The main difference between the discourse on body and the discourse on voice is that the partnership setting formally challenges the rhetoric of voice by creating specific, contained spaces where the female voice is allowed, while the rhetoric on body remains intact.

The patriarchal stance toward women's voice found some particularly striking expressions in the partnership synagogue, in a way that overlapped with
issues around women's knowledge. Although women are allowed to lead certain parts of the service, many men still assume that women are less capable.
Larry said that certain men "roll their eyes when women get up to read, or take
out a book to read until a man steps up." Some regularly take women aside after
services to correct them. Some women who have been reprimanded have chosen not to lead again. Melissa ironically once reported that Gvir said, "You are
the only woman in the synagogue who knows how to read Torah properly." In a
biting e-mail to the congregation, Gvir patronizingly wrote, "Not anybody can
lead services, especially not *Hallel* [The Song of Praise]. If any woman wants to
lead, I would be happy to teach her." Teenage girls have run out of the sanctuary
crying for being overly reprimanded during or after their reading. I once told
Yuval that I noticed that Gvir squirms when he learns that I am leading Friday
night services, to which he responded, "Yes, me and Gvir both."

Men's discomfort with women leading services has created new practices
among the men. Robby explained what happens at Shira Hadasha:

> When it's a woman who doesn't do well, I respond to it emotionally in different
> ways from the way I respond when it is a man who doesn't do it well. There is a
> much more forgiving response for men to start off with, because there's this sense
> of men davening or carrying on a tradition that has been engrained for a very long
> time, and that women davening are taking on something that is new. . . . A lot of
> the time I feel like that I am the safety net, and I am holding it up, and I am
> catching the ball when it gets dropped, and filling in and supporting and doing
> quite a lot of the singing, particularly when the women are davening, to kind of
> hold it. It's a different feeling from what happens when the men are davening,
> because we have got like a kind of a team that stands together around the *shlichei
> tzibur*. There is a group of us that take up positions around the *shlichei tzibur*, and
> with the men there's a kind of a boys' club that are supporting each other in *tefillah*,
> and we all hug each other afterward, that kind of thing. And the feeling when the
> women are davening is that the support, it's got a different feeling to it, it's more
> kind of helping out rather than participating with. . . . I do it lovingly, because it's
> very important for the *kehilla*. But there is a side of me that gets frustrated with it,
> and annoyed with it.

Robby describes a patronizing male gaze on women's leadership based on their
perceived lack of knowledge and skill. Men have a "club," but women need "help."

He also said that none of the women in Shira Hadasha "have really got a *nusach*," which makes him "uncomfortable." In fact, "there is a certain aesthetic about the women's davening that turns me off, that even when a man's davening is bad, it does not turn me off." This is a gender hierarchy of knowledge, skill, and power embedded in the synagogue culture based on men's reactions to women's voice.

Women's Status

The gender hierarchy in the synagogue finds expression in many aspects of synagogue life, in and out of the sanctuary. Jerry said his wife stopped attending his previous synagogue because not only are women forbidden to vote, but the women were actually thrown out of a meeting she attended. The inherent gender hierarchy, which is way beyond halakhic practices, is sometimes couched in language of "rights" versus "privileges." According to Ilan, for example, although women have the "capacity to do all sorts of things, it's not a given." Equal opportunity, he says, is not "about rights" but about "honor and privileges. I do not hold that women should just be allowed to lead services irrespective of the obligations they take on." Ilan sees women as *hafifnikim*, people who are not pulling their weight, and therefore should have "privileges" of leading taken away from them. The language of "privilege" as opposed to "right" implies that it can be revoked easily and not given automatically. Ilan's position that only women who demonstrate supreme religious observance should be allowed to lead—a position with a clear gender double standard, since there is no such filtering system for men, and even a completely nonobservant man will count for a quorum before a woman—is not merely theoretical but forms the basis of synagogue policy. He previously severed ties with a Conservative synagogue as a result of his proposal to implement his position as policy. The male gaze on women's behavior creates an all-encompassing gender hierarchy imposed by men.

The idea that women need to "prove" themselves in order to obtain the same "privilege" that is automatically accorded to men was echoed by other men as well. Yehiel is so disturbed by women's assumptions of "rights" despite an appearance of lack of commitment that he has voted against granting more rights to women in the synagogue. "The feminist revolution will demand many more things before we give equal rights," he said, adding that he was horrified to learn that a woman read from the Torah and then walked out of the sanctuary, where she told her friends "Wow, what fun, I read from the Torah." "What's going on here?" Yehiel asked. "You can't go up to the Torah and get that right and not feel obligated to the system." Yehiel, like Ilan, is watching and measuring the women, to assess their worth in receiving "rights." Here, too, the discourse of "rights" versus "obligations" supersedes the language of equality, creating a status for women like that of a child, someone who is being watched, measured, and perhaps punished with the revoking of privileges that were thought to be natural rights. It designs a masculinity that has the ultimate power and control to decide women's lives.

The language of women's punishment and infantilization found expression in other synagogue forums as well. The sections of the service that women are allowed to lead are the same ones reserved for boys under bar mitzvah age. As Asher said, in partnership synagogues "women are basically told that they are like children." In fact, Darchei Noam formally voted to alternate these roles between women and children. "Anyway, it's hard to get women to take these roles because they don't come early," Moshe, a *gabbai* in charge of assigning jobs, told me, justifying the decision. The gaze on women's punctuality was often used as a pretense for limiting their participation. Many informants reported on the discourse of women's punctuality in their congregations. At Darchei Noam, for example, Gary and Yuval often stood up and offered reprimands about the importance of punctuality, especially directed at women. At several synagogue meetings, both men and women took turns offering lectures on women's punctuality. In Shira Hadasha, the discourse of women's punctuality takes a particularly punishing form, what Nachshon calls a "failure of feminism." Women who do not come on time, Nachshon says, are letting down the mourners obligated to recite *kaddish* who do come on time. "That's not feminism," he says. "If you can't do it, if you can't see the orphan, who are you anyway?" Women's lack of punctuality makes them hypocritical "nobodies," not deserving of any special "rights." Nachshon speaks about women, not about men, who are watched, measured, and judged based on their arrival time at synagogue.

Some men are emphatically resentful toward women because of these issues. In the partnership synagogue in Los Angeles, for example, when no women volunteered to be called up to the Torah, one of the leading men reprimanded them, saying, "'All the guys here, we could be davening at another *shul* this morning. I hiked out two miles to go to this service so that women can lead things, and none of the women are getting up and doing it. Why should I haul out two miles?" Ilan, listening to this speech, said he wanted to scream out, "Right on!" Eitan expressed occasional regret about the decision to give women equal roles. "When we had the first meetings [to build the synagogue], someone came and said, 'If we do this, will you come, or will you be at home with the kids?'" he recalled. "You should have heard the women saying, 'What do you mean? You don't give us the chance!' So I say to myself, it's very painful for me that we are giving a chance. Here's your chance, and where are they?" Then he directed his response to me personally. "You are not doing it," he reprimanded. Women's lack of punctuality makes it "painful" for Eitan that women are being "given a chance." "Women have not internalized their commitment," he concluded. The unabashed disappointment that men have with women who come late came up in many interviews. "I look at my daughters, and they are not active," Yehiel said, almost with shame. "I go in the morning, at 8 AM, to synagogue, and they come late. So of course you can blame me that my chauvinistic education does not push them the way I push my son, etcetera. That is all true, I agree. I push my son more than my daughters. You can blame me. But still, I am talking here about something communal and not just familial." Even though Yehiel admits that he acted out different expectations with his sons and daughters, he sidesteps that issue by calling it "communal." It's not his fault; it's a widespread community problem. All the women in the community come late.

In the partnership synagogue, where men are presumably working to change gender roles in their society, the focus often remains on women's changes rather than on men's changes. Rather than focusing on the ways in which male gaze harms people, men continue to abide by the "be a man" box, and in turn superimpose it on women. Rather than question the entire use of male power wielding among Orthodox men, some men now exert forces on women to try to turn them into obedient men. Women are expected to be as meticulous, punctual, and emotionless in their conforming performance as men are. Rather than questioning the wisdom of the box, men are punishing women. Rather than deconstructing the gender hierarchy and working to understand how such social hierarchies impact people, some men settle into their roles as men whose job it is to keep the hierarchies in place. They seem to be saying, if we have had to suffer through the expectations of cold, emotionless, punctual performance, women who want equality should first have to suffer as well. For women to be included and counted, first they have to abide by the norms of Orthodox masculinity.

Women's Lives

Another way that the gender hierarchy remains firmly in place is in issues of child care. At Shira Hadasha, for example, babies are not welcome, and mothers with babies have been asked to leave. At Darchei Noam, where this is not the custom, there is a certain ambivalence among some men about women and babies. When Eitan asked women, "Are you going to come to synagogue or stay home with the baby?" he was both assuming that baby care is female, and punishing women for abiding by that role. Women's entry into public life is meant to balance roles, but assumptions of women's child care leave women vulnerable to the accusation that they are not fully internalizing their commitment, creating an unwinnable catch-22 situation for women.

This double bind that leaves women vulnerable is illustrated by a story that Yehiel told about a holiday weekend with his extended family, when a decision to hold the morning services at home required that they count women in the quorum. "In the middle of *kedusha* [when a quorum is needed] one of the children was crying outside and the mother just went outside," Yehiel said. He was mortified. "We're in the middle of *kedusha*! She's the tenth person in the *minyan*. She can't go outside! She did not understand that at all. That was the moment I realized that I made a mistake. . . . You can't make revolutions when the culture of the group does not yet understand what we're doing here. . . . She did not understand that she has something else to do here now, that she has to wait. If my child is crying and the mother was not there, I would gesture to the child to wait a second. He can cry another few minutes, and then I would go outside. It's no big deal." This story reveals a powerful tension between male and female socializations. The man is socialized into ignoring or putting off the child's cry, into assuming that a woman is there to take care of the crying child, into making his top priority staying inside as part of the quorum, into being unfailing and uncompromising in his commitment to the prayer, no matter what. By contrast, the woman is socialized into responding to a child's cry. The woman who wants to take part in the public culture is reproached for not completely assimilating the male socialization, despite the fact that she adhered perfectly to her female socialization. Her lack of "male" knowledge is considered a flaw, one that justifies depriving her of equal participation and putting brakes on "the revolution." Yehiel betrays no reflection on the relative worth of female versus male socializations and does not consider the possibility that the female socialization of care is superior to the male socialization of unimpeded performance. He considers a crying child waiting for attention "no big deal," while nine men waiting for an "*amen*" is the biggest deal in the world. The legal-halakhic needs of the quorum come before the emotional needs of a child. Yehiel does not entertain the possibility that the woman fully understands that she is the tenth man, as it were, but chooses to place the child's needs ahead of those of the quorum. In the woman's world, a child's pain is more important than the abstract notion that God needs ten people to hear a prayer. But this conceptualization of life, emotions, and relationships is foreign to Orthodox masculinity, and perhaps beyond Yehiel's understanding.

The language of reprimanding women for tardiness fails to take into account women's roles in enabling Orthodox masculinity. In order for a man to freely go to synagogue three times a day unencumbered by crying children or anything else, someone *else* is presumably going to be looking after the children and everything else during that time. Orthodox masculinity is possible only under the unspoken assumption that women are cooking, cleaning, and doing child care. Women's equal participation leaves a gaping hole: who is going to attend to the crying child, or prepare the meal, or set the table? Men's views of women's lives and cultures, therefore, form the backbone of the punishing rhetoric that seeks to limit gender transformations in Orthodoxy.

The Young Face of Punishing Patriarchy

When Lisa, a thirty-two-year-old high-tech human resource director and mother of three, was asked to lead services in Darchei Noam one Friday night, she happily agreed, despite the fact that she had also generously agreed to host the visiting scholar and his wife. She was so busy preparing meals and lodgings on that winter day that she did not make it to the synagogue on time. As a result, at the last minute, an eleven-year-old boy led the services in her stead.

At the synagogue meeting the next night, when Yuval proposed changing the synagogue format for the weekend of his son's bar mitzvah, Lisa's absence the night before became a central talking point. "If women don't even come to synagogue on time," the argument went, "why should we work so hard to maintain their right to do it?" The fact that Lisa was expected to work, look after children, prepare for Shabbat in her own home, host the rabbi and his wife, and then make it to the synagogue ready to lead services—that is, the complexity of women's gender roles—was not addressed.

The language of the debate highlights the significant tensions between the cultures of patriarchy-Orthodoxy-masculinity and the culture and ideology of feminism and social change. Following that fateful meeting, Maya wrote an e-mail to Yuval and some community members saying that he, Yuval, was "harming the whole community of women" and that she was "shocked and angered" by his request, which will "will hurt the community, not just now but in the future." Yuval's response to Maya ignored her expression of pain and said simply that "there are those (more than one) who think that there is room for a discussion, so please respect that." In other words, Yuval not only ignored Maya's ideas and emotions, but also replaced the idea that *she* was speaking for many with the claim that *he* was the one speaking for many, thereby creating a tug of war over who represents "the community." In addition, he tried to shut down the emotionally charged aspect of the discussion by asking for a bottom-line tactical decision. This is perhaps the new young face of Orthodox patriarchy: educated, intellectual, seemingly mild-mannered, put-together, dual-careerist, well versed in philosophy, and gently charming, but also coldly crushing of women's needs and emotions using a language of religious discipline and commitment, a language that masks a deep-seated attempt at emotionless control.

There are also significant epistemological implications from this new, young patriarchy. Yuval, whose BA happens to be in philosophy with a specialty in postmodernism, has recruited a sleek postmodernist ideology to substantiate his patriarchal needs. In the week following his proposal, we had many conversations as he tried to maneuver my position into one of support. I tried to explain, not as a researcher but as a community member and friend, that it felt as if I was being asked to go back to prison. I said that it would undo everything I have been trying to teach my children, that after two years of telling them that the partnership synagogue was not *less* religious but *more* religious for not discriminating against women, how would I explain to my daughter the reversal he had in mind (i.e., silencing women during his son's bar mitzvah)?

"Isn't tolerance an educational value as well?" Yuval asked me.

There it is, I thought, exactly what Sara Delamont and so many other feminist thinkers described about the postmodernist oppression of women. We can oppress women for one week, or two, or a hundred, in order to accommodate the preferences of those who believe in the legitimacy of women's oppression. In my courses on gender and education, I have devoted entire units to this topic. I contemplated the oft-discussed tension between tolerance and feminism, as I looked at my bookshelf with books such as Susan Moller Okin's *Is Multiculturalism Bad for Women?*[11] (*Yes*, I thought, *it really is*), and Martha Nussbaum's *Women and Human Development*,[12] in which she argues for universal values, especially within the context of traditional religious communities. Yet, despite all that theoretical knowledge, here I was, engaged in an emotionally charged, deeply personal debate on this topic with a man from my community asking the women in this community to give up our belief in our own partner status in the name of tolerance. In this conversation with Yuval, I had to figure out how to translate this entire worldview into a sound bite, and in the guise not of lecturer, researcher, or expert in gender theory, but in the guise of friend and community member.

"Not necessarily," I responded with a deep breath. "I don't believe in tolerance as the ultimate value, nor that all values are equal." My answer surprised him, given his penchant for postmodernism, and our discussion came to a halt.

At that moment, I made a critical decision. In order to preserve my research, I decided to step out of this particular conversation and accept whatever the community collectively agreed to, and take a step back to role of researcher. Over the coming months I continued my research but eventually became less involved as a participant in the services. The intensity of my own involvement on so many levels, coupled with the crushing realization that the synagogue was not what I had thought it was, that some of the men were not who I had assumed they were, gave me pause.

The Boundaries of Male Feminism

These stories reveal the complexity, and ultimately the boundaries, of the Orthodox male encounter with feminism. Men who practice gender resistance in some areas will still hold on to practices and rhetorics that promote old patriarchal concepts with a newer model. In fact, at times those very acts of resistance rest on patriarchal foundations.

One of the most glaring avenues of resistance to Orthodox masculinity that comes into conflict with feminism is the resistance via community. Men's need for community to counteract the cold, individualistic, emotionless performance was expressed by many informants, in earlier chapters. For some men, "community" implies a community of men and often has no bearing on social activism. This stands in stark contrast to feminist models of community in which people come together in order to create a more just society and alleviate human suffering.

The idea that "community stability" supersedes the objective of alleviating the pains of patriarchy was strongly expressed by some men in response to Yuval's proposal. Hillel, for example, supported Yuval because "we are a *kehilla* [community] first and foremost, and we are first of all to be flexible and adapting and help each other out. So to me it's very, very, inappropriate not to help out a family who wants to have a *simcha*." For Hillel, community as a network of people supporting one another's needs is the paramount value. In order to understand the extent of this value, I asked Hillel how he would react, in comparison, to a family asking not to say the prayer on behalf of the state of Israel during their family's event. "No, that goes against the ideals of our *shul*. But to have only men is not going against the ideals of our *shul*." In other words, community trumps gender equality. All else is up for discussion. Community, then, which in its ideal form is a central feminist ideology, is also a rhetorical tool co-opted in the process of suppressing gender equity. This idea of gender as threatening to "community" places gender equality at the lowest end of the social-cultural scale of priorities.

Like the concept of "community," certain rhetorics of "balance," also a prominent feminist value in its ideal form, are co-opted to repress women's equality. "I'm glad that feminism isn't up on some pedestal," Ehud said, justifying the practice of giving young boys roles that were once designated for women. "Some days we have women leading many sections, and some days we don't. It's balanced." This dubious balance, in which women are still precluded from leading many parts of the service, and share many jobs with children, also masks entrenched masculinity.

The language of casual indifference, as in, "It's no big deal," is also co-opted to mask entrenched masculinity. Reuven said, "If one Shabbat is all boys, what do I care? It's the same as if a girl would do everything one Shabbat. Why not?" In seeking out a balance and perhaps tolerance, Reuven makes the outrageous claim that Yuval's proposal has an opposite possibility; but there is never a time when "a girl does everything," even in a partnership synagogue. This indifference turns a blind eye to the gender hierarchies that remain firmly in place.

Moshe also uses the language of "compromise" and "nonconfrontation" with casual indifference to preclude gender change. "I agree with compromise," he said, suggesting that women should be less demanding of equal participation. "Gender equality is less important. I don't see it as such a principled thing." He freely admits that he does not hold up gender equity as "a flag," as something that is so important to him that he is willing to fight for it. Compromise and indifference are more comfortable positions than wrestling with gender transformation.

Finally, men supporting entrenched patriarchy sometimes find rhetorical ways to contort the male gaze into an expression of compassion toward women. In describing his disappointment that Yuval would not be able to make his son's bar mitzvah in the synagogue, Gary said that not only are some values "more important than women's participation" and that therefore there should be "room for compromise," but also that the synagogue had an obligation to accommodate Yuval in particular because of his commitment to women's equal participation. "He has very much internalized, maybe more than anyone I know, what it means for men and women to share equal roles," Gary said, explaining that Yuval is "bothered by the fact that women have not internalized the fact that they need to take as equal of a role in the *shul* as the men." Gary claimed that Yuval wants to see "a whole mental reshaping of our minds of what it means for women and men to be equal partners," which is reflected in his insistence on women coming on time. This "mental reshaping" is of course a task for women, not men, in that women should be adapted to the "be a man" box, not that men should be challenging their received socializations into Orthodox masculinity. Gary said that "under certain circumstances we may have to curtail women's participation in order to allow people to have their *smachot* [celebrations]." In this hierarchy of values, gender equity is trumped by language of community, by language of compromise, and by Yuval's demonstrated status as fighter for women's equality.

Gary's exploration of Yuval's proposal confirms that Yuval is seen not only as the quintessential man, the leader of the synagogue and a very important member of the congregation, but also as the proponent of gender equality because of his whipping gaze on women. Haggai echoed this sentiment. "[Yuval] is a pillar, and he's not there because of his wife. . . . He completely lives this, 100 percent, more than me." For these men, Yuval's presence gives legitimacy to the model, and he is seen as fully committed to gender equality (as opposed to, tellingly, those who are "here for my wife"). By idealizing Yuval, they are idealizing the entrenched masculinity that he represents.

Responses to Yuval reveal the shifting and inconsistent nature of changing masculinity. On the one hand, men are staking claims to values such as community, balance, tolerance, care, flexibility, and thoughtfulness, all of which have traditionally been outside Orthodox masculinity. It may even be argued that this resistance via tolerance and community is a purposeful rejection of the cold, performative masculinity that they were socialized into. On the other hand, men are reluctant to part with masculinity as a power status that allows them to gaze upon and control women. Men's change in response to their own pains of patriarchy is ultimately much more of a priority than change in response to the pains of women. Men will be compromising, caring, thoughtful, communal, and even ambivalent when it comes to issues that benefit men, but not necessarily for issues that benefit women. Of all the aspects of the box that men are willing to change, the one most difficult is the abdication of power vis-à-vis women.

Feminist Men Revisited

Although many men halt their own processes of change, and although gender power struggles remain entrenched in many settings, this is not the entire story. Alongside power-wielding men are other men who are truly willing to abdicate their power and stake their own status and identity in order to bring about justice and fairness. Feminist men, whose stories were told in earlier chapters, are in some ways more inspiring than feminist women, because they are not only willing to stand up for equal rights, but also willing to abdicate their own positions of power and simultaneously able to withstand pressure to adhere to social expectations. Given the intensity of pressures to conform, these are no small feats.

Isaac, one of the men in Darchei Noam to take a strong stand against Yuval's proposal, places gender equality as a centerpiece of synagogue life. "After experiencing Darchei Noam, when I go into another Orthodox *shul*, I think, this is not a complete *shul*, because it is not giving rights," he said. "If we saw a *shul* that said that they don't want Sephardim, we wouldn't stand for it. But we do that for other people, for women." He takes the position that equality is just as important a value as *halakha*, a position unheard of in Orthodox masculinity, where *halakha* is paramount. "The halakhic part of the *shul* means nothing if you don't have the equality part," he said. "I won't compromise. I won't have a *shul* where women aren't doing stuff. I can't. It's so logical to me." Equality, or the quest for equality, is as fundamental to Isaac's identity as *halakha*. He compares a "normal" synagogue to a *mezuzah* (a ritual object on Jewish doorposts), where the decorative container that everyone sees is empty, lacking the actual scroll of text that is the essence of the *mezuzah*. "You can't have *mezuzah* without a parchment in it, and that's what it is. Orthodox *shuls* are just a *mezuzah* without the parchment in it." To Isaac, Judaism without equality is just an empty shell.

Other men expressed a similar unequivocal commitment to equality as fundamental to their identities. Noam also takes issue with the language of "rights." "The participation of women is not a right; it's an obligation. It's my obligation to ensure that you have that right. I won't force you to act on it, but I have to ensure that you have that right." Nathan frames the participation of women as an issue of "the dignity of the congregation," thus employing the rhetorical device that was originally used to keep women *out* of the sanctuary to ensure them a place *in* the sanctuary. "If a group of people think that equality is important, then the congregation has to accept it. That is the true meaning of dignity of the congregation." Michael believes that this is the way forward, and men's resistance to change is going "backward." "Just because someone doesn't like it, or a guest would be uncomfortable, we do not have to go back," he said.

In short, although change is met with bumps and stalls, some men are able to courageously and honestly let go of the power issues of masculinity and deconstruct social hierarchies for the sake of fairness, justice, and equality. They are unapologetically dedicated to transforming gender—starting with themselves—in order to challenge the construction of the "be an Orthodox man" box. As Elitzur Bar-Asher Siegal said, "The singing doesn't interest me, I'm not here to make new friends and feel like I'm belonging. I'm here to right a wrong, to create a society that promotes equality as much as is possible. This is feminist resistance, and it stands alone as a form of resistance. It is about transforming the entire structure of male-female relationships in Orthodox society." These men are heroes.

Conclusion

The partnership synagogue is a place where men's identities are shifting as they negotiate the impacts of feminism in the Orthodox world. Joining the synagogue was one of the actions that signaled change—change in gender relationships, change in religious identity, and change in the composition of Orthodox society. The synagogues on the border of Orthodoxy created ripple effects within the entire Orthodox community, as women began to look from the side and to contemplate the possibilities, as men's yeshivas everywhere began to ask the question, "Is the partnership synagogue part of us?" As the partnership synagogues began to take their place in scattered places, locations shifted, some men began moving, and men settled into their places on the borders, reevaluating the meaning for their own identities, reestablishing their own relationships vis-à-vis the Orthodox world—in or out, center or side, moving or staying. Creating a partnership synagogue in the middle of Orthodoxy became an event, like a tremor in the earth that caused many around to move.

As these changes settled down, another process began to emerge—the force of restricting change. In some ways this is understandable. Change is scary, especially something as fundamental to an Orthodox man as religious identity, or masculinity. The forces that resist change began to emerge, one by one, marking boundaries, exerting force, and reminding all that Orthodox men are Orthodox, and that they are men.

Yuval's proposal highlighted the fragility of this masculinity in transition, the depth of the patriarchy in Orthodox masculinity, and the many forms that embedded patriarchy takes, and demonstrated that Orthodox men and women have, for the most part, not yet begun to unravel the real impact of Orthodox masculinity on their religious culture. It is perhaps easier to unravel the public issues—that is, women's cantorial roles—than the multiple pulls on men's identity.

As men begin to reassert both their masculinity and their Orthodoxy, new forms of patriarchy are in formation. The most obvious conclusion from this research is that identity is fluid and not static, and that men seeking to retain masculinity are creating identity markers, not merely resting on the delusional "the way it has always been." The demand for women to come on time, for example, introduces new layers of male gaze onto the female experience. The dismissiveness about women's inability to master men's knowledge keeps many women from stepping up. The punishing male voice about women's insufficient observance has also created new rhetorics for keeping women inferior. And some men have introduced new tactical maneuvers—whether by creating a herd of men around the *hazzanit* or by pushing female layners aside to create women-free zones—to reassert their power.

What I have discovered is that while men who attend partnership synagogues are changing themselves and creating communal change toward redefining gender in Orthodox culture, many have not yet begun the process of unraveling meanings of masculinity and femininity and are still trapped within the patriarchal structures that hurt both men and women.

I have also discovered, however, that despite these enormous pressures on Orthodox men to perform and conform, there are men who are in an active negotiation over these elements of their identity. Despite these conflicts of identity, many truly caring, compassionate, and feminist Orthodox men have demonstrated an uncompromising resolve and dedication to broad change. These are the men who are taking these experiences as an opportunity to continue the process of change, to reflect on their experiences and their own shifting identities, and who have, even through the course of this research, begun to unpack masculinities and power. Men like Azriel, Jonathan, Isaac, Danny, Steven, Efraim,

Tom, Noam, Oren, Amitai, Zvi, Michael, and Zeev expressed a deep desire to improve human lives and alleviate oppression and suffering, to examine the real impacts of patriarchy on both women and men. These men, considering what surrounds them, should be noted for being ethically strong-minded, courageous, generous, and kind. They defy social convention in order to transform masculinity. Their identities and ideas left me with hope for the future. They are willing to stand up and be different kind of men. Given the portrait of Orthodox masculinity, those men are models of inspiration, the true heroes of this story.

Part IV ⟶ Reflections and Conclusions

Men, it has been well said, think in herds; it will be seen that they go mad in herds, while they only recover their senses slowly, one by one.

—CHARLES MACKAY

CHAPTER 9

Reflections on Orthodox Masculinities

~ THE MEN OF THE PARTNERSHIP synagogues are on the cusp. They are functioning within a shifting identity, in a new place on an ancient backdrop, negotiating past and present, masculinity and femininity, self and community. The men described are in and they are out; they are stable but they are moving; they are dwelling on a border but still living in the box; they are changing but trying desperately to maintain their presence in the world that they know so well. The partnership synagogue is a place where these men can unpack themselves and their identities. It is a place where men are fighting while embracing, challenging while accepting, struggling while finding the most comfort in the box called Orthodox masculinity.

Life on the cusp is unstable, shaky, and inconsistent. These men are uncertain and insecure as they negotiate new terrain. Committed to change but at times unaware that the change they are navigating is their own gender identity, these men are part of an incomplete and hesitant revolution. Few men are able to articulate the connection between women's liberation and men's liberation from patriarchal structures. There is little if any discourse of changing the way masculinity is done, such as a critical discussion about how perfectionism and punctuality form synagogue cultures. Many aspects of gender identity are still left unchecked, such as the relationship between child care duties and expectations of prayer performance. Few men have examined the relationship between power structures and their own mixed feelings vis-à-vis the process of change, and many partnership synagogues are not ready to engage in explorations of male liberation.

As the movement for change grows and develops, so does the movement to hold change back. The process of male liberation is in tension with the process of retaining a status quo, for both women and men. Men living on this border are pulled in two opposing directions; they are pulled back into the box as they are trying to pull themselves out. As they challenge the box and break free, they are still trapped in the male gaze that hurts them, but are often unable to break out of that pattern of judging and gazing.

This is perhaps why gender negotiation is more likely to take the form of imposing the standard male cultural model on women rather than challenging the entire box. The process of reaching gender equality is often interpreted as offering women an opportunity to internalize the practices of Orthodox masculinity in bits and pieces. Layn here, learn there, and be a meticulous, emotionless, perfect performer. The greatest gender shift is arguably that women's perfectionism and punctuality, rather than their child care abilities, are now seen as indicators of women's correctness. The man-on-man gaze has shifted to a man-on-woman gaze. Women's failure to adopt this masculinity is a pretense for punishing women, whether by voting against giving them more roles in synagogue, justifying the removal of all women's participation for an occasional Shabbat, bemoaning women's cantorial style, putting down tardy women as "failures of feminism," or publicly humiliating women. The pervasive and cross-national language of women's punishment for lack of adherence to the male model of performance suggests that Orthodox men have not challenged the supremacy of this model at all. The partnership synagogue is a place where men are reacting to gender hierarchies by inviting women to share their space as objects of a male gaze, perhaps to relieve some of their *own* pressures. They are bringing women into their box, maybe as a comforting presence.

Despite the lack of awareness of the processes at work, men have chosen to enter this border space for reasons that clearly relate to their need to alleviate the pressures of being an Orthodox man. Orthodox men are seeking out warmth, care, community, connection, spiritual fulfillment, and a flexible *halakha*, all outside the norms of Orthodox masculinity. Orthodox men are starved for relationships, for the ability to connect with other men in a format beyond sitting together for an hour or two reciting some verses. The standard Orthodox *shul* offers little emotional or social comfort to men. While the interviewees have little language to describe this emptiness, their descriptions of life as an Orthodox man and their reasons for coming to the partnership service belie this vital observation. They are thirsting for a female culture of interconnectivity.

Some men have begun to reflect on their own gender identities. Some are seeking out a place for equity and fairness, to resolve a certain "disconnect" in their lives, and to find a way to adhere to their religious heritage despite the embedded injustice. Some have even begun to ask the question, "What kind of masculinity have I been socialized into?" A handful of men have actively begun the process of rejecting the entire system of gender constructs, whether by becoming "sensitive men," taking on "women's" roles and professions, or engaging others in the conversation about masculinity and gender.

It is tempting to ask which is the more dominant model, the men who are drawn into the box with its old paradigms, or the men who are pulling themselves out of the box and evolving? While perhaps intriguing, the question misses the point. This research is not about counting numbers or quantifying trends, but rather about telling a story about identity in tension. This research is meant to provide all Orthodox men—actually, all *Jewish* men—with a language to understand the tensions and dynamics in their own identities and surrounding cultures and to begin to place them in the context of a story of the evolution of Jewish masculinity. This story is about men in process, men in movement, men in conversation with themselves and with the entire history of Jewish people in the modern era. The men described here are all somehow in dialogue with the "be a Jewish man" box that has been passed down throughout history. Even if it is not entirely accurate in all settings—even if, for example, certain aspects of the box are entirely Ashkenazi, or middle- to upper-class, or ignore nuances of particular cultures—I believe that Jewish men will be able to gain a framework with which to understand their own transitions and processes. I submit that all Jewish men will be able to relate to this story in one form or another.

This research, which seeks to unpack the identity of Orthodox men, paints a complex portrait of men who as a group are, perhaps more than anything, starving for connection. The experience of going to synagogue to be with other men is not necessarily a deep, relationship-building experience. Certainly men have their *kiddush* clubs, their jokes, and their conversations about sports and about money, and in some places they also have accompanying basketball leagues, what was described as a definitive attempt to create fun and energize men's spaces outside the sanctuary. They sit next to each other in pews, pat each other on the back, sometimes help network for better jobs and share the latest technology gadgets and stock tips. But they are not necessarily engaged in relationship building, friendship building, or in understanding one another's inner lives. Emotionally and spiritually, men go into synagogue alone and come out alone.

Orthodox Men and Others

This portrait of Orthodox masculinity is an eclectic combination of bourgeois, Western marketplace man, religious fundamentalism globally, and Orthodox Judaism in general:

Orthodox Man and Marketplace Man

The overlap between the Orthodox man and marketplace man goes beyond the middle-to-upper-class emphasis on professional models of "success" accompanied by competitive sportiness and models of man as cold, detached provider. Certainly the difficulties encountered by both single and homosexual men attest to the idea that suburban, nuclear-family life is as much a part of Orthodox masculinity as anything else. There is a deeper connection with marketplace man, however, in the aspirations to join the club. Just as the "company man" spends his life climbing the corporate ladder, always striving to prove himself to the men around him who are judging his performance, always trying to be accepted, to gain approval, to get ahead and get into the "club," whether the club of partners, managers, or millionaires, so, too, Orthodox man spends his life striving. He strives to be perceived by his peers as the best layner, the best speech-giver, the most knowledgeable, the most religious, the most halakhic, the most committed, or perhaps the most serious. He wants to be the most man in every way.

On the other hand, one of the main differences between marketplace man and Orthodox man is in something very profoundly Jewish: the cerebral. The Orthodox man takes the competitiveness of marketplace man and applies it to the realm of cold, intellectual analysis. I think that this cerebral twist on marketplace man is illustrative of another important aspect of the Orthodox man that may not have come across in the research but is true in life. Orthodox men, relative to most marketplace men, are "nice guys." That is, this sort of cerebral quality finds expression in an outward-facing gentleness and pensiveness. Religious boys and men often have an image of being kind and gentle, embodying a kind of nonviolence that one expects of clerics or professors. Many of the men I interviewed did indeed outwardly possess this studious, nonaggressive demeanor. It is a cerebralized version of marketplace man.

Yet intelligence and gentle speech can at times belie aggression and control. Soft-spoken men who embrace patriarchal views, who in their gentle voices reprimand women and other men, are no less threatening than men who scream. In some ways, the gentle aggressor is more effective, because the charm can be misleadingly dangerous. Some Orthodox men embody this form of patriarchy, the youthful, charismatic patriarchy of the charming intellect—aggression with a smile.

The Orthodox Man and Other Religious Men

The Orthodox man overlaps not only with marketplace man, but to a certain extent he also overlaps with fundamentalist men in other religions. The increase in religious fundamentalism across cultures, documented most vividly by Karen Armstrong,[1] creates a broader setting for Orthodox masculinity. Men around the world are being torn between modernity and fundamentalism, and that battleground is most intensely fought around gender. Men in Christianity, Islam, and elsewhere grapple with the conflicting demands to be "modern" on the one hand and "religious" on the other. Geraldine Brooks documents the increasing extremes of gender demands in Gaza, Saudi Arabia, Jordan, and elsewhere in the Muslim world as fundamentalism takes hold through gender iconography.[2] Meanwhile, a slew of Christian books aimed at reclaiming masculinity reject calls for men to be "nice" in favor of being a "hero" or "warrior" and showing women what "real" men they can be.[3] These are undoubtedly confusing times for men, caught between messages of returning to fundamentalist religious practice and pulls toward equality, feminism, and fairness. Men are under a broader pressure to be more religious at the same time that they are under pressure to be more "modern." The messages overlapping with religious fundamentalist trends globally make being an Orthodox man even more challenging. These tensions are in some ways from sources outside of Judaism and are indicative of world trends.

Orthodox Men and Orthodox Women

Certain aspects of Orthodox masculinity are not only about men but also about women. Like men, Orthodox women are expected to perform their duties meticulously, to be committed, serious, and halakhic, and to stay within their "box." In some cases, pressure on women can be fierce, such as the pressure to be "family women." That said, the bulk of the box is male and cannot readily be applied to women. Layning, *hazzanut*, *kippa*, *tefillin*, and *tallit* remain so unequivocally male in Orthodoxy that even suggesting otherwise brings out enormous discomfort to the men. In one focus group, Moshe argued that the box is not about men because *tefillin* is the same as women lighting Shabbat candles; but that claim proved difficult to uphold. As other participants in the focus group pointed out, *tefillin* is daily, candle lighting is weekly; *tefillin* is on the body, candle lighting is detached; *tefillin* takes time, candle lighting is quick; *tefillin* goes back to the written law of Sinai, candle lighting is of questionable origin. The most significant difference, however, which highlights the real difference between Orthodox man and Orthodox woman, is that men can easily light candles, but women wearing *tefillin* are seen as strange aberrations. The difference is in power relationships of gender, in that men ultimately have more freedom of movement, and more choices, than women.

Yet both Orthodox men and Orthodox women share the pressure to remain in the box, or in the "club," at all costs, to follow whatever rules are being transmitted at a given time and not to veer from them too much in any direction. Orthodoxy is not really about God or religion. Haym Soloveitchik describes the absence of God language in the philosophy of modern Orthodoxy.[4] I believe that the research here is a sociological counterpart to Soloveitchik's philosophical analysis. That is, the Orthodoxy that is spread and transmitted societally is not one of spirituality, God, and seeking out meaning as much as it is about staying with a social class, or a social club—the men's club for men, and the women's club for women.

Identity and Resistance

Perhaps the most fascinating question of all is: what makes men change? If the story of identity is that men are socialized into a box full of conventions and social expectations, and that they are picking and choosing aspects of the box to resist, what makes some people resist? This is, in some ways, the million-dollar question in identity formation. After all, we are all engaged in partial resistances to different aspects of our identities. We challenge some constructs and not others, and some people seem to be challenging much more than others. Why?

Although I hesitate to offer a definitive answer to this question, I do think that this research highlighted some compelling issues that offer insights into the overall process. For one thing, resistance has nothing to do with age or generation. Many people have asked me if young men are more open to change than older men, and the answer is unequivocally no. Some of the most open-minded, independent, and resisting men are retirees, and some of the most closed-minded, herd-following men are in their twenties and thirties. In this research, there is absolutely no correlation between one's generation and one's ability to think freely and break open the box.

There does seem to be some correlation between autonomous thought and profession. For some reason, the partnership synagogues seem to attract an unusually high number of academics—some 30 percent of the interviewees have PhDs, the overwhelming majority in the social sciences and liberal arts. It may be that these professions attract people who enjoy independent, creative thinking, which overlaps with a willingness to push boundaries. Still, this portrait may be misleading. Within the group of academics there are some who maintain strong patriarchal stances, even in the guise of being independents. Nachshon, Yuval, Robby, and Gary, for example, men who expressed some of the harshest patriarchal stances, are all academics who have created some of the freshest and most creative versions of the old patriarchy. They are also all under forty-five years old, arguably the "younger" generation. So, just saying that men are "creative thinkers" does not mean that they are truly challenging the box. They may be challenging cerebral formulations, but they are not necessarily breaking open their own identities.

There are, arguably, other professions that also require creative, independent thought but in a less cerebrally focused way, perhaps in a more deeply personal way. A profession that comes to mind in this regard is an artist. Artists have to be both independent minded and inward looking to unpack their identities, and skillful in intelligences that are less cerebrally focused. Significantly, there is only one artist in the group—Adin. He is also the only interviewee who asked me to speak more deeply about masculinity and gender identity, about what it means to be a man. I do not know if there is a correlation between the two points, but it is a good indication that while academics are creative and willing to explore cerebrally, they are not necessarily inward focused, nor are they necessarily unpacking masculinity. That is a pretty good overall picture of the male culture that dominates the partnership synagogue—willing to challenge ideas but not to be personally vulnerable.

Another claim worth examining is that American or "Anglo" men are more likely to resist patriarchy than Israeli men. There may be a certain truth to this, but it is not entirely clear from the research. In some cases, American men were more vocal and articulate than Israeli men and had a language of social change and pluralism that many Israeli men did not have. The civil rights movement, prominent in American education and public awareness, instilled a language that Israeli men lack. Nonetheless, some Israeli men, despite not having been brought up with the language of civil liberties, adopted a strong willingness and even eagerness to deconstruct their own identities. By contrast, some American men, fully aware of the social lingo, expressed surprisingly chauvinist ideas. Perhaps the American ideology of "life, liberty, and the pursuit of happiness" gives men permission to seek out their own identities, so that the process of resistance to the box is less foreign than it may be for Israeli men. While Israeli and "Anglo" men are equally capable of resisting or not resisting, non-Israeli men have an advantage of having been brought up with a language that invites personal quest and promotes social pluralism.

There is probably an additional issue at work here, and that is the role of Orthodox feminism. There has not yet been any major research comparing the two trends of American Orthodox feminism and Israeli Orthodox feminism, but it is needed. What I can superficially surmise is that the American Orthodox feminist movement is older than its Israeli counterpart by about a generation, having started in the 1970s, as opposed to the 1990s, and as such has had an influence on Orthodoxy, particularly the synagogue. The Orthodox women who are most likely to join a partnership synagogue are probably those who were influenced by this movement in one form or another, though this needs to be checked. Furthermore, I submit that the Israeli and American versions of Orthodox feminism, while sharing the same agenda, in practice focus on different issues. While Kolech, the Israeli feminist organization, focuses on the rabbinate, education, scholarship, and systemic advocacy, JOFA, its American counterpart, is much more synagogue and ritual focused. The notion of changing gender roles in Orthodox ritual performance may have become more mainstream in the United States than in Israel. This may be connected to the centrality of synagogue life in American Jewish culture generally, as opposed to Israeli culture. The only thing I can say for certain is that the difference between American Jewish feminism and Israeli Jewish feminism is a topic that begs further exploration.

Despite these caveats, I believe that there are certain basic characteristics of developing agency for resistance and change:

Trauma. Many of the most poignant stories of resistance involved some kind of personal trauma. Whether it was Yossi's lifetime of abuse followed by his mother's illness and riding the bus on Yom Kippur, Oren's discovery of his own profound unhappiness, or Reuven's insult at his son's bar mitzvah, many of the most engaging narratives have, at their core, a turnaround of identity that began with trauma. Reuven, in fact, said it as a plain fact: "Every man who comes here has undergone some trauma." He explained that every man has had some kind of experience that challenged something about the way he was socialized into religious identity and brought him to this strange border-dwelling place. For a person to take such a "radical" step requires some kind of jolt. Trauma sometimes spearheads awakening. Perhaps resistance is actually an attempt at healing.

Uncertainty or ambivalence. As counterintuitive as this may sound, agency is often not an act of definitively charging off in a particular direction but rather a reflection of uncertainty or ambivalence. Stability and safety are in some ways the foes of agency. By contrast, doubt and ambivalence move people away from the group. If trauma shakes up a person's life, uncertainty leads to searching. This is a vital point, because masculinity is constructed as such a powerful, controlling force that ambivalence itself has no place. An ambivalent man is by definition on the path to agency. He has already rejected an essential part of the box: infallibility.

Empathy. One of the most stirring elements of male resistance is the capacity for empathy. It is clear that the difference between men who continue to engage in the language of punishment and those who do not is the posture of empathy. A man who steps into a woman's shoes, whether that woman is a daughter, a wife, or a stranger, is already beginning to unpack his own sense of self. The ability and willingness to adopt the perspective of the other is a critical element in the process of resistance to one's received socialization. For some men, empathy is even stronger and forms a kind of moral outrage. Oren's shame at having to tell women that they cannot be with their bar mitzvah sons, Larry's sympathy for women struggling with many children, and Noam's fury at the way an entire congregation isolated a mourning father simply because of his leftist political views are just a few of the striking instances in which men detached from the box when they took on other people's pain and injustice.

Epistemological/theological unpacking. For some men, though not for all, questioning goes to the epistemological core of identity. They will reach questions such as, What is life? What am I here for? What is God? What is good and evil? and so on. Of all the items in this list, I think that this may be the least necessary for identity resistance. I say that because epistemological questioning, while profound in some ways, is still rather cerebral and as such can also keep men in the box. This may not be true in other cultures and societies. For the Orthodox man, however, epistemological and theological questioning may be more widespread than challenging one's entire identity. It is possible to be a "questioner" while still acting out the rules of the box. Nevertheless, some of the men who resisted most intensely described their journeys in theological and epistemological terms, such as, "This cannot be what God wants," or "This is not what it means to be a good person." There is room, therefore, to suggest that identity resistance is bound up in internal epistemological dynamics.

Courage. Perhaps this is obvious, but perhaps the most dominant characteristic of the process of resisting social conventions is a fearlessness that enables a person to buck the system. Resistance brings many undesirable results, especially in Orthodoxy. Social rejection, ostracizing, being construed as "weird"— these are not always easy to live with. More than anything else, the process of resistance entails letting go—letting go of the need for control, letting go of constant striving for approval, and letting go of one's fears.

The flip side of this question is, of course, what keeps men from resisting? I think the answer is readily apparent: *fear.* Men are afraid of an entire web of social processes. They are afraid of losing the masculinity that gives them presence, power, direction, and identity. The entire "be a man" box gives them a security in knowing who they are in this world. Deconstructing that is a huge threat. They risk being labeled as outsiders, not normal, nonreligious, or worse, Reform. If they shift masculinity, they lose that treasured identity marker of being part of the religious community.

I think, however, that there is a much deeper fear at work here: ultimately, men are afraid of being cast as *women.* Men who do not take themselves "seriously," who do not perform well, who are not powerful and aggressive, are deemed effeminate. This may not be said often out loud, but it is undoubtedly the underlying subtext. Men who step aside for women are rags, pushovers, wimps. The fear of being cast as wimpy or as a *hafifnik* I believe scaffolds this entire process, because at the end of the day, men know that they are men by virtue of the fact that they are not women. As Barrie Thorne demonstrates,[5] it is much easier for a woman to be "like a man" than it is for a man to be "like a woman." Being "like a woman" means going down in social status and facing complete societal rejection and ridicule. That scenario undoubtedly drives much of what is going on with men. They are not completely resisting masculinity because ultimately there is too much at stake.

The fearfulness was especially obvious at the last synagogue meeting in November 2008 at Darchei Noam, which was set up to finally discuss the "Orthodoxy" petition. Approximately forty people came, evenly split between men and women, for a three-hour discussion of the "controversial" aspects of the bylaws. The meeting was dedicated to two passages in the document, one that delineated the process by which the synagogue can change its halakhic "status quo" regarding women's participation, and one that described the synagogue as "halakhic-egalitarian" rather than "Orthodox." Regarding changing the "status quo," the document suggested that any issue can be raised at the annual general meeting, following extensive community-wide study, and that a vote of two-thirds majority is required to implement change. Several suggestions that were raised included changing the majority required for change to 80 percent, or to 100 percent; requiring a proxy of all members; requiring rabbinic approval; and creating an extensive document outlining the current status quo so that there would be no debate. In other words, the bulk of the discussion was figuring out ways to disable change. The very language of "status quo" marked a huge shift. A synagogue that was built on the idea of change and allowing as much change as possible within *halakha* was now cementing change into a formal written document and preempting dynamic evolution. The discussion about "Orthodoxy" took a similar tone. Some men discussed the importance of how a congregation appears to others and why it cannot be called "Reform," and Reuven expressed outrage at the fact that it took the *va'ad* ten months to respond to his petition to call his partnership synagogue "Orthodox."

Although there were few voices in disagreement—most notably Gary, who said there is no "status quo" but merely issues that have not yet been discussed, and Isaac, who said that changing the *shul* from "halakhic-egalitarian" to "Orthodox" was already a change in the status quo—the overwhelming tone of the meeting, among men and women alike, was fear of change. Even men who I think may not entirely feel that way did not speak up. Many of the men—the majority of whom were interviewees—did not voice any opposition to this fearfulness. Hillel, Judah, and Stuart sat silently while Gvir, Reuven, and Eitan dominated the discussion. Men who may have had something to say about flex-ibility and openness—such as Zvi, Tom, and Efraim—were not there. Not show-ing up is its own form of silence, and silence is fear, too. As Audre Lorde wrote, "And of course I am afraid, because the transformation of silence into action is an act of self-revelation, and that always seems fraught with danger. . . . In the cause of silence, each of us draws the face of her own fear—fear of contempt, of censure, or some judgment, or recognition, of challenge, of annihilation. But most of all, I think, we fear the visibility without which we cannot truly live."[6]

The day after the meeting, I had an illuminating discussion with Yair, Eitan's brother, whom I did not interview. "Who cares what we call ourselves?" he said. "We are not really Orthodox anyway," he smiled, thus placing himself outside the box, but appearing comfortable there. "I really don't care what other people say about me, anyway," he added, "but I'm pretty sure I'm the only Israeli who feels that way." While this comment certainly supported the claim that Anglo-Israeli cultural differences form a central part of the narrative, I actually thought that his claim was somewhat unsubstantiated—and notably unsupported—at the meeting. The only woman to express the position that "egalitarian" is vital to the synagogue was Galit, an Israeli woman who said, "I understand Ameri-cans who are afraid of being labeled Conservative, because they know what that is. But here in Israel? The Conservative and Reform movements hardly even exist! What are people so afraid of?" In response, Limor, who had initially been insistent upon "Orthodox" but over the year changed her mind, tried to ex-plain. "In Israel," she said, "everything is black and white. There is no flexibility. That's why it's so important." So while issues of what is "American" and what is "Israeli" form a central part of the narrative, it is still not entirely clear that these reflect coherent cultural constructs. They may in fact be perceptions, or even just excuses.

My conversation with Yair was enlightening in terms of Eitan as well. Eitan's pose of "older brother" to the wayward younger brother is an apt description of his role in the synagogue. His younger brother does not care if he is called Ortho-dox or not, he is not afraid of bucking what is meant to be "Israeli" religiousness, and he smiles about it. Eitan, on the other hand, is controlling, containing, and serious, perhaps seeing himself as the dam, holding back the rush of change—or perhaps the rush of emotion. This *is* Eitan's emotional expression.

My friend and colleague Dr. Ariella Zeller, who was also at the meeting, be-lieves that this was a moment of men trying to reverse the change of the past three to four years. She said that many men have a real ambivalence about their process of change and a visceral insecurity about this life on the cusp. On the one hand, they want to rebel and resist, but on the other hand, they are almost repulsed by their own resistance. The men at the meeting were saying that they have had enough of breaking away from the crowd and that we need to stop now. That's it, to here and no further. This is the reason to write down the status quo and to formalize and restrict future change with such severe limitations, as if to ensure that change will be limited, if at all. The brakes were put on—not just the brakes, but the emergency brakes—and that is exactly how it felt to them, as if this were in fact an emergency. It was a crisis of identity and defini- tion of who they were. This is why they needed to define themselves as Ortho- dox: to set the record straight. They were, they *are*, Orthodox and nothing else. They have looked at what is outside the box, and they are freaking out. The box represents safety, home, what they know. They are done resisting, and now they are symbolically running to the box. Ariella went on to argue that the men are fearful because they have stepped out of the box and are scared of the un- certainty of what it will all look like in the end. They are afraid of not knowing how to finish what they started. What Ariella is describing, of course, is male impotence. They are, indeed, profoundly afraid of losing their masculinity.

Although this is clearly a generalization that does not apply to all the men, I think it is an apt description of the process that Reuven, Gvir, and Eitan are leading. The fact that so many men were silent or did not come indicates that a viable alternative to the fearfulness is not readily apparent. The fact that so many men continue to view as leaders some of the most fearful of the men says that many of them lack a vision for their own process of liberation. I would argue that many men lack a consciousness of social processes altogether. Con- sider, for example, that all the other aspects of the bylaws, including issues of charity and social activism, were not even mentioned as a topic for discussion. In fact, Eitan read out loud the one sentence in the vision statement that says the congregation will be "active in charity and social causes" and responded, "Let's take that out. It's grandiose." His suggestion went into the agenda for the synagogue's annual general meeting without any objection. The entire vision of creating a just society was wiped out in one fell swoop, without even a murmur.

It seems, therefore, that the meeting indicated a critical turning point in the process of men's evolution here. If, until this point, men were expressing a cer- tain deliberation and ambivalence, a willingness to take a risk and be different from the "club," this meeting was a clear sign of reverting to the norm. In the battle between men's capacity for courage and their retreat into fear, it was clear that fear of being construed as outside the norms had firmly taken hold, wiping out the last remnants of the notion that this partnership *minyan* was a place of courage and resistance. It was perhaps a victory for some: the partnership *minyan* was now truly part of Orthodoxy.

Even here, there is a fearful obsession with the box. Even men in the partnership synagogue continue to dwell in the box and are struggling to find a language with which to break down the walls. In fact, I would argue that Yair is completely wrong when he says that the synagogue is "not really Orthodox." It is *precisely* Orthodox. What makes it Orthodox is that this meeting and the conversation about "are we Orthodox" is even taking place. Only people who are Orthodox are so obsessed with such a question. The only people who are afraid of being cast outside the box are those who most desperately need to be there.

Why Partnership?

The lingering question is, why would a man who is so steeped in patriarchy participate in a partnership synagogue? I believe there are several possibilities. One answer is that men are genuinely interested in doing gender differently, but they do not have the language or the tools to really unpack the entire system, or understand what bothers them. This research is the first attempt at giving Orthodox men a language to understand their own experiences of masculinity, and I hope it helps create conversations within Orthodox communities about masculinity.

A second possibility is that men feel compassion toward women but are reluctant to abdicate power. Most of the partnership synagogues, for example, have male leadership, offering men avenues to exert leadership and find new locations of power. They are starting a process that feels right to them but are afraid of how far it will go.

A third answer is perhaps a bit cynical, but hinted at in several interviews and other conversations. In some liberal-academic circles—the population that dominates this research group—the partnership synagogue is something of an "in" thing. If there is a new trend out there, some people like to ensure that they are part of it—even if they do not fully understand what it's about. That is certainly the case for many informants, some of whom told me, "Don't interview me; I'm not here for the reasons you think I am." They joined this synagogue for reasons of comfort, convenience, or colleagues without really understanding why it exists. Without truly appreciating the depth of the feminist struggle, they found themselves in a nice place without having to unpack their own identities and experiences.

Why Orthodoxy?

One cannot help but ask why resistance matters. After all, one can make the case that if a person's socialization is good and just, there is no reason to change it. Indeed, many aspects of Orthodoxy reflect desirable values. Commitment, for example, is a rare commodity amid a Western culture of superficial, lightning-speed impulse fulfillment. It may even be argued that perfectionism and punctuality are good things in that they demonstrate commitment and loyalty to the needs of a larger community.[7]

I agree that there are noble aspects to Orthodoxy. The point about resistance, however, is not necessarily to *reject* elements of the box as much as it is to *take ownership* of one's identity. Resistance is important not because commitment should be rejected but because people need to make their own choices. To simply accept one's socialization without ever trying to examine its cultural context is to not really live. Resistance is the stuff of life; it is the energy, the passion, the spiritual quest of finding oneself within social structures that seek to own us.

Orthodoxy, in particular, seeks to own its society members and inhibit resistance. The enormous corpus of regulations that increasingly saturates the culture seeks to maintain a system of blind obedience and preempt individual thinking and choice. The entire system of groupthink, fear, and ostracizing is meant to tell people to fit in and do not think for themselves. The language of God adds to the weight of this socialization. People from the youngest ages are told that the minutiae of practice come directly from God. The overbearing language of God's will that seeps through every aspect of Orthodox life makes independent thought difficult indeed.

The point of resistance is about ownership, not necessarily rejection. If a man decides that perfect performance of *trop* is a genuine expression of spirituality, then that may indeed be his expression of resistance—if it emerges from a process of cultural examination and introspection. But to aggressively impose it on others without reflection, and then criticize others who do not adequately conform—especially women seeking out justice and fairness—that is where personal resistance has not, in fact, taken place, and that causes a lot of unnecessary pain.

I would like to suggest that the question "Why be Orthodox?" be opened up by Orthodox men and women. It seems to me that if one takes a step back from the group socialization, the answer is just not so obvious. Asking the question and seeking out real answers may be an integral part of the advancement of Jewish life.

One of the informants did just that as he completed his rabbinical studies. He had grown up Conservative and landed in an Orthodox rabbinical school, but his teacher continued to challenge him on this issue. Are you sure you want to be Orthodox? His long and thoughtful response sheds light on some real, personal, and intensive deliberation, a model for other men. His letter to his teacher is too long to reproduce in its entirety, but I will excerpt a bit of it here:

> You asked me if I am still comfortable being called an Orthodox Jew, and further, an Orthodox Rabbi. My answer now, as then, is yes. As I reflect on what brought me to rabbinical school in the first place, I realize that it was my love of Talmud Torah. I love learning Torah, and I am passionate about sharing that love with other Jews. All of my adult life has been motivated by trying to make my life as meaningful as possible and to help others do the same. At first this took me into the world of the arts and culture, thinking that Beethoven and Mahler would provide that transformative, redemptive, possibility.
>
> But I came to realize that, though I see holiness and the possibility for transformation in great works of art and music, the greatest and most profound redemption can come through a life of Torah study and observance. Our creation in the image of God is a gift which can only be repaid by striving to actualize that image as deeply and widely as possible—morally, ethically, intellectually, and spiritually. And though I believe that listening to the Brahms Requiem is a spiritual experience, listening to it is not going to feed a hungry person, or liberate a Sudanese slave, or save a patient dying of cancer. These things can only be accomplished through the activation of the human capacity for altruism, which, as our teacher Rabbi Yitz Greenberg has preached, comes through the internalization that every human being is created *b'tzelem eloki* [in God's image], and is thus endowed with uniqueness, equality, and infinite value.
>
> Thus when I speak of my love of Talmud Torah, I do not limit the term to sitting in the *beit midrash* [house of study]. To me, Talmud Torah encompasses both study and practice, reflecting the value of *Hazal* that it is not enough to learn; one must also do—*lilmod u'la'asot* [to learn and to do]. The deepest and truest Talmud Torah reflects a synthesis of the intellectual, spiritual, moral, and ethical, connecting the worlds of heart, head, and body, the worlds of *beit knesset* [synagogue], *beit midrash, sadeh* [field]

and *shuk* [marketplace]. Just as we bring *ma'asim* from the world into our learning, we must bring our *hiddushim* [new insights] from our learning into the world.

The New Orthodoxy

To paraphrase Ruth Behar,[8] Orthodoxy is writing men while men are writing Orthodoxy. Orthodoxy has written, defined, and constructed masculinity, and these men in turn are rewriting Orthodoxy as they struggle to liberate themselves. They may not be aware of it, they may not do it coherently or consciously, but they are struggling and resisting as they dwell on the edge of the box. They come to the partnership synagogue, they negotiate with the women in their lives, and they risk taking actions that others in their society would call unorthodox and unmanly. They risk being lesser men in order to take part in the resistance. In many ways this is very radical, it is probably also very tough, and it is most definitely scary. The men are still coming week after week and listening to women layn. They still try to be good fathers, and they will even talk to a feminist researcher at length about topics that they may have never articulated before out loud, topics that they may not have even thought about before. Being part of this research, like going to the partnership *minyan*, entails becoming self-reflecting, and these are acts of courage.

This is the New Orthodoxy. The men who are stepping out of the box to create spaces that are redefining gender are engaged in the creation of a new identity, and arguably a new society. This cadre of men is constructing a new culture or perhaps subculture that is creating new rules and definitions of gender. The children who go to partnership *minyanim* are going to have a whole new box to contend with, one that will have a certain resemblance to the "be a man" box described here, but one that will also have different rules and expectations. It is being constructed as we speak by men who are rewriting Orthodoxy.

Not all partnership *minyanim* are conducting this negotiation in the same way. The stories of Darchei Noam in Modi'in are not the stories in other communities. Each man and each community will re-create masculinity in its own contextualized way, but they are all part of the same process. All the men in this New Orthodoxy are in conversation and negotiation with the box, and they have all done something significant enough to land in a brand-new space.

In this process, men should learn a bit from women. For the past few decades, women have been looking out at men's worlds and saying, "We want some of that." Women want freedom to be active, economically successful, working, assertive, and publicly visible. Women are working hard to redefine what it means to be a "woman" and giving themselves the freedom to be who they are. One side effect is that men have had to shift some notions of what it means to be a man. They take on more house and child care roles in order to enable women that freedom. Yet, in many places, men have not really begun a parallel process for themselves. Few men, especially Orthodox men, have moved aside the partition to see what is on the other side and said, "I want some of that." Yet women have quite a lot to offer men. Women do not have social status and clout, nor do they have the power that comes from competitive aggression. But women's culture can offer men a lot of what they are missing in their identities, including care, relationship, flexibility, nurturing, and profoundly connected friendships. Perhaps most important, women have the freedom to occasionally stop striving to be the best and just *be*. Men can most certainly use some of that.

I would like to suggest that men take lessons from women in the deconstruction of gender. Although men and women are both socialized into gender, the societal process of deconstructing "woman" is far more advanced than that of deconstructing "man." Western society is arguably engaged in an ongoing discourse about the "role of women." Women around the world, admittedly not all, can often create self-describing sentences to the effect of, "I was taught that women should be X, but I choose to be Y." I am not suggesting that the fight for women's rights is finished and done. Rather, I am saying that the language of gender identity for women exists in a popular, widespread form. Women know how to talk about how they were socialized into womanhood, even if they are still unpacking it all, or choosing to internalize it. For men, by contrast, the language is hard to come by. Certainly there are books, journals, and university departments here and there dedicated to men's studies, masculinity studies, and gender studies, as well as a range of men's awareness groups. Nevertheless, I would argue that the scope and extent of men's gender awareness is not nearly as advanced as women's gender awareness. This argument comes in part from Harry Brod's insights that men don't study masculinities, and that there will never be a full-scale men's feminist revolution, and in part from discussions with men for this study. The conversation about men's gender, in spite of the hard work of scholars of masculinity, is just beginning.

The liberation of men and the liberation of women should not have to be in tension with one another. Men should not see feminism as a threat but as a key to their own freedom. Feminism has a tremendous gift to offer men: fluidity in gender identity. It's time for men to stop worrying about being men and to start *being*.

Epilogue

There are women who truly and sincerely aspire and yearn to reach levels
of holiness, and closeness to God is good for them. . . . We should pull
them in with love and not send them wandering, and ostracize them, and
with that send them to graze in foreign fields. —DANIEL SPERBER

〜' IN NINETEENTH-CENTURY EUROPE, the Jewish world experienced a bizarre gender twist when girls were systematically sent to get well-rounded educations in order to prepare for a life of supporting their future yeshiva-student
husbands, but they were forbidden from learning Torah. By contrast, the boys
were forbidden to learn secular subjects but were exceedingly knowledgeable
about Talmud. What resulted, according to feminist scholar Dr. Debbie Weissman, was a situation in which young Jewish women understood, experienced, and
functioned well in the wide world but were treated as ignoramuses, or second-class
citizens, in their local Jewish cultures. By the turn of the century, many young
women were abandoning religious Judaism in favor of socialism, Marxism,
feminism, or any other ideology and lifestyle that would enable them to thrive
as intelligent, independent beings. According to Weissman, this trend is what
led Sara Shnirer to open up the first religious school for girls, Bais Yaakov, in
which girls could take ownership of religious knowledge, and, Shnirer hoped,
they would be motivated to stay religious.[1] At the time Shnirer was considered
heretical, but her vision proved to be revolutionary. When women are empowered, trusted, and well treated, they stay. Otherwise, they find the door.

I have been thinking about these trends as I reflect on the impact of this research on women in general and on me personally. There are a lot of parallels
between the situation for Jewish women then and now. Today, too, educated,
intelligent, independent, and passionate women are stifled by Orthodox culture. They lead double lives, in which they are able to fully function in the secular world but dwell in a religious lifestyle that places them behind the curtain as
if they are ignorant, incompetent, or merely bodies. I think it's only a matter of
time before we see trends among young religious women leaving Orthodoxy.

There is not much research on this.[2] The voices of girls' protest are thus far muted. Women may be already voting with their feet, but we would not even know.

Perhaps this explains the persistence of the argument that women don't seem to care that much. Some do not even protest their status in the synagogue. Or as some informants argued, women don't even show up on time to the partnership service, so clearly they are not at all interested in feminism. As much as these words seethe with misogyny, it is indisputable that Orthodox women's protest is not taking the form of their running en masse toward the partnership synagogue. Indeed, in a recent article in *Ynet*, Efrat Shapira-Rosenberg, a religious columnist in the Judaism department, wrote that she only goes to a partnership service "in my dreams." "I am of course a feminist," she declared, "but if I'm to be honest with myself, I am happy not to have all these other obligations of praying three times a day. I don't know if that's what I want." Some talkbacks responded with comments such as, "If that's the case, you're not a feminist," and "What do you expect? Orthodoxy will never change." What seems clear is that if a woman who is willing to call herself an Orthodox feminist is not going to this service, we may conclude that women are not embracing this particular form of feminist protest in droves.

Nevertheless, I think there is a much deeper point here than simply writing off women's resistance, one that became increasingly clear as I conducted this research. The relationship between Orthodoxy and feminism is more complicated than women running to *minyan* three times a day on time—acting like men, if you will. There is a whole slew of reasons why women do not come "on time" or perhaps at all—whether it's that they are still doing the bulk of child care and food preparation on Shabbat, whether they are still recovering from years of alienation and a private resistance that makes reading the paper on Shabbat morning very attractive, or whether they have internalized the message and the habit that if they don't count for *minyan*, it doesn't really matter if they come anyway. More than that, however, the assumption that feminist resistance entails women adopting male socialized behavior is misguided.

For one, everything that men are expected to do as Orthodox men, whether being "on time" three times a day or standing without talking from beginning to end of the service, assumes female servitude. The only reason men have been able to insist on "on time" and fulfilling all their other rigid, ritualistic obligations is that they have always been able to count on women to cook, clean, and watch the children. These assumptions persist today, and not only in Orthodoxy. It is not uncommon for young, upwardly mobile men to plan business trips without regard to home needs, to agree to work the longest hours they can, knowing that someone at home is picking up the slack, and by extension to accept without question the notion that they should be praying in a group of ten men three times a day despite the strain these assumptions place on female labor. To wit: Nachum's entire model for Orthodox masculinity is the *yeshiva bachur*, the single student whose every need is taken care of. But by whom? The community? The mother? The wife? It doesn't matter. There continues to be an idealization of religious practice that is fully dependent on the servitude of someone else, usually women. So if women want access to this experience and socialization, they have a problem. Who is serving *their* needs so they can freely and happily get to *shul*?

There is a more profound reason why women are not adopting the male model: *women find the male model absent of meaning*. Female cultures of spirituality are emotion filled, personal, engaging, musical, spontaneous, surrounded by people, connections, children, and friendships. Jews have been praying in more or less the same way from the same book with the same pages upon pages of words for recitation for a few thousand years, give or take. So when push comes to shove and women gain access to those practices, the celebration is short-lived. For this we struggled so hard? *This* is what we were looking for all this time? No wonder so many women say, okay, but no thanks. Women seeking access to this space from which they are systematically excluded are disappointed with their own culture. Because it is not really their culture; it is *men's culture*. The Orthodox synagogue, even when women are involved, remains a men's space based on the way men are socialized.

Ultimately, I think that the real reason why women are not running to the synagogue is found in the core of this research. If we look at Orthodox masculinity and compare it to Orthodox femininity (leaving aside for the moment the issue of hierarchy and the exercise of power from one to the other), on the simple level of gender as collection of characteristics, one that we will call "male" and the other that we will call "female," it becomes clear why women are not rushing into the male world. Women are socialized as carers, a role that entails servitude, physical restrictions, and enormous amounts of unpaid labor, but also involves love, warmth, friendship, relationship, care, flexibility, and home. Men, by contrast, are socialized as mechanistic performers, with all the accompanying status, power, and strength, but also with emotionless, connectionless, cold, and demanding behavioral expectations that leave little room for individual expression or even ambivalence. In fact, to be a man may provide personal power, and it certainly has physical, social, and monetary rewards, but it does not necessarily involve freedom. Being mounted with expectations of thrice-daily rote repetition and performance among emotionless peers and calling that prayer is not all that attractive. It is especially not attractive to women who have experienced something else. Women who have experienced friendship, sharing, deep caring, and the love between women look at what goes on between men and think, why would I want *that*? I think that's the real reason women aren't all that interested in running to do the man's thing in synagogue. At the end of the day, being a woman is much nicer than being a man.

Separating out the power aspects of this equation, however, masks a huge aspect of the story. After all, if being a woman is so great, why aren't men rushing to take on femininity? As Barrie Thorne writes, there are still many more girls who want to be like boys than boys who want to be like girls, and society is incredibly more tolerant of boy-like girls ("tomboys") than girl-like boys ("sissies"). Perhaps men are reluctant to abandon masculinity because of those stigmas. Alternatively, it may be tough to be a man, but there are infinite rewards: power, prestige, status, control, and, of course, choices. In Orthodoxy, men can take any role that they want. They can walk into any synagogue in the world and their place is counted, their "amen" indispensable. And if they know a tune or two, they can become king—king of the synagogue, king of the community, and king of the Jews. But to take on a female culture means abandoning all that. It is an abdication of privilege, and power and control are everything. Understandably, perhaps, men are not all that eager to give that up.

So the masculinity of the synagogue that keeps women away takes shape in the persistent ways that men exercise power and control. Even in this partnership-style *minyan* where men supposedly move over and abdicate privilege for women, male power is in full force. It may take other shapes and forms, it may be disguised as men being "nice" or perhaps even self-described "feminists." But I continuously encountered a male power that was not entirely ready to abdicate. Personally, it was very hard for me to be told off by men about the way I lead services and the time I get to synagogue. (In the middle of our interview, one man told me that I was being a bad mother and role model for coming late to *shul*.) It was hard to listen to men talk about women's lack of knowledge and incorrect singing. It was especially hard to see girls (including my own daughter) running out of *shul* crying while the men who caused their pain did not even notice. It was hard to listen to the language men used to put women down, sometimes subtle and sometimes overt and aggressive. And it was especially hard for me to hear Judaism and *halakha* being invoked as a rationale for hurting women.

There are some wonderful Orthodox feminist women who are no longer able to make themselves at home in an Orthodox synagogue, not even in a partnership *minyanim*. My Australian feminist friend who was asked by Nachshon to leave the sanctuary because she was holding a baby in the back is one example. Another friend who was the *gabbait* in a partnership synagogue was aggressively nudged out of her synagogue because she wasn't "precise" and "perfectionist" enough in the way she took the role.

Orthodox men have found some creative, sometimes passive-aggressive, and sometimes quite biting ways of maintaining their own power and keeping women down, which make the Orthodox synagogue a place that is not really safe for women.

This research ended up being much harder for me, personally, than I anticipated. I started off thinking that I was going to be exploring gender liberation from a new perspective, from the perspective of men abdicating power in order to build a compassionate community. In the end, I didn't entirely find that, and it was a very painful realization. In this research, I was perhaps the quintessential vulnerable observer. My observations permanently altered my own identity.

I have been to many women's prayer services, and there is something extremely comforting in an all-women's presence. I know that in the women's space, I will not be pushed around by a bullying man. I will not be made to feel like an observer of someone else's work. I am also not a sex object—there are no men looking at my body to see if I'm offensive or suggestive (though there are arguably enough women who have internalized that gaze and continue to judge the apparel of other women). Perhaps most important, every job is available to women. There is not a single job in the service that men come and take away from women. Even *hagba*, the lifting of the Torah, a practice I have never seen or heard of a woman doing in a partnership synagogue, is always done by women in the all-women's service. Women's bodies are allowed to be strong when there are no men present. The women's service is potentially a place for a certain radical feminism, even though in practice few women go there with radical feminism in mind. Still, I find myself thinking, perhaps an all-women's space is really the best place for a woman. It is, without question, the safest.

Despite that, women's services are unfulfilling. What is taken away from women remains invisible, outside of the service, but still there. We are not allowed to say certain parts of the service because even if there are one hundred women in the room, we are not counted as a group. Even alone, we are not considered people. At a recent women's Torah reading, I got an *aliyah* and was about to say the blessings when I was told, "Don't say *barchu* because we're not a *minyan*." I knew all of that—I've done the blessings many times—and yet the statement was so very jarring. I looked at the hall full of women and thought, how can we internalize this incredible insult, even among ourselves? Are we not people? Are we not a group? We have been observers of this tiny little ritual thousands of times, answered *"amen"* to men thousands of times, and yet we are not even allowed to answer *"amen"* to ourselves? It made me want to cry.

I started my story with a great passion and desire for taking ownership of the Jewish liturgy and especially Torah reading, with an enormous, burning desire to have a place in synagogue. I got part of my wish, and while it was certainly liberating for a time, it was also profoundly disillusioning. The problem with Orthodoxy, I came to realize, is not just that women are forbidden from doing what men do. The problem is in the entire set of assumptions around men, the idealization of a masculinity that, really, is not what I want in life. Orthodoxy is not really a place for women.

More than that, Orthodoxy is a by definition a male construct. Orthodoxy is *men*. The way to be a complete Jew in Orthodoxy—from the bris to the bar mitzvah to giving a woman a ring and maybe giving her a *get* (divorce)—is to be a man. I know, lots of wonderful feminists have been pointing this out for decades. I am not merely saying that Judaism is a patriarchal culture. What I'm saying is that *Orthodoxy as a construct is male*. Orthodoxy is not only a creation of men, built upon the actions of men and the groupings of men, led and maintained by men, but it is also a culture that rests on idealized images of human existence that can only really be fulfilled by men. *As a woman, I can never really be truly Orthodox*. I can be the wife or daughter of Orthodox. I can be an observer of Orthodox. But as a woman, I am never quite inside the culture. Because to be Orthodox in its full meaning ultimately means being a man.

The question then becomes, what is Orthodoxy without masculinity? I'm not sure, but it's not my question to answer. That question is for the men. It's up to men to reconstruct a religious life without the unwanted and undesirable constructs. I hope that this book can be part of the first step in that process.

From my perspective, I would like the Orthodox community to develop a gender-neutral spiritual culture. If a characteristic is deemed to be of value, it should belong to men and women alike. If the community considers child rearing important, let both men and women take part equally. If emotional connection and warmth are important, let everyone take ownership, and let it be placed high up on the scale of priorities, in real terms. If music is important, let both men and women sing. Similarly, let us let go of those characteristics that, upon close inspection, are really not connected to spirituality and religiousness at all. We have a nearly two-thousand-year-old Talmudic tradition that prides itself on such punctuality, precision, and perfectionism that the precise words of the *Shema* must be recited at a certain time. But, really, is that what makes us godly? Or is it just an expression of men seeking control in a world of chaos who measure, cut, and calculate every movement so as to avoid having to actually feel emotions such as fear, uncertainty, and pain? I am hardly the first person in history to take issue with the possibly Germanic and possibly Talmudic overemphasis on perfectionism at the price of emotional expression. Hassidism, Kabbalism, and arguably Reform Judaism took issue with some of these same cultural practices of rigid inflexibility that preempt genuine spiritual expression. My contribution to the discussion is this: the reason that these practices remain in place in Orthodox culture is that they have become intricately linked to the meanings of being a *man*. So what I would really like to see is men beginning to let go of all this. If a man veers from the norm, says the *Shema* late, sings the *trop* slightly differently, or perhaps speaks to God in silence and tears rather than in prescribed words, he will still be a man. In my view, he will likely be an even better man.

I find myself revisiting John Stoltenberg's *Refusing to Be a Man.* For Orthodoxy to be less hurtful, less oppressive, and less damaging to the well-beings of both men and women, Orthodoxy has to be reconstructed by men. That is, the men have to challenge the masculinities within themselves and, as Stoltenberg suggests, simply refuse to be that way.

In order for men to make changes in the community, they have to first unpack their own masculinities, and that is undoubtedly the greatest challenge. That was the purpose of this research, to help unpack Orthodox masculinity so that there can be less pain in Orthodoxy. If men begin to take ownership of these constructs, if they start to examine their own processes of socialization and learn to actively and consciously resist, then real change can happen. Men have to refuse to partake in the hurting of women, and of themselves. If that begins to happen, then I have hope.

The research process led me on some unexpected paths and forced me to look at issues from close up, with a magnifying glass and a mirror, and face things that I am not sure I would have wanted to face. *Vulnerable observer indeed.* But the research is not about me. It's about the men. I hope that the mirror I held up for the men helped them in their own journey of identity. If my research helps men tease out that which is beautiful and meaningful in their religious identities while letting go of that which is hurtful, then my work here is done.

Appendixes

Appendix A

Notes on Methodology

I obtained interviewees in a variety of ways.* At Kehillat Darchei Noam in Modi'in, where the membership list is freely available and widely distributed each year, I went through the list and called one man after another. I explained that I was a postdoctoral lecturer in education and that I was interested in the gender identities of Orthodox men, specifically men in partnership or "Ortho-egal" synagogues. Of the approximately seventy members of the synagogue, I interviewed twenty-eight, nearly half. Only one man in the synagogue gave me an aggressive "no," saying that he would not give a view that was "favorable." His resistance apparently was based on the assumption that I was writing a syna-gogue puff piece, though my description of the research was purposefully clin-ical. In Shira Hadasha, where the synagogue list is not freely available, I con-ducted ten interviews, reaching each person through word of mouth. Most are English speakers, though not necessarily American, and all are heavily involved "regulars" and not in transit, though it is not clear what portion of the commu-nity they represent. For the rest of the interviewees, I sent e-mail requests to the synagogues through their leaders or list-serves and got from one to three inter-views per community, a sampling from around the world. The method is there-fore somewhat self-selecting and would not survive any thorough statistical analysis. It is not meant to offer statistics, but rather an ethnographic portrait of border-dwelling men in Orthodoxy. Nonetheless, the Modi'in informants rep-resent a hefty chunk of the research community.

Each interview took a different course and had its own dynamic. Some were in men's homes, some at their workplaces, some at cafés, and some via Skype. All the interviews were digitally recorded and professionally transcribed, and all the participants gave permission to use the interview for research purposes. I offered all of them the opportunity to review their transcripts in order to edit, change, or censor. I did not use a set script of questions but rather a loose list of topics around their religious, professional, and personal backgrounds, their history with Orthodoxy and their synagogues, and their gender relationships and issues. At first I also included a topic called "meanings of masculinity," in which I would ask a question like, "What does it mean to be a man?" but the reactions were mostly silence or dumb stares. Only a small handful of men voluntarily addressed the issue of their own meanings of gender. After an entire hour of talking about the above topics, one man said, "I thought you were going to ask me about gender," after which he delightfully explored his own journey learning not to be like the men in his early life. He was remarkable in his ability to have that conversation. Most interviewees could not, a finding that is in and of itself interesting.

During the course of the research, after I had collected approximately forty interviews and had begun analysis, I conducted two focus groups in Modi'in. I invited many of the men who had been interviewed in Modi'in (approximately twenty), to one of two evenings in which I presented a Power Point presentation representing early versions of some of the chapters. These focus groups were also recorded and transcribed, and the discussions are included in the analysis.

I should also note that I interviewed my own spouse—twice, actually, because the first time it took a good ten to fifteen minutes before he began to take the interview seriously. By the end, he treated me like an interviewer and gave long, honest, and thoughtful answers. The interview in fact revealed ideas and emotions that were possibly more honest and thought through than those that emerge in the hustle and bustle of everyday life. That experience shed tremendous light on the dynamics of the interview process and the power of nonjudgmental listening. It also gave me new and surprising insights into a masculinity that I thought I knew well.

In terms of religious upbringing, the overwhelming majority of the men come from Orthodox homes. Forty men were brought up Orthodox, nine were brought up Conservative, and the remainder were either secular or "traditional." This runs counter to the impression that many of these *minyanim* attract large numbers of formerly Conservative Jews. In fact, a mere one-sixth of informants were brought up in the Conservative movement, and very few, if any, landed in the partnership synagogue straight from a Conservative synagogue. For all but two men, the synagogue experience immediately preceding membership in the partnership synagogue was Orthodox. In that sense, this research is unequivocally about Orthodoxy.

In the synagogues in Israel, there is a commonly held perception that most of the people who join partnership congregations are of American or "Anglo" origin. This perception was validated with regard to Shira Hadasha, where only one informant was born in Israel—and he tellingly declared that he chose to be involved because he felt the place needs "some native Israelis." (To be fair, one of the Shira Hadasha potential informants with whom I failed to find a suitable interview time was also Israeli, though I was given his name by someone who said, "You should try and find some Israelis to interview.") In the other *minyanim*, however, this was not the case. In the Baka Shivyoni *minyan*, for example, all three of the informants and all the potential informants were Israeli born, though the sample is clearly too small to make any generalizations. In Modi'in, the situation is a bit more nuanced, though not entirely. Sixteen of the Modi'in informants were born in English-speaking countries—though three came to Israel as children or babies, and twelve informants were born in Israel. While there is certainly a strong English-speaking component, there is also a strong Israeli representation, eliminating the theory that this is not a genuinely Israeli movement. Nonetheless, the cultural relationship between "Anglo" Israelis and native Israelis begs further analysis.

Note

* The research method was a combination of feminist ethnography and naturalistic inquiry, based on an eclectic blend of outlooks, including those of Ruth Behar, Lincoln and Guba, Shulamit Reinharz, and others. Yvonne S. Lincoln and Egon G. Guba, *Naturalistic Inquiry* (Beverly Hills, Calif.: Sage, 1986); Shulamit Reinharz, *Feminist Methods in Social Research* (New York: Oxford University Press, 1992); Ruth Behar and Deborah A. Gordon, *Women Writing Culture* (Berkeley: University of California Press, 1995). For an exploration of the interview process from a classic perspective see James P. Spradley, *The Ethnographic Interview* (Orlando, Fla.: Harcourt Brace Jovanovich, 1979). For a discussion of some of the feminist dilemmas involved in this research, see Judith Stacey, "Can There Be Feminist Ethnography?" in *Women's Words: The Feminist Practice of Oral History*, ed. Sherna Berger Gluck and Daphne Patai, 111–20 (New York: Routledge, 1991); and Elaine Campbell, "Interviewing Men in Uniform: A Feminist Approach?" *International Journal of Social Research Methodology* 6, no. 4 (2003): 285–304. The latter was particularly relevant to this research, as it explored the dynamics of a female feminist researcher in a patriarchal setting, a situation with significant parallels to this research. To understand the methods I used for textual analysis, see Nita Schechet, *Narrative Fissures: Reading and Rhetoric* (Madison, N.J.: Fairleigh Dickinson University Press, 2005). I was lucky enough to have Dr. Schechet as a lecturer for one of my many methods courses as a graduate student. Her brilliant approach, coupled with a keen eye for textual nuance, formed the cornerstone of my approach toward analysis.

Data on Interviewees

The following is a breakdown of the basic data on interviewees:

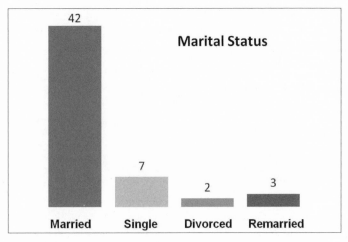

FIGURE Appendix B.1

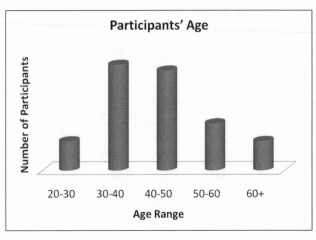

FIGURE Appendix B.2

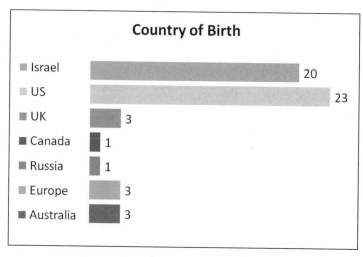

FIGURE Appendix B.3

Profession	Participants
Academic	14
Non Profit	3
Teacher	4
Writer	1
Lawyer	2
Hi-Tech/Computers	10
Psychology	3
Doctor	1
Business	1
Rabbi	2
Student	2
Retired	3
Sales/Marketing	4
Other	4

FIGURE Appendix B.4

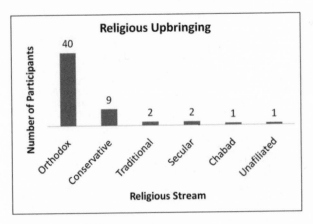

FIGURE Appendix B.5

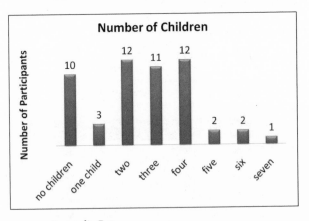

FIGURE Appendix B.6

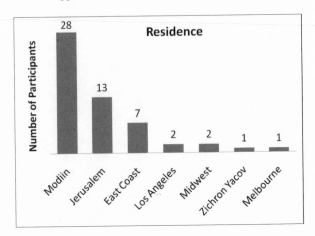

FIGURE Appendix B.7

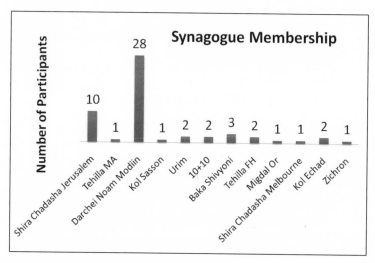

FIGURE Appendix B.8

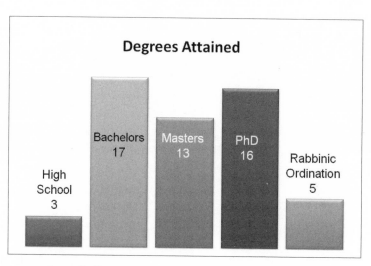

FIGURE Appendix B.9

Glossary

aliyah/aliyot. Call-up (sing./pl.). The Torah, the five books of Moses, is divided into fifty-four *parshas*, or *parshiyot*—that is, portions—such that one portion is traditionally read aloud each week in synagogue with special cantillations that have been orally transmitted through the generations. Each portion has a designated week, so that every synagogue in the Orthodox world is reading the same verses all around the world. Each weekly *parsha*, or Torah portion, is further divided into seven portions, or *aliyot*, and the blessing on the Torah is recited in between each *aliyah*. The blessing is made by seven different people, each of whom is "called up," or receives an *aliyah*. During the time of the Talmud, the person called up also read the accompanying portion—something that today is rarely practiced. In some synagogues, one person reads the entire portion, and in other synagogues there are multiple readers, not necessarily the ones who recite the blessing on each section. A congregation in formation, often casually calling itself a "*minyan*" to distinguish itself from a more-established synagogue or "shul," is more likely to have seven different readers than one reader for the whole portion. This is because reading an entire portion requires tremendous skill (a topic covered at length in chapter 2), and a small group is likely to have fewer members with that skill set and willingness, since it takes many hours to prepare a Torah reading, and a certain degree of intense concentration to layn, a practice discussed at length in this research.

amidah. The standing prayer, the central prayer of the liturgy recited three times a day during the week, four times on Shabbat and holidays, and five times on Yom Kippur

An'im Zemirot. A song at the end of the service traditionally led by boys, but in partnership synagogues, girls also lead

Ari'zal. Seventeenth-century kabbalistic leader

Ashkenazi. Of European heritage or lineage

ba'al. Literally "owner," the traditional Hebrew word for husband

ba'al keriya. Literally, "owner of the reading," i.e., Torah reader, someone who knows the cantillations

bentsch. Yiddish term meaning, literally, "bless," referring to the recitation of the "Grace after Meals" (see *birkat hamazon*)

b'mhera b'yameinu amen. A classic ending of traditional blessings is "And may the third Temple be built quickly and in our time, amen." Rabbis who wish to turn biblical interpretation of their sermons into a moralizing message will often end with this phrase.

bracha/brachot.   Blessing (sing./pl.)

Bracha Achrona.   A very short "Grace after Meals" recited at meals that do not include bread

Birkat Hamazon.   Complete "Grace after Meals"

bris.   Ritual circumcision

davening.   A Yiddish usage for "praying"

derekh.   The "path"; used in the expression "off the *derekh*," to refer to people who abandon strict Orthodoxy

dvar/divrei Torah.   (sing./pl.) Literally means "word of Torah." Sermon/sermons, a speech in synagogue with a message from the Bible. In congregations with rabbis, this role is generally relegated to the rabbi, whereas synagogues that do not have rabbis—which is the overwhelming majority of partnership *minyanim*—either do not have speeches or designate the role to rotating members of the community. Also, the overwhelming majority of Orthodox synagogues do not allow women to give the *dvar Torah*, and the partnership synagogues do.

eitz hayim.   The tree of life

eruv.   A boundary around a town or city, resembling electrical wiring, that permits the residents to carry items on Shabbat, which would otherwise be forbidden. This symbolic fence, signifying that the community is of singular ownership and thus similar to private property, is a legalistic loophole aimed at eliminating the duress of the prohibition against carrying in the public sphere on Shabbat. However, the practice has been a source of tremendous controversy in some communities.

gabbai/gabbait.   (masc./fem.) A kind of cross between manager, stagehand, and master of ceremonies of the prayer service. The jobs of the *gabbai/gabbait* include assigning readers and cantors, standing at the podium during the service, and calling people up to the podium when it is their turn to "perform." One of the innovations of the partnership synagogue is that there are two people in this role, one man and one woman, who stand on either side of the podium during Torah reading, so that the *gabbai* can manage the men and the *gabbait* can manage the women.

gever.   Hebrew word for "man," related to the words *gvura* (strength) and *l'hitgaber* (to overcome)

gvura.   Strength or courage

hafifnik.   Modern Hebrew slang for a slacker; *hafif* is a modern adjective meaning sloppy or haphazard

haftarah.   The passages from the Prophets read aloud in synagogue each week

halakha.   Jewish law

Hallel.   The Song of Praise, a series of psalms recited on holidays

haredi/haredim.   Ultra-orthodox Jew (sing./pl.)

hazzan/hazzanit. Cantor (masc./fem.)

hechsher. · Seal of kosher approval

hevreman. Hebrew slang referring to a male socialite, a man who is friends with everyone

hiloni/hilonim. Secular Jew (sing./pl.)

Kabbalat Shabbat. Friday evening prayers

kacha. "Just because." A slang response to a question of "why" that is more like a non-response

kaddish. Mourner's prayer; requires a quorum

kashruth. Laws of keeping kosher

kavana. Intent or sincerity in prayer

kavod hatsibur. Literally, "the dignity of the congregation"—a legalistic rationale for limiting women's roles in synagogue

Kedusha. Literally, "holiness"; the title of a significant section of the standing prayer (*amidah*) that requires a quorum in order to be recited

kehilla. Community

kiddush. Literally, "sanctifying"; refers to a prayer said over wine to open the Sabbath meal. In many congregations, the morning service is followed by a communal buffet, casually referred to as a *kiddush*, because it opens with someone saying the *kiddush* prayer.

kippa. Skullcap

layn/layning. Reading from the Torah with cantillations

Lecha Dodi. A medieval poem that forms a central component of the Friday night prayer service (see *Kabbalat Shabbat*)

l'hitgaber. To overcome

l'hitparnes. To earn a living or "provide"

l'hitragesh. To be emotional (it may mean to be excited, anxious, nervous, or simply overcome with emotion)

l'taktek. To be quick and efficient, like the sound of a person typing on a typewriter

Ma'ariv/Arvit. Evening prayers

mehitza. Partition

mezuzah. Ritual scroll hung on doorposts

m'gabesh. Bringing group cohesion

midrash. Biblical interpretation or exegesis

mincha. Afternoon prayers

minyan/minyanim. (sing./pl.) The literal meaning of "*minyan*" is "quorum" from the root "M-N-I," which means "count" or "appoint." According to traditional Jewish law, or *halakha*, a quorum is composed of ten Jewish men over the age of thirteen. The Conservative movement has allowed women to be counted since 1973, as does the Reconstructionist movement, but the Reform movement has eliminated the requirement of *minyan* altogether. *Minyan* has also taken on a less formal meaning, which is a "synagogue in formation," a congregation that is small, new, and not established enough to consider itself a full-blown synagogue.

mitzvah, mitzvoth. Commandment (sing./pl.)

neshama. Soul or spirit

nusach. This has two meanings that are somewhat related. It may refer to a cultural "version" of a prayer, or the way a particular ritual is practiced according to a certain heritage. There are several different versions of how phylacteries are laid, for example— Ashkenazi and Sephardi. The word *nusach* may also refer to a version of a melody for a prayer, with connotations of correctness. The usages are related but not identical.

parsha/parshiyot. Portion (sing./pl.). The Torah, the five books of Moses, is divided into fifty-four *parshas*, or *parshiyot*—that is, portions—such that one portion is traditionally read aloud each week in synagogue with special cantillations that have been orally transmitted through the generations. Each portion has a designated week, so that every synagogue in the Orthodox world is reading the same verses all around the world. Each weekly *parsha*, or Torah portion, is further divided into seven portions, or *aliyot*, and the blessing on the Torah is recited in between each *aliyah*. The blessing is made by seven different people, each of whom is "called up," or receives an *aliyah*. During the time of the Talmud, the person called up also read the accompanying portion—something that today is rarely practiced. In some synagogues, one person reads the entire portion, and in other synagogues there are multiple readers, not necessarily the ones who recite the blessing on each section. A congregation in formation, often casually calling itself a *minyan*, to distinguish itself from a more-established synagogue or *shul*, is more likely to have seven different readers than one reader for the whole portion. This is because reading an entire portion requires tremendous skill (a topic covered at length in chapter 2), and a small group is likely to have fewer members with that skill set and willingness, since it takes many hours to prepare a Torah reading, and a certain degree of intense concentration to layn, a practice discussed at length in this research.

Rosh Hashana. Jewish New Year

sabra. Native Israeli; a metaphor based on the sabra fruit that is prickly on the outside, soft and sweet on the inside

Sephardic. Of North African heritage

Shabbat/Shabbos. The Sabbath

shaharit. Morning prayers

shaliach/shlichat tzibur. (masc./fem.) Literally, "messenger of the congregation," a euphemism for cantor

shul. Synagogue

simcha/smachot. (sing./pl.) A special occasion, such as a wedding or birth

Simchat Torah. Literally, "celebration of the Torah"; the final festivity during the High Holiday season. It includes much singing, dancing, and levity and a somewhat chaotic ritual of giving every member of the community an opportunity to get called up to the Torah to recite the Torah blessings. In most Orthodox synagogues, "every member" means "every man," but in the partnership synagogues, it means every man and every woman. In order to make this possible, several "stations" are set up simultaneously around the sanctuary, and the five-part Torah portion is read over and over until everyone has been called up.

smartut.   Dishrag; the metaphorical equivalent of a doormat

smicha.   "Getting *smicha*" is the act of receiving rabbinic status, the equivalent, say, of "passing the bar" for lawyers

sruga.   Knitted or crocheted, as in "*kippa sruga,*" a knitted skullcap

tallit.   A large, rectangular prayer shawl that has ritual fringes, or *tzitzit.* It is worn during the prayer service.

tefillah/tefillot.   Prayer (sing./pl.)

tefillin.   Phylacteries, or leather straps connected to two small boxes containing parchments with biblical verses inside. The phylacteries are bound to the arm and the head and are traditionally worn during weekday morning prayers, or *shaharit.*

tikkun olam.   Repairing the world, a mission of social justice

Torah.   Five books of Moses

treif.   Not kosher

trop.   Cantillations

tzibur.   Public, or congregation

tzitzit.   Ritual fringes

va'ad.   Executive committee

yahrzheit.   Anniversary of someone's death

yarmulke.   Skullcap

yeshiva/yeshivot.   House of study (sing./pl.)

Yigdal.   Poem recited at the end of services, usually by a child

Notes

Prologue

1. The literal meaning of "*minyan*" is "quorum," from the root "M-N-I," which means "count" or "appoint." According to traditional Jewish law, or *halakha*, and Orthodox practice, a quorum is composed of ten Jewish men over the age of thirteen. The word *minyan* is also used to mean "congregation," as is the Yiddish word *shul*.

2. Sara Delamont, *Changing Women, Unchanged Men? Sociological Perspectives on Gender in a Post-Industrial Society* (Buckingham, UK: Open University Press, 2001).

1. Jewish Men on the Borders

1. Jeffrey Salkin, *Searching for My Brothers: Jewish Men in a Gentile World* (New York: Perigee, 1999), 3.

2. Aviva Cantor, *Jewish Women, Jewish Men: The Legacy of Patriarchy in Jewish Life* (San Francisco: Harper, 1995).

3. Daniel Boyarin, *Unheroic Conduct: The Rise and Fall of Heterosexuality and the Invention of the Jewish Man* (Berkeley: University of California Press, 1996).

4. Oz Almog, *The Sabra: The Creation of the New Jew* (Berkeley: University of California Press, 2000).

5. See for example Michael Kimmel, "Judaism, Masculinity and Feminism," in *A Mentsch among Men: Explorations in Jewish Masculinity*, ed. Harry Brod, 153–57 (Freedom, Calif.: Crossing Press, 1988).

6. Admiel Kosman, *Men's Tractate: Rav and the Butcher and Other Stories—On Manhood, Love and Authentic Life in Aggadic and Hassidic Stories* (Jerusalem: Keter, 2002) [Hebrew].

7. Warren Rosenberg, *Legacy of Rage: Jewish Masculinity, Violence and Culture* (Amherst: University of Massachusetts Press, 2001), 1.

8. Harry Brod, ed., *A Mentsch among Men: Explorations in Jewish Masculinity* (Freedom, Calif.: Crossing Press, 1988), 181.

9. Michael G. Holzman, *The Still Small Voice: Reflections on Being a Jewish Man* (New York: URJ Press, 2008), xix.

10. Samuel C. Heilman, *Sliding to the Right: The Contest for the Future of American Jewish Orthodoxy* (Berkeley: University of California Press, 2006).

11. "Orthodox man" or "religious man" is perhaps misleading from an ethnic perspective, especially in Israel, where an entire group of "traditional" Jews has no formal place in the black-and-white religious-secular cultural dichotomy. Many men who regularly attend *minyan* are not necessarily comfortable calling themselves "religious." The term "religious" or "Orthodox" is arguably an Ashkenazi usage, based on the strict black-and-white identification within the Ashkenazi culture. Charles Liebman, in *The Ambivalent American Jew: Politics, Religion, and Family in American Jewish Life* (Philadelphia: Jewish Publication Society of America, 1973), claims that denominations are an Ashkenazi phenomenon rooted in Eastern European immigration to the United States, when men needed to redefine what it means to be Jewish. It is possible that the entire discussion of denominational shifts applies almost exclusively to Ashkenazi communities.

12. Samuel C. Heilman and Steven M. Cohen, *Cosmopolitans and Parochials: Modern Orthodox Jews in America* (Chicago: University of Chicago Press, 1989), 1–2.

13. For an example of a particularly heated debate on this subject, see the popular Jewish blog "The Canonist," by Steven I. Weiss, where he reviews Heilman's book (negatively), and Heilman responds by vociferously defending his claims. http://www.canonist .com/?p=1327 (accessed January 1, 2010).

14. Heilman and Cohen, *Cosmopolitans and Parochials*, vii.

15. *National Jewish Population Survey, 2000–01* (New York: United Jewish Communities, 2003); Heilman, *Sliding to the Right*. Precise figures are difficult to ascertain because of the reluctance of certain Orthodox communities to take part in surveys, secular studies, and/or Jewish Federation projects.

16. Steven M. Cohen, *American Modernity and Jewish Identity* (New York: Tavistock, 1983), 12.

17. Liebman, *Ambivalent American Jew*, 43.

18. Cohen, *American Modernity*, 23.

19. Bernard Lazerwitz et al., *Jewish Choices: American Jewish Denominationalism* (New York: SUNY Press, 1998), 5.

20. Heilman and Cohen, *Cosmopolitans and Parochials*, 17–21.

21. Sylvia Barack Fishman, *Jewish Life and American Culture* (New York: SUNY Press, 2000), 1.

22. Fishman, *Jewish Life*, 22.

23. See, for example, Jane Eisner, "Women of the Wall Leader Interrogated by Police," *The Forward*, January 6, 2010, http://www.forward.com/articles/122754/ (accessed January 10, 2010).

24. Marc D. Stern, "Egalitarianism and Halakha: An Introduction," in *Formulating Responses in an Egalitarian Age*, ed. Marc. D. Stern, 1 (Lanham, Md.: Rowman & Littlefield, 2005).

25. Stern, "Egalitarianism," 8–9.

26. These figures are a bit misleading and imprecise, mostly because large communi-

ties of Orthodox Jews are reluctant to engage in the research, out of their ideological commitment to the antimodern end of the spectrum.

27. Steven M. Cohen, "Members and Motives: Who Joins American Jewish Congregations and Why," *S3K Report* 1 (Fall 2006): 1. For an expansion of these ideas about the particular dynamics of Orthodox affiliation, see Jonathan Sacks, *Traditional Alternatives: Orthodoxy and the Future of the Jewish People* (London: Jews' College Publications, 1989).

28. Thanks to Dr. Jonathan Rynhold for astute analysis that helped sharpen this section.

29. Yair Sheleg, *The New Religious Jews: Recent Developments among Observant Jews in Israel* (Jerusalem: Keter, 2000) [Hebrew].

30. Asher Cohen, "The Weakness of Progressive Judaism in Israel: A Social-Cultural Analysis," unpublished paper, 2008 [Hebrew].

31. Yizhak Geiger, "Between the New Religious Zionism and Traditional Religious Zionism," *Tsohar* 11 (Summer 5762): 129–32 [Hebrew].

32. Tamar El-Or, *Next Year I Will Know More: Literacy and Identity among Young Orthodox Women in Israel* (Tel Aviv: Am-Oved, 1998).

33. Thanks again to Dr. Jonathan Rynhold for help with this analysis.

34. See, for example, Shraga Fisherman, *Noar Hakippot Hazerukot* (Youth of the Strewn Skullcaps) (Michlelet Orot Yisrael: Elkana, 1999) [Hebrew].

35. Literally, "path of pleasantness." It should be noted that the informants from Darkhei Noam clearly emphasize that they did not form in response to Shira Hadasha but rather formed as a result of their own processes.

36. JOFA (The Jewish Orthodox Feminist Alliance) dedicated a session in its 2007 conference to this topic.

37. William Kaplowitz, "Partnership *Minyanim* in the United States: Planning Theory in Action" (master's thesis, University of Michigan, 2008), 18.

38. Mechon Hadar, http://www.mechonhadar.org/ (accessed June 1, 2010).

39. Mendel Shapiro, "Qeri'at Ha-Torah by Women: A Halachic Analysis," *Edah Journal* 1, no. 2 (2001): 1–52.

40. For a detailed analysis of the halakhic texts see *Women and Men in Communal Prayer: Halakhic Perspectives*, ed. Chaim Trachtman (Jersey City, N.J.: Ktav Publishing House, 2010).

41. Rabbi Daniel Sperber, interview with the author, May 2, 2008.

42. Mendel Shapiro, interview with the author, March 4, 2008.

43. Elitzur Bar-Asher Siegal, interview with the author, August 22, 2008.

44. Tova Hartman, *Feminism Encounters Traditional Judaism: Resistance and Accommodation* (Waltham, Mass.: Brandeis University Press, 2007).

45. Rabbi Shai Held, Rabbi Elie Kaunfer, and Rabbi Ethan Tucker.

46. Heilman and Cohen review in their introduction all the research that they claim had been done on Orthodoxy until that point (1989), and here is their list of authors:

Charles Liebman, Egon Mayer, Chaim Waxman, William Helmreich, David Ellenson, Jeffrey Gurock, and Reuven Bulka—*all men*. Similarly, Jeffrey Gurock, in *The Men and Women of Yeshiva: Higher Education, Orthodoxy, and American Judaism* (New York: Columbia University Press, 1988), writing about "Orthodoxy," devotes ten chapters exclusively to men and one chapter at the very end to "The Women of Stern College." Note that the book is titled *The Men and Women of Yeshiva*, when in fact it's almost entirely men. Similarly, when he writes that the administration was disappointed to learn that only 7 percent of YU students were considering rabbinical school or teaching, it does not occur to the writer to mention that the ones considering rabbinical school were obviously men. The survey was obviously done on men. Examples of this phenomenon—in which Orthodox leaders, thinkers, or writers say "people" when they mean "men"— abound. Shraga Fisherman's book *Noar Hakippot Hazerukot* (Youth of the Strewn Skullcaps), examining the psychological processes of youth leaving Orthodoxy, interviewed only boys—but generalized onto all youth. The late Motti Bar-Lev, noted sociologist of Israeli Orthodoxy, also used to use all-male samples, asking questions about identity such as, "Will your wife cover her hair?" (Motti Bar-Lev, "Cultural Characteristics and Group Image of Religious Youth," *Youth and Society* 16, no 2 (1984): 153–70). Finally, Gurock, in his acknowledgments, says about his son, "His literary horizons for now include works for boys on Dave Winfield and Rickey Henderson. But then again, isn't that where so many of us began?" The "us" he refers to are men, who began as "normal" American boys playing baseball. The conflation of sports and religion here is telling. The implications for Orthodox male gender identity that emerge from these types of vignettes will be explored in later chapters. The point here is that for a very long time, the "default" religious person has been a man. Thus, Orthodoxy was created by men, is run by men, and is studied and evaluated predominantly by men.

47. These interviews all took place between September 2006 and August 2008 and ranged in length from forty-five to two hundred minutes. Each interview took a different course and had its own dynamic. Some interviews were in men's homes, some at their workplaces, some at cafés, and three took place in my home, for reasons of logistical ease. With a handful of informants, I conducted multiple interviews at different points in the research. Interviews were digitally recorded and professionally transcribed. All identifying details are disguised to protect informants. Pseudonyms were chosen to maintain the ethnicity and culture of the informants (e.g., Itai might be changed to Ofer; Brian might be changed to Steven; Zevulun might be changed to Yissachar). Details that reveal a distinctness, such as if an informant were known as the only Japanese member of his congregation, the only bricklayer, or a father of twelve in his community, are left out here. (More details on research methods can be found in Appendix A.) The ages of the men interviewed are somewhat imprecise because the research was collected over two years. Ages recorded are based on the men's reported ages at the time of interview, but they may not correspond relative to one another. The vast majority were in their

thirties or forties, with an average age of approximately forty-two. The overwhelming majority—forty-four men—are parents, with an average of 3.3 children each. (More details can be found in appendix B.) Finally, there are two interviewees who do not regularly pray in these services. I interviewed them because they have either participated in the past or played a role in establishing such a congregation.

48. Shlomo Deshen and Moshe Shokeid, *Generation in Transition: Change and Continuity in the World of North African Émigrés* (Jerusalem: Yad Ben-Zvi, 1999) [Hebrew].

49. Although I learned that several informants later lost their jobs, after the research was completed.

50. Much has been written on the subject of reliability and validity in qualitative research. The implications of these discussions are particularly intriguing regarding feminist men interviewing men in patriarchal structures. See for example Judith Gardiner, ed., *Masculinity Studies and Feminist Theory: New Directions* (New York: Columbia University Press, 2002) and Elaine Campbell, "Interviewing Men in Uniform: A Feminist Approach?" *International Journal of Social Research Methodology* 6, no. 4 (2003).

2. The "BOMB": The "Be an Orthodox Man" Box

1. R. W. Connell, *Gender and Power* (Stanford, Calif.: Stanford University Press, 1987).

2. R. W. Connell and James W. Messerschmidt, "Hegemonic Masculinity: Rethinking the Concept," *Gender and Society* 19, no. 6 (2005): 832.

3. Michael Kimmel, *The History of Men: Essays in the History of American and British Masculinities* (Albany, N.Y.: SUNY Press, 2005).

4. Bob Connell, "Men at Bay: The 'Men's Movement' and its Newest Best-Sellers," in *The Politics of Manhood: Profeminist Men Respond to the Mythopoetic Men's Movement (and the Mythopoetic Leaders Answer)*, ed. Michael S. Kimmel, 75–89 (Philadelphia: Temple University Press, 1995).

5. Michael A. Messner, "Boyhood, Organized Sports, and the Construction of Masculinities," in *Masculinities: Interdisciplinary Readings*, ed. Mark Hussey, 140–52 (Englewood Cliffs, N.J.: Prentice Hall, 2003).

6. Gary Alan Fine, *With the Boys: Little League Baseball and Preadolescent Culture*, (Chicago: University of Chicago Press, 1987).

7. Susan Faludi, *Stiffed: The Betrayal of the American Man* (New York: William Morrow, 2003).

8. Paul Kivel, "The 'Act Like a Man' Box," in Hussey, *Masculinities*, 69–72.

9. *Tefillin*, or "phylacteries," are leather straps connected to two small boxes containing parchments with biblical verses inside. The phylacteries are bound to the arm and the head and are traditionally worn during weekday morning prayers, or *Shacharit*. The *tallit* is a large, rectangular prayer shawl that has ritual fringes, or *tzitzit*, on it. This, too,

is worn as part of the prayer service. *Kippa* is a skullcap. All these forms of garments are predominantly worn by men, though throughout history there have always been women keeping the tradition as well (see Judith R. Baskin, *Jewish Women in Historical Perspective* [Detroit: Wayne State University Press, 1991]). Moreover, women's wearing of these ritual objects is one of the issues that the Conservative and Reform movements have actively changed in their practice.

10. Tamar Rapoport and Yoni Garb, "The Experience of Religious Fortification: The Coming of Age of Religious Zionist Young Women," *Gender and Education* 10, no. 1 (1998): 5–20.

11. This quote is translated from the Hebrew. Approximately one-third of the interviews were conducted in Hebrew, and the translations are mine. Where translation can be ambiguous, I included the Hebrew transliteration as well.

12. Interestingly, after I completed this analysis, a movie came out about Orthodox men, titled *A Serious Man*. Although it's a comedy, much of the movie's message about socialization into Orthodox masculinity is validated by this research.

13. All Hebrew interviews were translated solely by me. Occasionally, when I had a question about a translation, I consulted with one of my native Israeli informants. Where the translation is still imprecise, as translation so often is, I have included the Hebrew as well for original reference. Here, for example, *me'az u'mitamid* has a much harsher implication in Hebrew than "always."

14. See, for example, Danny Kaplan, *Brothers and Others in Arms: The Making of Love and War in Israeli Combat Units* (New York: Haworth Press, 2003); Edna Lomsky-Feder and Eyal Ben-Ari, *The Military and Militarism in Israeli Society* (New York: SUNY Press, 2000).

15. Ariel Hirschfeld, "Gvarim b'gvarim," *Mishkafayim* 22 (1994): 9–15 [Hebrew].

16. Sara Helman, "Militarism and the Construction of the Life-Worlds of Israeli Males: The Case of the Reserves System," in *The Military and Militarism in Israeli Society*, ed. Edna Lomsky-Feder and Eyal Ben-Ari, 191–224 (New York: SUNY Press, 2000); Amia Lieblich, *Transition to Adulthood during Military Service: The Israeli Case* (Albany, N.Y.: SUNY Press, 1989).

17. Almog, *New Jew*.

18. Yael Ben-Zvi, "Blind Spots in Portraiture: On Oz Almog's *Ha-tsabar—Dyokan, Sabra: The Creation of the New Jew*," *Jewish Social Studies* 7, no. 1 (2000): 167–74.

19. Ben-Zvi, "Blind Spots," 170.

20. Edna Lomsky-Feder, "A Woman Studies War: Stranger in a Man's World," in *The Narrative Study of Lives*, ed. Ruthellen Josselson and Amia Lieblich, 233 (London: Sage, 1996).

21. A classic ending of traditional blessings is "And may the third Temple be built quickly and in our time, amen." Rabbis who wish to turn biblical interpretation of their sermons into a moralizing message will often end with this phrase, a practice noticed by this informant, which he sees as a kind of cookie-cutter religious message.

22. Michael L. Satlow, "'Try to Be a Man': The Rabbinic Construction of Masculinity," in *Men and Masculinities in Christianity and Judaism: A Critical Reader*, ed. Björn Krondorfer, 264 (London: SCM Press, 2004).

23. Haym Soloveitchik, "Rupture and Reconstruction: The Transformation of Contemporary Orthodoxy," *Tradition* 28, no. 4 (Summer 1994): 64–130.

24. Significantly, Deshen and Shokeid, in *Generation in Transition*, offer a very similar analysis to describe the differences between Ashkenazi and Sephardic cultural heritage. That is, they argue that Sephardic transmission has remained largely oral, familial, and communal, while Ashkenazi transmission has become cerebral, cold, and text-based. Soloveitchik's contribution to this idea is that Ashkenazim have not always been this way, and that it's a result of the Holocaust and the destruction of the communal and familial structures necessary for transmission. In any case, it confirms that this portrait of Orthodox masculinity is Ashkenazi, and that Sephardic men may in fact demand a separate study.

25. Yochai Hakak, *Vocational Training for Ultra-Orthodox Men* (Jerusalem: Florsheimer Institute for Policy Studies, 2004) [Hebrew].

26. For an interesting analysis of how ultra-Orthodox masculinity contrasts with Western culture around male breadwinning, see Orna Blumen, "The Performative Landscape of Going-to-Work: On the Edge of a Jewish Ultraorthodox Neighborhood," *Environment and Planning D: Society and Space* 25, no. 5 (2007): 803–31. See also Nurit Stadler, "Is Profane Work an Obstacle to Salvation? The Case of Ultra-Orthodox (Haredi) Jews in Contemporary Israel," *Sociology of Religion* 63, no. 4 (2002): 455–74.

27. See, for example, Laurence Kotler-Berkowitz, "Poor Jews: An Analysis of Low Income in the American Jewish Population," *Contemporary Jewry* 29, no. 3 (2009): 241–77; Eli Berman, "Sect, Subsidy, and Sacrifice: An Economist's View of Ultra-Orthodox Jews," *Quarterly Journal of Economics* 115, no. 3 (2003): 905–53.

28. Gwen Ackerman and Alisa Odenheimer, "Israel Prosperity Seen Unsustainable as Haredim Refuse to Work," Bloomberg, August 2, 2010, http://www.bloomberg.com/news/2010-08-01/israel-prosperity-seen-unsustainable-as-haredim-refusal-to-work-takes-toll.html (accessed August 3, 2010).

3. On Hippies, Heretics, and Hafifniks

1. Solomon E. Asch, "Opinions and Social Pressure," *Scientific American* 193 (1955): 31–35. He would have his subject enter a room with a group of people and show them three lines of different lengths with obvious differences. Then he would ask the subject to match a line in a different box with the one of identical length in the first box. Little did the subject know that everyone else in the group was an actor, asked to lie and furiously insist that lines that are obviously not the same length are equal. Asch wanted to see how people would respond to the pressure to be like everyone else, even when it went against their natural judgment. As it turned out, 37 percent agreed with the lying

group, changing their opinion to match the opinion that is obviously wrong but held by "many people" or perhaps "important" people, and only 29 percent absolutely refused to join the bogus majority. The rest wavered somewhere in the middle. A full 79 percent conformed at least once during the series of trials.

2. As I was completing this manuscript, the film *A Serious Man* was released, a comedy about an Orthodox man that confirms this analysis in humor—and seriousness.

3. For a classic analysis of internalizing gaze see John Berger, *Ways of Seeing* (Gloucester, Mass.: Peter Smith, 1972).

4. See, for example, Gil Ronen, "Rabbi Shapira: Time to Fight Neo-Reformists in Our Midst," *Israel National News*, July 5, 2009, http://www.israelnationalnews.com/News/News.aspx/132217 (accessed October 5, 2009).

5. Rabbi Steven Greenberg, *Wrestling with God and Men: Homosexuality in the Jewish Tradition* (Madison: University of Wisconsin Press, 2004), 1–2.

6. *Kiddush*, literally "sanctifying," refers to a prayer said over wine to open the Sabbath meal. In many congregations, the morning service is followed by a communal buffet, casually referred to as a *kiddush* because it opens with someone saying the *kiddush* prayer. More about the significance of the *kiddush* in the final chapter.

7. This seemingly innocuous act—of carrying in one's hands, on one's shoulders, or even in one's pockets—reflects sometimes bitter disputes in Orthodox communities over the issue of *eruv*, a halakhic loophole that allows people to overcome the rabbinic prohibition against carrying on Shabbat.

4. Orthodox Men Creating Partnership

1. Sylvia Barack Fishman and Daniel Parmer, "Policy Implications of the Gender Imbalance among America's Jews," *Jewish Political Studies Review* 20, no. 3–4 (Fall 2008).

2. Steven M. Cohen and Arnold M. Eisen, *The Jew Within: Self, Family, and Community in America* (Bloomington: Indiana University Press, 2000).

3. Amy Klein, "Are Jewish Boys in Crisis?" JTA, August 3, 2009, http://jta.org/news/article/2009/08/03/1006967/are-jewish-boys-in-crisis (accessed January 1, 2010).

4. Susan Weidman Schneider, "From the Editor," *Lilith* 34 no. 3 (Fall 2009): 3.

5. Melanie Weiss, "Missing. . . ." *Lilith* 34, no. 3 (Fall 2009): 17.

6. Alan Haber, "Egalitarian *minyanim*? Not authentic, Not Orthodox," *Jerusalem Post*, February 26, 2008, http://www.jpost.com/Home/Article.aspx?id=93257 (accessed July 10, 2010).

7. Rabbi Isaac Luria (1534–72), or Arizal, was a leading rabbi and mystic in Safed and is considered the father of contemporary Kabbalah.

8. The late Rabbi Shlomo Carlebach, an American, Hassidic, musical, eccentric, and controversial but creative and emotional religious leader, composed many melodies for the prayers, mostly simple tunes that are most effective when sung repeatedly by a room

full of swaying chanters. His songs tend to be in sections of the service that were traditionally recited quickly, thus creating a tension between those who want a lot of singing and those who want a quick service.

9. A song at the end of the service traditionally led by boys, but in partnership synagogues, girls also lead.

10. Thanks to Dr. Ariella Zeller for elucidating this point.

5. Jocks, Dads, and Homebodies

1. For more on the role of the sharing of household chores in gender identity shifts, see, for example, Francine M. Deutsch, *Halving It All: How Equally Shared Parenting Works* (Cambridge, Mass.: Harvard University Press, 1999).

2. The rest of the interviewees are either single, have no children, have older children, or the information on this topic is sketchy.

3. Two years after Gad said in his interview that he would never consider quitting his job because his wife, though a higher-paid engineer, is the woman and more "naturally" suited to child care, he actually did leave his job and take a part-time job closer to home. He described many considerations for this move (not the least of which was that he hated his boss and did not have many alternative options), but two of the major rationalizations—which he shared in an elaborate Facebook message—were that his wife could now work more and he could be a more active father. He now takes and picks up his children from school every day. So, even as I conducted this research, identities were shifting. Men are changing as I type these words.

4. Deborah Tannen, *You Just Don't Understand: Men and Women in Conversation* (Ballantine: New York, 1990).

5. *Kavana* is intent, focus, or sincerity in prayer.

6. The Talmud.

7. John Stoltenberg, *Refusing to Be a Man: Essays on Sex and Justice* (Evanston, Ill.: Northwestern University Press, 1999).

6. Men Encountering Feminism

1. Michelle Fine, "Contextualizing the Study of Social Injustice," in *Advances in Applied Social Psychology*, ed. Michael Saks and Leonard Saxe (Hillsdale, N.J.: Lawrence Erlbaum, 1985).

2. Shulamit Reinharz, *Feminist Methods in Social Research* (New York: Oxford University Press, 1992).

3. See, for example, Janice McCabe, "What's in a Label? The Relationship between Feminist Self-Identification and 'Feminist' Attitudes among U.S. Women and Men," *Gender and Society* 19 (2005): 480.

4. Peter F. Murphy, ed., *Feminism and Masculinities* (Oxford: Oxford University Press, 2004).

5. Michael Kimmel and Thomas Mosmiller, *Against the Tide: Pro-Feminist Men in the U.S., 1776–1990* (Boston: Beacon Press, 1992).

6. Michael Kimmel, "Judaism, Masculinity and Feminism," in *A Mentsch among Men: Explorations in Jewish Masculinity*, ed. Harry Brod, 153–57 (Freedom, Calif.: Crossing Press, 1988).

7. Steven P. Schacht and Doris W. Ewing, eds., *Feminisms and Men: Reconstructing Gender Relations* (New York: NYU Press, 1998).

8. Geraldine Fabrikant, "Would You Hire Your Husband?" *New York Times*, June 29, 2008, http://www.nytimes.com/2008/06/29/business/29hubby.html (accessed July 1, 2008).

9. Shapiro, interview.

10. Cohen and Eisen, *Jew Within*, 206.

11. Holzman, *Still Small Voice*, xx.

12. Ibid., xxxiii.

13. Ibid., xxxvi.

14. Ibid., xxxviii.

15. Rona Shapiro, "The 'Boy Crisis' That Cried Wolf," *The Forward*, January 5, 2007, http://www.forward.com/articles/9792/ (accessed January 6, 2007).

16. Holzman, *Still Small Voice*, xxviii.

7. "Just Not Reform"

1. At one point, some members of the *va'ad* were concerned there would be too many people involved and demanded that anyone who wants to participate must commit to attend the whole series of meetings. I was not involved with that decision, a measure meant to make an important conversation closed to some people. Nonetheless, the rule meant that by the end of the process, the group had been whittled down to around twelve people from the original forty.

2. Although it is disingenuous to clump Reform and Conservative together, for the purpose of this chapter they are one category, because in Israeli Orthodox culture that is how they are overwhelmingly seen. I apologize for the offense, and I hope readers understand that my usage reflects the informants' narratives, not my own.

3. There are an estimated fifty Conservative synagogues in Israel, and another twenty-five or so Reform congregations, and the Conservative movement claims to have fifty thousand members, which is less than 1 percent of the Jewish population in Israel. Moreover, like Shira Hadasha, the Conservative and Reform movements are deemed "American," or an "imported product," and as with Shira Hadasha, this image is not without some basis in fact: 40 percent of the members of the Conservative movement in Israel

are English speakers, in contrast to an estimated 10 percent of English speakers in Israel generally. http://www.masorti.org/.

4. It is worth pointing out that not all things American are seen as illegitimate in Israel. After all, pop culture, fashion, movies, television, high-tech, and the Internet all have strong English-language and American components that Israeli society completely thrives on and certainly does not reject for being "American." Yet, somehow, the narrative that the Conservative and Reform movements are not native to Israel and are therefore "out" has taken hold. This begs explication and analysis.

5. *Bracha Achrona* is a truncated "Grace after Meals," used at small meals that do not involve bread.

6. I would like to emphasize that I am not claiming that the entire goal of Conservative Judaism is to resist Orthodoxy. Obviously, every member of the Conservative movement has her or his reason for belonging. That is a different topic. Here, because the context of this study is expressions of cultural resistance of Orthodox men, this section deals with the issue of resistance, and thus the subject is Orthodox men, not the internal dynamics of Conservative Judaism.

8. *The New Patriarchy*

1. Feminists promote use of the words word *ish* ("man," parallel to *isha*, "woman," the word for "wife") or *ben-zug* (partner) instead of *baal*, words that are less ownership oriented and thus less offensive to women.

2. Michael Kimmel, *Manhood in America: A Cultural History* (New York: Free Press, 2006), 1.

3. Jeff Hearn, "From 'Hegemonic Masculinity' to 'The Hegemony of Men,'" *Feminist Theory* 5, no. 1 (2004): 49–50.

4. Harry Brod, Gendertalk Radio. Nancy Nangeroni and Gordene O. MacKenzie interviewers, program no. 371, August 5, 2002, http://www.gendertalk.com/radio/programs/350/gt371.shtml.

5. John Stoltenberg, "Healing from Manhood: A Radical Meditation on the Movement from Gender Identity to Moral Identity," in *Feminism and Men: Reconstructing Gender Relations*, ed. Steven P. Schacht and Doris W. Ewing, 90 (New York: NYU Press, 1998).

6. Stoltenberg, "Healing from Manhood," 92.

7. John Stoltenberg, "Toward Gender Justice," in Murphy, *Feminism and Masculinities*, 49.

8. Hearn, "'Hegemonic Masculinity,'" 51.

9. Michael S. Kimmel, "From Conscience and Common Sense to 'Feminism for Men': Pro-feminist Men's Rhetorics of Support for Women's Equality," *International Journal of Sociology and Social Policy* 17 (1/2): 8–34.

10. Quoted in Kimmel, "Judaism, Masculinity and Feminism," 36.

11. Susan Moller Okin, *Is Multiculturalism Bad for Women?* (Princeton, N.J.: Princeton University Press, 1999).

12. Martha Nussbaum, *Women and Human Development* (Cambridge: Cambridge University Press, 2000).

9. Reflections on Orthodox Masculinities

1. Karen Armstrong, *The Battle for God: A History of Fundamentalism* (New York: Ballantine, 2001).

2. Geraldine Brooks, *Nine Parts of Desire: The Hidden World of Islamic Women* (New York: Anchor Doubleday, 1995).

3. John Eldredge, *Wild at Heart: Discovering the Secret of a Man's Soul* (Nashville, Tenn.: Thomas Nelson, 2006); Eric Ludy, *God's Gift to Women: Discovering the Lost Greatness of Masculinity* (Sisters, Ore.: Multnomah Publishers, 2003).

4. Soloveitchik, "Rupture and Reconstruction."

5. Barrie Thorne, *Gender Play: Girls and Boys in School* (New Brunswick, N.J.: Rutgers University Press, 1993).

6. Audre Lorde, *Sister Outsider* (Freedom, Calif.: Crossing Press, 1984), 42.

7. Special thanks to Kenneth Quinn for pressing me on this point.

8. Ruth Behar, "Out of Exile," in *Women Writing Culture*, ed. Ruth Behar and Deborah A. Gordon, 1–31 (Berkeley: University of California Press, 1995).

Epilogue

Epigraph drawn from Sperber, *The Path of Halakha: Women Reading Torah: A Case of Pesika Policy* (Jerusalem: Reuven Mas Publishers), 49–50 [Hebrew].

1. Deborah Weissman, "The Education of Religious Girls in Jerusalem during the British Mandate." (doctoral dissertation, Hebrew University, Jerusalem, 1993).

2. *Noar Hakippot Hazerukot* (Youth of the Strewn Skullcaps), the book by Shraga Fisherman considered pivotal in understanding why young people leave Orthodoxy, is exclusively about boys and men.

Bibliography

Almog, Oz. *The Sabra: The Creation of the New Jew*. Berkeley: University of California Press, 2000.

Armstrong, Karen. *The Battle for God: A History of Fundamentalism*. New York: Ballantine, 2001.

Asch, Solomon E. "Opinions and Social Pressure." *Scientific American* 193 (1955): 31–35.

Bar-Asher Siegal, Elitzur, and Michal Bar-Asher Siegal. "Guide for the 'Halachic Minyan.'" http://minyanurim.com/uploads/Guideline%20for%20Halachic%20Minyanim%20January%2019%20-%20English.pdf (accessed July 1, 2008).

Barth, Fredrick, ed. *Ethnic Groups and Boundaries: The Social Organization of Culture Difference*. Long Grove, Ill.: Waveland Press, 1998.

Baskin, Judith R. *Jewish Women in Historical Perspective*. Detroit: Wayne State University Press, 1991.

Behar, Ruth. "Out of Exile." In *Women Writing Culture*, edited by Ruth Behar and Deborah A. Gordon, 1–31. Berkeley: University of California Press, 1995.

Behar, Ruth, and Deborah A. Gordon. *Women Writing Culture*. Berkeley: University of California Press, 1995.

Ben-Ari, Eyal. *Mastering Soldiers: Conflict, Emotions and the Enemy*. Oxford: Berghahm, 1998.

Benhabib, Seyla. "The Generalized and Concrete Other." In *Situating the Self: Gender, Community and Postmodernism in Contemporary Ethics*, edited by Seyla Benhabib, 148–77. Cambridge, UK: Polity Press, 1992.

Ben-Zvi, Yael. "Blind Spots in Portraiture: On Oz Almog's *Ha-tsabar—Dyokan*, Sabra: The Creation of the New Jew." *Jewish Social Studies* 7, no. 1 (2000): 167–74.

Berger, John. *Ways of Seeing*. London: British Broadcasting Corp. and Penguin Books, 1972.

Berman, Eli. "Sect, Subsidy, and Sacrifice: An Economist's View of Ultra-Orthodox Jews." *Quarterly Journal of Economics* 115, no. 3 (2003): 905–53.

Blumen, Orna. "The Performative Landscape of Going-to-Work: On the Edge of a Jewish Ultraorthodox Neighborhood." *Environment and Planning D: Society and Space* 25, no. 5 (2007): 803–31.

Boyarin, Daniel. *Unheroic Conduct: The Rise and Fall of Heterosexuality and the Invention of the Jewish Man*. Berkeley: University of California Press, 1996.

Brod, Harry. Gendertalk Radio. Nancy Nangeroni and Gordene O. MacKenzie interviewers, program no. 371, August 5, 2002. http://www.gendertalk.com/radio/programs/350/gt371.shtml.

——, ed. *The Making of Masculinities: The New Men's Studies*. Boston: Allen & Unwin, 1987.

——, ed. *A Mentsch among Men: Explorations in Jewish Masculinity*. Freedom, Calif.: Crossing Press, 1988.

——. "Studying Masculinities as Superordinate Studies." In *Masculinity Studies and Feminist Theory: New Directions*, edited by Judith Gardiner, 177–90. New York: Columbia University Press, 2002.

Brooks, Geraldine. *Nine Parts of Desire*. New York: Anchor Doubleday, 1995.

Campbell, Elaine. "Interviewing Men in Uniform: A Feminist Approach?" *International Journal of Social Research Methodology* 6, no. 4 (2003): 285–304.

Cantor, Aviva. *Jewish Women, Jewish Men: The Legacy of Patriarchy in Jewish Life*. San Francisco: Harper, 1995.

Cohen, Asher. "The Weakness of Progressive Judaism in Israel: A Social-Cultural Analysis." Unpublished paper, 2008 [Hebrew].

Cohen, Steven M. *American Modernity and Jewish Identity*. New York: Tavistock, 1983.

——. "Members and Motives: Who Joins American Jewish Congregations and Why." *S3K Report* 1 (Fall 2006): 1.

Cohen, Steven M., and Arnold M. Eisen. *The Jew Within: Self, Family, and Community in America*. Bloomington: Indiana University Press, 2000.

Connell, R. W. *Gender and Power*. Stanford, Calif.: Stanford University Press, 1987.

——. *Masculinities*. Cambridge, UK: Polity Press, 1995.

Connell, R. W., and James W. Messerschmidt. "Hegemonic Masculinity: Rethinking the Concept." *Gender and Society* 19, no. 6 (2005): 829–59.

Dahan-Kalev, Henriette. "Mizrahi Feminism: The Unheard Voice." In *Jewish Feminism in Israel*, edited by Kalpana Misra and Melanie S. Rich, 96–112. Hanover, N.H.: University Press of New England / Brandeis University Press, 2003.

Delamont, Sara. *Changing Women, Unchanged Men?* Philadelphia: Open University Press, 2001.

Denzin, Norman K., and Yvonne S. Lincoln. *Collecting and Interpreting Qualitative Materials*. Thousand Oaks, Calif.: Sage, 2004.

Derrida, Jacques. *Writing and Difference*. Chicago: University of Chicago Press, 1978.

Deshen, Shlomo, and Moshe Shokeid. *Generation in Transition: Change and Continuity in the World of North African Émigrés*. Jerusalem: Yad Ben-Zvi, 1999 [Hebrew].

Deutsch, Francine M. *Halving It All: How Equally Shared Parenting Works*. Cambridge, Mass.: Harvard University Press, 1999.

Eldredge, John. *Wild at Heart: Discovering the Secret of a Man's Soul*. Nashville, Tenn.: Thomas Nelson, 2006.

El-Or, Tamar. *Next Year I Will Know More: Literacy and Identity among Young Orthodox Women in Israel.* Tel-Aviv: Am-Oved, 1998.

Faludi, Susan. *Stiffed: The Betrayal of the American Man.* New York: William Morrow, 2003.

Fine, Michelle. "Contextualizing the Study of Social Injustice." In *Advances in Applied Social Psychology,* edited by Michael Saks and Leonard Saxe, 103–8. Hillsdale, N.J.: Lawrence Erlbaum, 1986.

Fisherman, Shraga. *Noar Hakkipot Hazerukot* (Youth of the Strewn Skullcaps). Michlelet Orot Yisrael: Elkana, 1999 [Hebrew].

Fishman, Sylvia Barack. *Jewish Life and American Culture.* New York: SUNY Press, 2000.

Fishman, Sylvia Barack, and Daniel Parmer. "Policy Implications of the Gender Imbalance among America's Jews." *Jewish Political Studies Review* 20 (Fall 2008): 3–4.

Frank, Aaron. *Toward an Understanding of Male Gender Identity in Contemporary American Orthodox Judaism.* Jerusalem Fellows final project, 2002.

Gardiner, Judith, ed. *Masculinity Studies and Feminist Theory: New Directions.* New York: Columbia University Press, 2002.

Geiger, Yizhak. "Between the New Religious Zionism and Traditional Religious Zionism." *Tsohar* 11 (Summer 5762): 129–32 [Hebrew].

Greenberg, Steven. *Wrestling with God and Men: Homosexuality in the Jewish Tradition.* Madison: University of Wisconsin Press, 2004.

Gurock, Jeffrey. *The Men and Women of Yeshiva: Higher Education, Orthodoxy, and American Judaism.* New York: Columbia University Press, 1988.

Hakak, Yohai. *Vocational Training for Ultra-Orthodox Men.* Jerusalem: Florsheimer Institute for Policy Studies, 2004 [Hebrew].

Hartman, Tova. *Feminism Encounters Traditional Judaism: Resistance and Accommodation.* HBI Series on Jewish Women. Hanover, N.H.: University Press of New England / Brandeis University Press, 2007.

Hearn, Jeff. "From 'Hegemonic Masculinity' to 'The Hegemony of Men.'" *Feminist Theory* 5, no. 1 (2004): 49–72.

Heilman, Samuel C. *Sliding to the Right: The Contest for the Future of American Jewish Orthodoxy.* Berkeley: University of California Press, 2006.

Heilman, Samuel C., and Steven M. Cohen. *Cosmopolitans and Parochials: Modern Orthodox Jews in America.* Chicago: University of Chicago Press, 1989.

Heller, Craig. "A Paradox of Silence: Reflections of a Man Who Teaches Women's Studies." In *Teaching What You're Not: Identity Politics in Higher Education,* edited by Katherine J. Mayberry, 228–41. New York: NYU Press, 1996.

Helman, Sara. "Militarism and the Construction of the Life-Worlds of Israeli Males: The Case of the Reserves System." In *The Military and Militarism in Israeli Society,* edited by Edna Lomsky-Feder and Eyal Ben-Ari, 191–224. New York: SUNY Press, 2000.

Henkin, Yehuda H. "Qeri'at Ha-Torah by Women: Where We Stand Today." *Edah Journal* 1, no. 2 (2001): 1–7.

Hesse-Biber, Sharlene Nagy, and Patricia Leavy. *Feminist Research Practice.* Thousand Oaks, Calif.: Sage, 2007.

Hirschfeld, Ariel A. "Gvarim b'gvarim." *Mishkafayim* 22 (1994): 9–15 [Hebrew].

Holzman, Michael G. *The Still Small Voice: Reflections on Being a Jewish Man.* New York: URJ Press, 2008.

hooks, bell. "Men: Comrades in Struggle." In *Feminism and Men: Reconstructing Gender Relations,* edited by Steven P. Schacht and Doris W. Ewing, 265–80. New York: NYU Press, 1998.

———. *The Will to Change: Men, Masculinity, and Love.* New York: Atria Books, 2004.

Hussey, Mark, ed. *Masculinities: Interdisciplinary Readings.* Englewood Cliffs, N.J.: Prentice Hall, 2003.

Kaplan, Danny. *Brothers and Others in Arms: The Making of Love and War in Israeli Combat Units.* New York: Haworth Press, 2003.

———. *The Men We Loved: Male Friendship and Nationalism in Israeli Culture.* New York: Berghahn Books, 2006.

Kaplowitz, William. "Partnership *Minyanim* in the United States: Planning Theory in Action." Master's thesis, University of Michigan, 2008.

Kimmel, Michael. "From 'Conscience and Common Sense' to 'Feminism for Men': Profeminist Men's Rhetorics of Support for Women's Equality." In *Feminism and Men: Reconstructing Gender Relations,* edited by Steven P. Schacht and Doris W. Ewing, 21–42. New York: NYU Press, 1998.

———. *The Gendered Society.* New York: Oxford University Press, 2000.

———. *The History of Men: Essays in the History of American and British Masculinities.* Albany, N.Y.: SUNY Press, 2005.

———. "Judaism, Masculinity, and Feminism." In *A Mentsch among Men: Explorations in Jewish Masculinity,* edited by Harry Brod, 153–57. Freedom, Calif.: Crossing Press, 1988.

———. *Manhood in America: A Cultural History.* New York: Free Press, 1996/2006.

———. "Masculinity as Homophobia: Fear, Shame, and Silence in the Construction of Gender Identity." In *Theorizing Masculinities,* edited by Harry Brod and Michael Kaufman. Thousand Oaks, Calif.: Sage, 1994.

———, ed. *The Politics of Manhood: Profeminist Men Respond to the Mythopoetic Men's Movement (and the Mythopoetic Leaders Answer).* Philadelphia: Temple University Press, 1995/2005.

———. "Teaching a Course on Men: Masculinist Reaction or 'Gentlemen's Auxiliary'?" In *Changing Men: New Directions in Research on Men and Masculinity,* edited by Michael Kimmel, 278–94. Thousand Oaks, Calif.: Sage, 1987.

Kimmel, Michael, and Thomas Mosmiller. *Against the Tide: Pro-Feminist Men in the U.S., 1776–1990.* Boston: Beacon Press, 1992.

Kivel, Paul. "The 'Act Like a Man' Box." In *Masculinities: Interdisciplinary Readings,* edited by Mark Hussey, 69–72. Englewood Cliffs, N.J.: Prentice Hall, 2003.

Kosman, Admiel. *Men's Tractate: Rav and the Butcher and Other Stories—On Manhood, Love and Authentic Life in Aggadic and Hassidic Stories.* Jerusalem: Keter, 2002 [Hebrew].

Kotler-Berkowitz, Laurence. "Poor Jews: An Analysis of Low Income in the American Jewish Population." *Contemporary Jewry* 29, no. 3 (2009): 241–77.

Lazerwitz, Bernard J., Alan Winder, Arnold Dashefsky, and Ephraim Tabory. *Jewish Choices: American Jewish Denominationalism.* New York: SUNY Press, 1998.

Lieblich, Amia. *Transition to Adulthood during Military Service: The Israeli Case.* Albany, N.Y.: SUNY Press, 1989.

Liebman, Charles. *The Ambivalent American Jew: Politics, Religion, and Family in American Jewish Life.* Philadelphia: Jewish Publication Society of America, 1973.

Lincoln, Yvonne S., and Egon G. Guba. *Naturalistic Inquiry.* Thousand Oaks, Calif.: Sage, 1986.

Lomsky-Feder, Edna, and Eyal Ben-Ari. *The Military and Militarism in Israeli Society.* New York: SUNY Press, 2000.

Lorde, Audre. *Sister Outsider.* Freedom, Calif.: Crossing Press, 1984.

Ludy, Eric. *God's Gift to Women: Discovering the Lost Greatness of Masculinity.* Sisters, Ore.: Multnomah Publishers, 2003.

McCabe, Janice. "What's in a Label? The Relationship between Feminist Self-Identification and 'Feminist' Attitudes among U.S. Women and Men." *Gender and Society* 19 (2005): 480.

McDavid, Alex. "Feminism for Men 101: Educating Men in 'Women's Studies.'" In *Feminist Teacher* 3, no. 3 (1988): 25–33.

Messner, Michael. "Boyhood, Organized Sports, and the Construction of Masculinities." In *Masculinities: Interdisciplinary Readings*, edited by Mark Hussey, 140–52. Englewood Cliffs, N.J.: Prentice Hall, 2003.

———. *Politics of Masculinities: Men in Movements.* Oxford: AltaMira Press, 2000.

———. "Radical Feminist and Socialist Feminist Men's Movements in the United States." In *Feminism and Men: Reconstructing Gender Relations*, edited by Steven P. Schacht and Doris W. Ewing, 67–87. New York: NYU Press, 1998.

Motsafi-Haller, Penina. "'You Have an Authentic Voice': Anthropological Research and the Politics of Representation outside of the Researched Society." *Te'oriaU'Bikoret* 11 (1997): 81–98 [Hebrew].

Murphy, Peter F., ed. *Feminism and Masculinities.* Oxford: Oxford University Press, 2004.

Naples, Nancy. *Feminism and Method: Ethnography, Discourse Analysis, and Activist Research.* New York: Routledge, 2003.

National Jewish Population Survey, 2000–01. New York: United Jewish Communities, 2003.

Nussbaum, Martha. *Women and Human Development.* Cambridge: Cambridge University Press, 2000.

Okin, Susan Moller. *Is Multiculturalism Bad for Women?* Princeton, N.J.: Princeton University Press, 1999.

Rapoport, Tamar, and Yoni Garb. "The Experience of Religious Fortification: The Coming of Age of Religious Zionist Young Women." *Gender and Education* 10, no. 1 (1998): 5–20.

Reinharz, Shulamit. *Feminist Methods in Social Research.* New York: Oxford University Press, 1992.

Rosenberg, Warren. *Legacy of Rage: Jewish Masculinity, Violence, and Culture.* Amherst: University of Massachusetts Press, 2001.

Sacks, Jonathan. *Traditional Alternatives: Orthodoxy and the Future of the Jewish People.* London: Jews' College Publications, 1989.

Salkin, Jeffrey. *Searching for My Brothers: Jewish Men in a Gentile World.* New York: Perigee, 1999.

Satlow, Michael L. "'Try to Be a Man': The Rabbinic Construction of Masculinity." In *Men and Masculinities in Christianity and Judaism: A Critical Reader,* edited by Björn Krondorfer, 261–76. London: SCM Press, 2004.

Sawyer, Jack. "On Male Liberation." In *Feminism and Masculinities,* edited by Peter F. Murphy, 25–28. Oxford: Oxford University Press, 2004.

Schacht, Steven P., and Doris W. Ewing, eds. *Feminisms and Men: Reconstructing Gender Relations.* New York: NYU Press, 1998.

Schechet, Nita. *Narrative Fissures: Reading and Rhetoric.* Madison, N.J.: Fairleigh Dickinson University Press, 2005.

Shapiro, Mendel. "Qeri'at Ha-Torah by Women: A Halachic Analysis." *Edah Journal* 1, no 2 (2001): 1–52.

Sheleg, Yair. *The New Religious Jews: Recent Developments among Observant Jews in Israel.* Jerusalem: Keter, 2000 [Hebrew].

Soloveitchik, Haym. "Rupture and Reconstruction: The Transformation of Contemporary Orthodoxy." *Tradition* (Summer 1994): 64–130.

Sperber, Daniel. *The Path of Halakha: Women Reading Torah: A Case of Pesika Policy.* Jerusalem: Reuven Mas Publishers [Hebrew].

Spradley, James P. *The Ethnographic Interview.* Orlando, Fla.: Harcourt Brace Jovanovich, 1979.

Stacey, Judith. "Can There Be Feminist Ethnography?" In *Women's Words: The Feminist Practice of Oral History,* edited by Sherna Berger Gluck and Daphne Patai, 111–20. New York: Routledge, 1991.

Stadler, Nurit. "Is Profane Work an Obstacle to Salvation? The Case of Ultra-Orthodox (Haredi) Jews in Contemporary Israel." *Sociology of Religion* 63, no. 4 (2002): 455–74.

Stern, Marc D. "Egalitarianism and Halakha: An Introduction." In *Formulating Responses in an Egalitarian Age,* edited by Marc. D. Stern. Lanham, Md.: Rowman & Littlefield, 2005.

Stoltenberg, John. "Healing from Manhood: A Radical Meditation on the Movement from Gender Identity to Moral Identity." In *Feminism and Men: Reconstructing Gender Relations*, edited by Steven P. Schacht and Doris W. Ewing, 146–60. New York: NYU Press, 1998.

———. *Refusing to Be a Man: Essays on Sex and Justice*. London: UCL Press, Taylor and Francis Group, 1989/2000.

———. "Toward Gender Justice." In *Feminism and Masculinities*, edited by Peter F. Murphy, 41–49. Oxford: Oxford University Press, 2004.

Tannen, Deborah. *You Just Don't Understand: Men and Women in Conversation*. Ballantine, New York, 1990.

Thorne, Barrie. *Gender Play: Girls and Boys in School*. New Brunswick, N.J.: Rutgers University Press, 1993.

Trachtman, Chaim, ed. *Women and Men in Communal Prayer: Halakhic Perspectives*. Jersey City, N.J.: Ktav Publishing, 2010.

Weissman, Deborah. "The Education of Religious Girls in Jerusalem during the British Mandate." Doctoral dissertation, Hebrew University, Jerusalem, 1993.

Wexler, Phillip. *Becoming Somebody: Toward a Social Psychology of School*. Washington, D.C.: Falmer Press, 1996.

Index

Page numbers in italic refer to figures and tables.